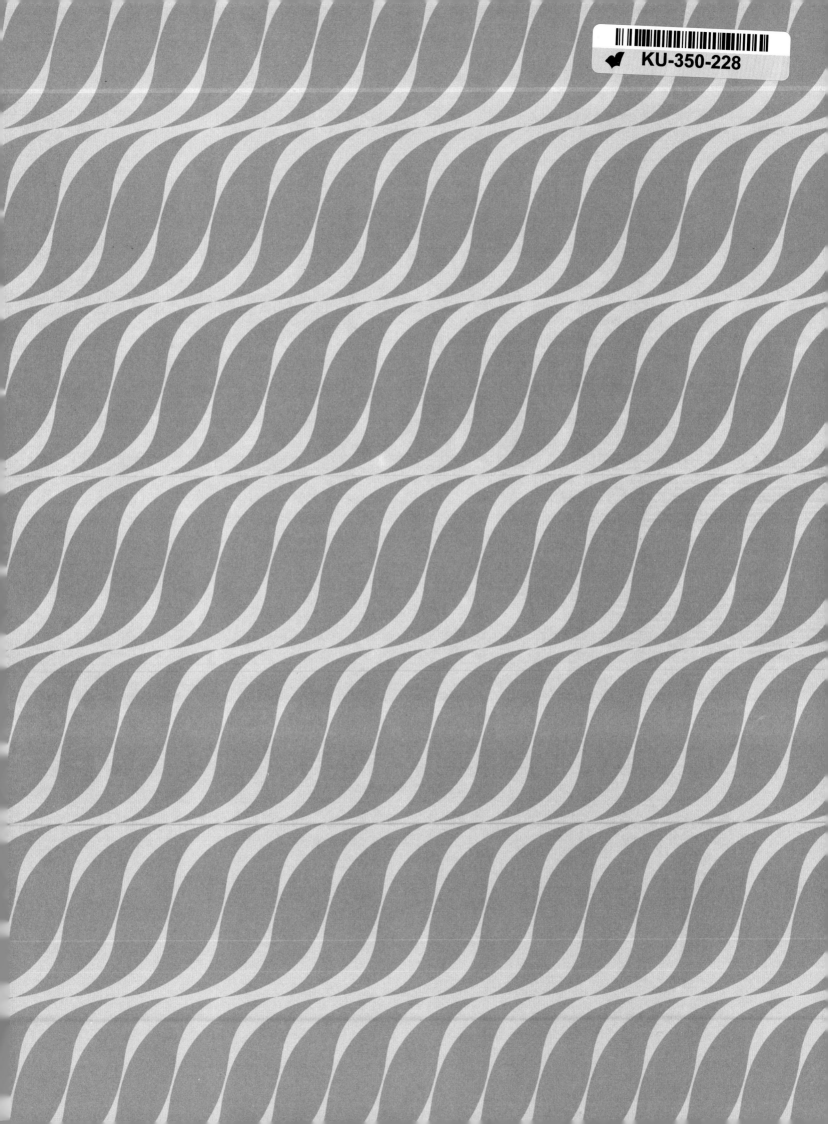

THE CHILDREN'S ILLUSTRATED BIBLE

THE OLD TESTAMENT

THE CHILDREN'S ILLUSTRATED BIBLE

THE OLD TESTAMENT

Retold by VICTORIA PARKER
Consultant: JANET DYSON

southwater

CONTENTS

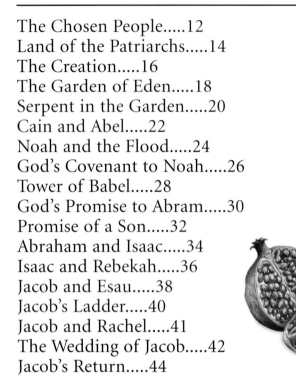

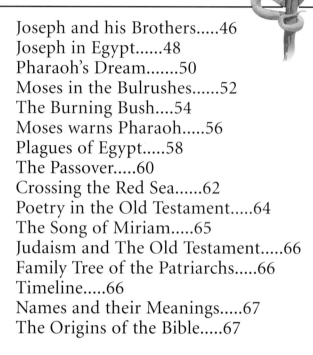

LOOK OVER JORDAN.....68

THE GREAT KINGS.....126

EXILE AND RETURN.....184

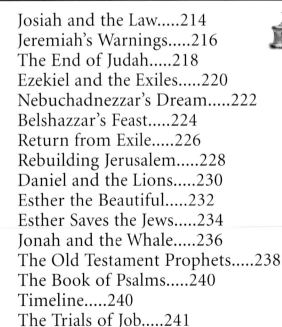

Introduction

NOAH'S ARK
Early in the history of the world, God brought a great flood which covered the Earth. This medieval wall-painting shows Noah's Ark, in which humans and animals survived the flood to people the Earth again.

If you enjoy reading books, you'll enjoy reading the Bible. It doesn't matter whether you are a Muslim, Jew, Christian, Budhist, or have no religious beliefs at all. After all, the word Bible is from the Greek 'biblos', meaning 'book'. And the Bible is exactly that –a whole library of different types of books for you to dip into. Most people enjoy reading the story books best. But the Bible also contains beautiful poetry and songs; hundreds of wise proverbs and laws; and many fascinating letters, and diaries.

For many people, the Bible is a vital way of getting to know God. Others read it simply because they enjoy its wonderful pieces of writing or its fascinating tales of centuries of history. Either way, the Bible can remind us of the lessons of the past, inspire us with hope for the future, and help us to find the right way forward in our own lives. The books of the Bible are usually divided up into two sections: the Old Testament and the New Testament.

From Creation to the Prophets

The stories of the Old Testament span thousands of years, and recount the history of the Jewish people from the very beginning of the world almost to the days of the Roman Empire. The writings also prophesy the coming of a Messiah, or saviour. The Jews believed that the Messiah would be a person who, through pain and suffering, would lead the Jews to great glory and would establish the mightiest of all kingdoms. So the books of the Old Testament are the Scriptures, or sacred writings of the Jews.

GOD'S CREATIONS
The Book of Genesis, the first book in the Bible, tells how God created the Earth and all the animals that live there. The camel, ass and wild goat were among the animals that the peoples of the Old Testament domesticated (bred for human use). The camel and ass carried heavy loads for long distances. Goats provided hair that could be spun and woven into clothes and blankets.

The Messiah

The stories of the New Testament tell of the life of Jesus Christ and the establishing of his church of followers through the world (a time span of only sixty or seventy years). Christians believe that Jesus Christ was the Messiah promised by the Scriptures. The New Testament books therefore do not just record the life of an extraordinary religious leader, they also show the fulfilment of all the promises in the Old Testament books.

Many voices, many words

The 66 books that make up the Old and New Testaments were written by people who lived over a period of several thousand years. However, many of the Old Testament books lived in people's memories and were handed down by word of mouth long before scribes actually wrote them down. Then the Old Testament stories were carefully copied word for word onto parchment – a type of paper made from animal skin. They were written entirely in Hebrew (the Jewish language) except for a very few passages, which were written in

SACRED SCROLLS

The first five books of the Bible are sacred to the Jewish people, who call them the Torah. The books are written as scrolls (lengths of paper wound on wooden rollers). The words of the Torah are written in Hebrew, the language of the Jewish people, as seen in the photograph on the left. The alphabet used to write the Torah is the Jewish alphabet, not the Roman alphabet in which the words in this book are written.

UNDER THE LASH

The people of Israel who lived in Egypt in Moses' time were treated very harshly by the Egyptians. They worked long hours for little food and were often beaten by overseers. The Egyptians built huge monuments such as the Pyramids and used their slaves to drag the loads of stone from which the monuments were made.

IN THE LAND OF EGYPT

The Book of Exodus tells how Moses led the Israelites out of Egypt, where they had been slaves, completely subject to the rule of the Egyptians. Moses was found as an abandoned baby and adopted into the Egyptian royal family where he was treated as an equal. This allowed him to speak directly to the Pharaoh. He is shown here asking Pharaoh, the ruler of Egypt, to recognize the Israelite God and let the Israelites become a free people.

SLAIN ENEMIES
The Israelite hero David kills his Philistine enemies and shows the bodies to Saul, his king.

another ancient language, called Aramaic. In this collection of stories you can read a story called *Josiah and the Law*, which shows how difficult it was for people to keep these precious Scriptures safe through the centuries. For convenience the books of the Old Testament are usually grouped together like this:

> ***Genesis, Exodus, Leviticus, Numbers, Deuteronomy***
> The Law of Moses
>
> ***Joshua, Judges, Ruth, 1 Samuel, 2 Samuel, 1 Kings, 2 Kings, 1 Chronicles, 2 Chronicles, Ezra, Nehemiah, Esther***
> The Books of History
>
> ***Job, Psalms, Proverbs, Ecclesiastes, Song of Solomon***
> The Books of Poetry and Wisdom
>
> ***Isaiah, Jeremiah, Lamentations, Ezekiel, Daniel***
> The Books of the Major Prophets
>
> ***Hosea, Joel, Amos, Obadiah, Jonah, Micah, Nahum, Habakkuk, Zephaniah, Haggai, Zechariah, Malachi***
> The Books of the Minor Prophets

FOREIGN KINGS
For a time the Israelites were ruled by the Babylonians, who had a great empire. This sculpture shows Gilgamesh, one of the great Babylonian heroes.

The Chosen People

The first five books of the Old Testament are traditionally accepted to have come from a great prophet called Moses, who wrote down the words of God. Moses' books tell the story of the creation of the world and how God chose Abraham to be the father of the Jewish people. They tell how the Jews escaped from slavery in Egypt at the hands of the Pharaoh and journeyed to find the land God had promised them for a home. They also contain God's teachings to the Jewish people of who He was and how He wanted them to obey his laws. For Jews, these five books are the most important part of the Bible, and they call them the Torah.

FALLEN IDOL
The Philistines stole the Israelites' holiest object, the Ark of the Covenant. When the Ark was put beside the statue of Dagon, the Philistines' god, the statue broke.

SACRED LIGHT
This type of seven-branched candlestick, called a menorah, was first made by Moses to light the Tabernacle, the holiest of Jewish places.

Land and leaders

The twelve Old Testament books of history follow the story of the Jews over the next thousand or so years. The books tell how the Jews eventually won the promised land, and were ruled first by leaders called judges and then by kings. The people fell into sin and the country was split by civil war. Then Israel was conquered by Babylon and the Jews spent decades living under foreign rulers before finally returning home.

Words of wisdom

The remaining books of the Old Testament fit into the timespan of the first 17 books. The books of poetry (for example *Job* and *Psalms*) speak beautifully of God, life, loss and love, sorrow and joy. The books of prophecy, such as Isaiah and Jeremiah, tell how God communicated with human beings during the years when kings ruled the divided nation of Israel and Judah. This volume will lead you through the Old Testament by retelling over one hundred of the most important stories.

These include tales of heroes and villains (such as *David and Goliath*), great warrior leaders (such as Joshua in *Fall of Jericho*), magical miracles (in *Crossing the Red Sea*), bad kings (such as Ahab and Belshazzar) and beautiful queens (as in *Wealth and Splendour*).

The variety of stories in the Bible does not end there, however. *Noah and the Flood* tells of the awe-inspiring events that almost ended humanity's life on this Earth. In *Jonah and the Whale* there is spine-tingling adventure. There are also joyful love stories (such as *Isaac and Rebekah*) and heart-rending tragedies (such as *Jepthah*); gory battles between nations (such as *The Longest Day*); sagas of betrayal and brutality (as in the Samson stories) together with uplifting tales of courage and triumph (such as *Daniel and the Lions*). We hope you enjoy them.

ROYAL NAME
The Egyptians wrote in hieroglyphics (picture-words). This carving shows how they wrote the name of the Pharaoh Rameses II.

ABANDONED KING
This sculpture shows Rameses, believed to be Pharaoh at the time the Israelites fled Egypt.

THE CHOSEN PEOPLE

*From the Garden of Eden to the Israelites'
departure for the land promised to them by God*

The Chosen People

THE Bible is a collection of 66 books which were written over a period of nearly 1,600 years, starting from around 1400BC. Many of the stories in the Bible had been passed down from one generation to another by word of mouth and were well known for a long time before they were written down. Different books were written by different authors, and as time went by they were gradually all put together into one bigger book. This big book became the Bible. The word "Bible" comes from the Greek word "biblia", which simply means "books". The stories are all linked, together they form the story of God's relationship with his people.

As well as forming the first part of the Christian Bible, the Old Testament is also the sacred book of the Jewish people. The 39 books of the Old Testament, that tell the story of the people of ancient Israel over many centuries, appear in both the Jewish and the Christian holy texts, but in a slightly different order.

This section covers the first part of the Bible, from God's creation of the world, to the Israelites' crossing of the Red Sea. It includes the first stories of the Bible, from the Creation to the story of Adam and Eve's temptation in the Garden of Eden. This is a very important story in the Bible as it tells of the first sin in the world. It shows how Adam and Eve, even while they were still living in the Garden of Eden, disobeyed God, and were cast out of Paradise into the world.

Their two sons, Cain and Abel, were the first people born into the world, and the first people born after Adam and Eve left Eden. Cain commits a sin when he kills his younger brother Abel, and his punishment is worse than God's punishment of Adam. Cain is told he must wander the world for the rest of his life, and that the ground will no longer grow crops for him. God also puts a mark on him, to remind him of his sin, and warn other people to leave him alone.

After Cain and Abel we find the story of Noah and the mighty flood, which happens because the descendants of Adam and Eve have abandoned God,

Jewish *Torah*
The book shown above is the Torah. It contains the first five books of the Old Testament that make up the Jewish religious laws. There is also a prayer shawl, and a *dreidel*, used in games played at the Hanukkah festival, the only time that the Jews can play games of chance.

and no longer live a good life. So for the only time in history God decides to wipe all life from the face of the planet. He spares only Noah and his family, who have maintained their belief in God and tried to live their lives as God wished. He seals them away, along with pairs of all the animals of the world, in the Ark that God instructed Noah to build, and He saved them from the flood.

The story called 'God's Promise to Abraham' marks the start of the most important part of the Old Testament. After the flood, Noah's descendants, just like the descendants of Adam before him, have abandoned and neglected God. Rather than destroy the world, God chooses Abraham and his descendants to become His own people, His special race on earth. The story tells how God makes an agreement, or covenant, with Abraham. If Abraham follows God's instructions, and continues to have faith in Him, Abraham's descendants will become a great people and will one day inherit the land of Canaan, called the promised land. Abraham has faith in the promise of God, and packs up his family to move to Canaan, where he settles with his family.

God's covenant with Abraham is re-established with his descendants, we see the birth of his son, Isaac, and his grandson, Jacob, and we see how God speaks to these men when they grow up, and reminds them of the promise He made to Abraham. God promised Abraham that his descendants would become a great nation, as many people as there are stars in the sky, and with Jacob we see this start to come true. Jacob fathers twelve sons who eventually become the forefathers of the twelve tribes of Israel. One son, Joseph, is sold by his brothers and taken to Egypt. The Israelites' 400 years of exile, as God told Abraham would happen, begin with Joseph's arrival in Egypt. Jacob and his family follow Joseph there to escape a terrible famine, and while they are living there, firstly as free people but later as slaves, their numbers multiply.

God said to Abraham that his descendants would live in Egypt for 400 years, and would be led to freedom and to the promised land, and we see this come miraculously true when the great leader, prophet and law-giver Moses leads the great nation to freedom across the Red Sea.

Many of the stories illustrate God testing the faith of His people. Some pass the test, like Abraham who is prepared to sacrifice his own son if it is God's will. Others, such as Cain, are weaker. But, here and throughout the whole of the Old Testament, God continues to forgive His people for their sins. He realises that the people that He created are not perfect, and is willing to accept wrong-doing from them if they remain faithful to Him and are truly sorry for their sins. Then, through His chosen leaders, He guides them to the promised land.

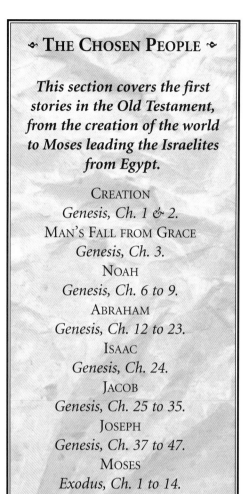

❧ THE CHOSEN PEOPLE ❧

This section covers the first stories in the Old Testament, from the creation of the world to Moses leading the Israelites from Egypt.

CREATION
Genesis, Ch. 1 & 2.
MAN'S FALL FROM GRACE
Genesis, Ch. 3.
NOAH
Genesis, Ch. 6 to 9.
ABRAHAM
Genesis, Ch. 12 to 23.
ISAAC
Genesis, Ch. 24.
JACOB
Genesis, Ch. 25 to 35.
JOSEPH
Genesis, Ch. 37 to 47.
MOSES
Exodus, Ch. 1 to 14.

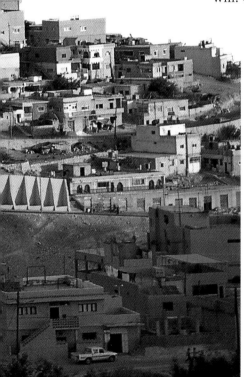

Wadi-Musa, Jordan
This town, on a hillside in what is now the country of Jordan, is Wadi-Musa. It lies directly on the route that the Israelites would probably have taken on their exodus from Egypt, heading north towards the promised land.

Illuminated letter
Bibles have always been regarded as very important books that contain the words of God to His people, so great care used to be taken in making the Bible look very ornate. The letter above would have taken someone a very long time to do.

Lands of the Patriarchs

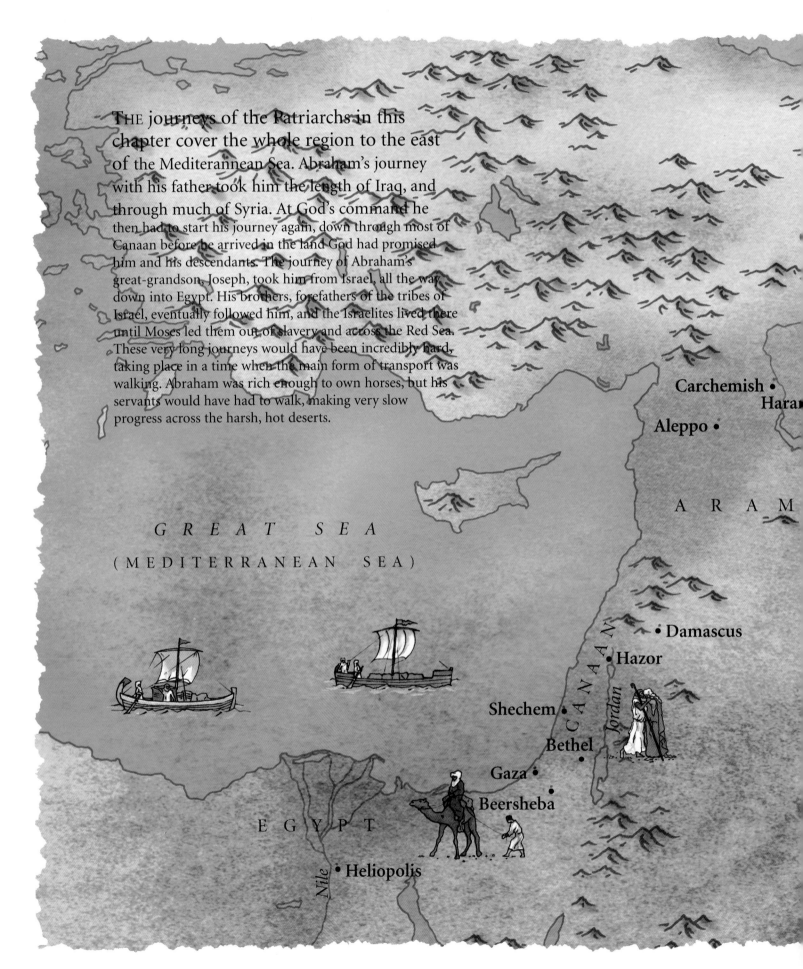

THE journeys of the Patriarchs in this chapter cover the whole region to the east of the Mediterannean Sea. Abraham's journey with his father took him the length of Iraq, and through much of Syria. At God's command he then had to start his journey again, down through most of Canaan before he arrived in the land God had promised him and his descendants. The journey of Abraham's great-grandson, Joseph, took him from Israel, all the way down into Egypt. His brothers, forefathers of the tribes of Israel, eventually followed him, and the Israelites lived there until Moses led them out of slavery and across the Red Sea. These very long journeys would have been incredibly hard, taking place in a time when the main form of transport was walking. Abraham was rich enough to own horses, but his servants would have had to walk, making very slow progress across the harsh, hot deserts.

Carchemish •

Harar

Aleppo •

A R A M

GREAT SEA

(MEDITERRANEAN SEA)

• Damascus

Hazor

Shechem •

Bethel
•

Gaza •

Beersheba
•

E G Y P T

Nile

• Heliopolis

Mt.Ararat

HYRCANIAN
SEA

A S S Y R I A

Mari •

Euphrates

• Accad

Tigris

• Babylon

B A B Y L O N I A

Ur •

LOWER
SEA

The Creation

IN the beginning, nothing existed except God's Spirit, hovering over a darkness and never-ending water. Then God spoke. "Let there be light," He said, and suddenly there was brightness all around. God thought that the light was good, and He separated it from the darkness. He called the light Day and the dark Night. God looked on as evening drew in and watched as morning arrived. He had formed the very first day.

On the second day, God said, "Let there be skies to divide the watery wastes. Some waters will float above the skies and some will lie below." It all happened just so, and God called the skies Heaven.

Next God said, "Let all the waters under heaven be gathered into one place, so that dry land may appear. I name the waters Sea, and the dry land Earth." God looked at His work and was pleased. He commanded things to grow and at once tiny green shoots began to sprout all over the earth. As plants of all kinds took root, leafy tendrils uncurled and stretched, stems burst into bushes and trees sprang upwards. Then evening came once again and morning, making the third day.

"Let there be lights in the skies to shine on the Earth," said God. "They will mark out the passing days, months, seasons and years." He made the burning sun to rule over the day and the cooler moon to govern over the night, together with the stars. Then He set them all moving in the heavens. God was again happy with what He had done, and the fourth day came to an end.

The stars
God created the stars, along with the sun and the moon, to mark out the passing days. People have since learned how to tell the time from the sun, and mark the seasons by the movement of the stars. In the Bible, the word 'star' is used to describe any light in the sky, other than the sun and moon.

What is a day?
In the Bible, the word 'day' can mean a period of 24 hours, or an indefinite period of time. In the Creation story, everything happens in six days. Some people think this is using 'day' in its sense of 'period of time'. Others believe it is just a way of expressing God's creative energy. Finally, others believe that Creation took place in literally six days.

"Let living creatures swim in the seas and birds fly through the skies," said God, on the fifth day. Instantly, coral covered the sea beds, crabs burrowed into sand and limpets clung to rocks, shoals of fish darted through rivers and beneath waves, and sea monsters lurked in the deep. Above the Earth, flocks of birds spread their wings for the first time and began to flap and flutter, soar and swoop. And God thought it was all good work. He blessed every single creature and told them to fill the waters and the skies He had given them for their homes.

On the sixth day, God said, "Now for the living creatures of the Earth – from tiny creeping things to the largest wild beasts." He made creatures with fur, scales and hair; beasts that grunted, growled and snorted; animals

> *And God saw everything that He had made, and behold, it was very good.*

with claws, paws, hooves, and tails; living things that galloped and slithered. God made animals of every kind and sent them out to live in the land that He had made. He watched them and thought He had done well.

Last of all, God made people - men and women - that looked just like Him. "You shall rule over the fish of the sea and the birds of the air and the animals of the land," He told them. "You own the Earth," He said, and He blessed them. "Go and fill the whole world. I am giving the plants to you and all the living creatures for food."

As the sixth day drew to a close, God looked all around at everything He had done, and He was very pleased. The heavens and the Earth were finished, and everything had happened just as He had wished. The seventh day came and God was tired. He rested, and blessed the seventh day of the week as a holy time of rest for all people.

The animals
When God had made the land and the sea, He made the animals which lived there. The only animals named in this story are whales. Otherwise, animals are listed in very general terms. From the air come birds, from the water all the fish and animals of the seas, and from the land come cattle, beasts and creeping things. These descriptions are supposed to cover all animals, from the tiniest to the most enormous, from ants to elephants.

❖ ABOUT THE STORY ❖

The Creation story tells of how the world began. In simple language, it describes the wonder of the universe, and God's power in creating it.

There is a great deal of repetition of key phrases, which mirrors the orderly way in which God created the world. The Creation story can only be understood by believing in God, not by science. The world was created by God and depends on Him for its continued existence.

The Garden of Eden

AFTER God had gathered the waters together into the sea and commanded the Earth to appear on the third day of Creation, He had been pleased with His work. But when He had looked all around Him, God had seen that the land was dry and brown. He had not yet brought rain to water the land, so nothing could grow. And besides, God had not yet created people to plough the earth, to sow crops and to care for flowers and trees.

As God thought of all these things, He sent a fine mist up from the ground. Gradually, drops of wetness drifted down and covered the face of the Earth. Then God scooped up some of the damp dust and began to shape it. Very carefully He formed a figure, until He was happy with the way it looked. Then God breathed into the figure's nostrils a deep, long breath - the breath of life. The figure blinked awake and the first Man became a living being. God looked at him with love and called him Adam.

Next, God created a special garden in a place called Eden. He ordered water to spring from the ground, and at once a river appeared. It flowed right through the garden to the edge of Eden, before bursting over the boundary and becoming four smaller rivers. The river Pishon flowed around the land of Havilah. The second river, the Gihon, circled the land of Cush. The Tigris wound its way east of Assyria. The fourth river was the mighty Euphrates.

God set about planting trees of many different kinds. All were rich with fruit, but none was more beautiful than the trees at the centre of the garden: the Tree of Eternal Life and the Tree of the Knowledge of Good and Evil.

THIS SECOND DESCRIPTION OF CREATION IS WRITTEN FROM A DIFFERENT POINT OF VIEW, THIS TIME FOCUSING ON MAN. IT TALKS OF GOD SPECIFICALLY IN RELATION TO THE PEOPLE HE CREATED.

Adam naming the animals
God brought all the animals to Adam so he could give them names. It is possible that this was so that Adam could get to know all the different animals over which God had made him master. Adam could learn which would work for him, like horses and sheep, cows and pigs, and which would run free, like lions and tigers.

God took the man He had made and placed him in Eden. "You may eat all the fruit you wish from any of my trees except the Tree of the Knowledge of Good and Evil," God warned him. "If you taste a mouthful of the fruit from that tree, you will become mortal and will one day die." Then He gave Adam His beautiful garden to care for.

God created all the animals of the earth, and all the birds that fly in the skies. He brought them to Adam to see what he would call them. One by one Adam gave them all names: the lion and the lioness, the bull and the cow, the peacock and the peahen, giraffes, zebras and antelopes . . . God ordered that from that day onwards, and ever after, every living creature on the earth should be called just as Adam had said that day.

❝ *Out of the ground God made to grow every tree that is good for food.* ❞

God looked at each pair of animals and birds and saw that they were content together. But Adam stood alone and God realized that he was lonely. "It is not good for the man to be on his own," He thought to Himself. He sent Adam into a deep sleep, took out one of his ribs, and mended the wound. Then God tenderly shaped the rib until He was pleased with the figure He had created - the very first Woman. Then God woke Adam from his dreams and gave him his companion. Adam was delighted. "At last!" he cried. "I have something just like myself!" And Adam and Eve lived happily in God's garden of paradise.

The rivers of Eden
Of the four rivers named in this story, only the Tigris and the Euphrates are known today. There have been many attempts to identify the others as, for example, the Nile and the Indus. However no one knows for certain. The picture here shows part of the Euphrates, the largest river in western Asia.

God makes Adam
This picture shows a statue of God imagining Adam. Although it looks like Adam is looking from behind God's head, this is the sculptor's way of trying to show the picture of Adam that existed in God's mind before Adam was made, and shows how God made Adam in His own image. He formed his body from dust, just like a potter is able to make jugs from clay.

Serpent in the Garden

OF all the hundreds of creatures God had made, the snake was by far the most wily. One day he saw that Eve was going for a walk through the Garden of Eden without Adam, and he seized the chance to talk to her. "Did God tell you not to eat anything in the garden?" he asked Eve.

"We're allowed to eat any fruit except from the tree in the middle," Eve said. "God says that if we do, we will die."

"Of course you won't die!" the snake mocked. "God has told you not to eat it because it has the power to make you just like Him. You already know goodness, but when you eat from the Tree of Knowledge, you will know evil too."

Eve went to see the Tree of the Knowledge of Good and Evil for herself. How beautiful it was! Its branches were heavy with fruits. "What could be so wrong about wanting to be wiser?" she wondered. Eve reached out and plucked a plump globe. It looked and smelled so good, surely it must be delicious to eat! She took a bite, and it was the most wonderful thing she had ever tasted! Soon there was nothing left but the seeds and stalk. "I must take some to Adam," she thought, and they both ate until they were full.

Straight away, Adam and Eve realized that they had made the most dreadful mistake. Now they knew what it meant to disobey God. They suddenly felt ashamed of their nakedness and covered themselves up with fig leaves.

When Adam and Eve heard the Lord approaching they ran off. How could they face God after the terrible thing they had done? "Where are you?" the Lord asked.

Adam knew he had to tell the truth. "I heard you coming," he replied, "and I was afraid because I was naked."

Tree of Knowledge
This picture shows the Tree of the Knowledge of Good and Evil, also called the Tree of Wisdom. There are many different views as to what 'the knowledge of good and evil' might mean. One view is that it means the knowledge of right and wrong. Another is that it means the knowledge of everything in the universe. Yet another view is that the tree was just an ordinary tree, chosen by God to provide a test of man's obedience to Him.

Which fruit?
The fruit growing on the Tree of the Knowledge of Good and Evil is not named in the Bible. Most people represent it as an apple, but is more likely to be a pomegranate, like in the picture.

God roared like thunder. "Who told you that you were naked?" He demanded. "Have you eaten the forbidden fruit?"

"It was Eve who gave it to me!" Adam protested.

God turned to Eve and, with great sadness, said, "Tell me what you have done."

Eve hung her head in misery. "The snake tricked me into eating it," she cried.

Adam and Eve knew that they had filled the Lord with unhappiness and they stood before Him in utter despair.

First, God punished the snake. "You will be the most cursed of all creatures," He said. "You will crawl on your belly and eat dirt all your life."

Next God told Eve, "Childbirth will be painful, yet you will long to be with your husband and master."

> ❝ *'Cursed is the ground because of you, in toil you shall eat of it all your life.'* ❞

To Adam He said, "Because you listened to your wife rather than listening to my commands, the very ground itself will be cursed. You will work hard to grow crops, and you will need to fight weeds. After a life of hard work, you will die and return to the dust from which I made you."

Finally, God made clothes for Adam and Eve. "Now you know both good and evil, I cannot let you stay here," He explained. "If you also ate fruit from the Tree of Eternal Life, you would have to live with the pain of your shame for ever." Then God drove Adam and Eve out of Eden, and set angels with flaming swords to guard the entrance.

ADAM AND EVE HAVE SINNED AGAINST GOD, AND THEY SUFFER BECAUSE OF THIS. THE PUNISHMENT FOR THEIR SIN IS SEPARATION FROM GOD AND EXPULSION FROM THE GARDEN, OUT INTO THE WILDERNESS. ❧

The Fall of Man

Adam and Eve's disobedience to God and their expulsion from the Garden of Eden is often called The Fall, or The Fall of Man, which represents all mankind's later sins. This picture shows Adam and Eve fleeing from the garden. Above them, an angel whirls a flaming sword and nearby stands a skeleton, symbolizing death.

❧ ABOUT THE STORY ❧

God gave Adam and Eve everything they needed to live happily together. However, they destroy the peace and innocence of the Garden of Eden by giving in to temptation and doing the one thing God has forbidden. God punishes them for their disobedience. Instead of having the eternal life God originally promised, Adam will be turned back into the dust from which he came, which means that he will eventually die.

Cain and Abel

After the Lord had thrown Adam and Eve out of paradise, in time Eve gave birth to a son. Cain was the very first baby to be born into the world, and Eve was delighted and amazed. "With the help of the Lord, I have created a new life!" she cried. Imagine her happiness later on when she had another baby – a brother for Cain, called Abel.

The two boys grew up together into strong young men. Cain chose to be a farmer and looked after the land, while Abel preferred the life of a shepherd and cared for his flock. The day came when they had to choose the best of their efforts to offer to God. Cain picked the fattest ears of corn and vegetables he had grown, while Abel took some of the first lambs that had been born in his flock. Both the men were satisfied with the fruits of their labours.

First, the Lord examined Abel's gifts and was pleased with them. But to Cain's horror, He didn't accept the older brother's presents. Cain's face fell and his heart filled with rage. What made Abel's offerings any better than his own?

The Lord said to him, "What has made you so angry? Why do you look so gloomy? You know that if you do good, I will be pleased. If you don't, sin is there waiting for you. You must always be ready to fight off evil, or it will leap at you and eat you up."

Cain should have crushed his hurt pride and made up his mind to be a better person. Instead, he found it easier to wallow in self-pity, blaming God for being unfair. Because Cain hadn't listened to the Lord's words, he didn't notice that the warning was coming true. Gradually, he

Farmers and wanderers
Cain was a farmer who works the land to grow crops. To punish him for killing Abel, God decreed that the land would no longer produce any crops for Cain, and ordered him to leave his home. This was even worse than the punishment God had imposed upon Adam, which had been to work land that was choked with weeds and thistles. Instead of living the settled existence of a farmer, Cain was condemned to a lonely life of wandering through the desert, without a home to shelter him, or a family to support him. 'Nod', the name of the faraway place Cain was banished to, means 'wandering' in Hebrew. Today, there are still tribes of wandering people, called nomads, living in desert areas of the Middle East.

Abel's sacrifice
Here, Abel has built an altar to burn his offerings to God. Later in the Bible, it becomes an offence against God if anyone other than a priest builds an altar.

grew more and more jealous of his younger brother until wickedness swallowed him, and he began to dream up plots to get Abel out of the way. One day, Cain asked his brother to go out into the fields with him. Cain found himself alone with Abel, and seizing the opportunity, he attacked his brother by surprise and killed him.

Cain was sure that no one had seen what he had done, but he was wrong. God sees everything that happens everywhere. God called to him and asked, "Cain, where is your brother, Abel?"

Cain's reply was sullen and sarcastic. "I don't know," he lied, brazenly, "I'm not my brother's keeper!"

Then the Lord accused him of his crime. "Cain! What have you done?" God was furious. "I can hear your brother's blood crying out to me from the soil where you spilled it! The very earth itself is condemning you for this terrible deed, and it will no longer grow things for you. Instead of farming your land, you must now be homeless. Go away, out of my sight, and spend the rest of your life wandering from place to place!"

Cain was devastated. "Lord! This is more than I can bear," he wept. "You, my God, are cursing me and no longer want anything to do with me. I am being sent away from the land I know and cast out among strangers. I might well die!"

"If anyone kills you," commanded the Lord, "they shall face an even more terrible punishment." He put a mark on Cain's forehead so that anyone he came across would recognize him and know to leave him alone. Then Cain was banished eastwards to a faraway place called Nod, which lay at the very edge of the world.

> *And when they were in the field Cain rose up against his brother Abel, and killed him.*

⊶ ABOUT THE STORY ⊷

This story contains the first mention of sin. Cain is given a chance to lead a good life, but he lets jealousy get the better of him. Instead of behaving as a loving brother should, he commits a terrible crime. When God punishes him, he protests and is unrepentant. God sends him away, having first put a mark upon him. The mark serves both to protect Cain from enemies, and to remind him always of his sin.

Why did God reject Cain's offering?
In this story, no explanation is given as to why God accepts Abel's offering and rejects Cain's. However, elsewhere in the Bible, God tells Moses that all first-born animals must be sacrificed to Him (Exodus 13:2) and that the first fruits of a harvest must be offered to Him (Leviticus 23:10). The events in this story suggest that Abel was careful to make the correct offering but that Cain was not.

Noah and the Flood

IN the early days of the world, people lived much longer than they do now. Adam reached the age of 930 years old! He and Eve had many hundreds of children between them, all of whom lived for 800 years or more and who had many hundreds of children of their own. Over the centuries, each family grew. . . and grew. . . and grew. . . until men and women were everywhere throughout the world. But wickedness spread with them all over the Earth.

God watched as, one by one, people forgot about Him. He saw that they went about their own business, with no thought for anyone else, and that they carried only evil in their hearts. How it pained Him to look on the beautiful

world He had made and see that it had turned so bad! God regretted having given people life. They had spoiled everything He had so lovingly created. Very sadly, God came to a fearful decision. "I will wipe out the human race and get rid of all living creatures from the face of the Earth," He thought, " – except for Noah."

> 66 *The Lord saw that the wickedness of man was great in the Earth.* 99

Out of all the millions of men and women, Noah was the very last good man on the Earth – the only person who tried to live his life as God wished. Because of this, the Lord loved Noah and wanted to spare him and his family. "The world is full of evil and I am going to destroy all the people and creatures in it," God told Noah. "I am going to drown every living thing apart from you, your wife, your three sons Shem, Ham and Japheth, and their wives. Do as I tell you and you will be saved. I want you to build a huge ship out of gopher wood, 300 cubits long, 50 cubits wide and 30 cubits high and make it watertight. Shape it into an ark by covering it with a roof, put a door in the side, and give it three decks with lots of separate compartments. When the time comes, load up a male and female of every animal and bird, take plenty of food for yourselves and all the creatures, and I will shut the door."

Noah did exactly as God had told him, ignoring the people who laughed at such a seemingly ridiculous task. Then the Lord locked them all safely away. For a week they

---

❧ ABOUT THE STORY ❧

As time goes by, people begin to forget about God. They are no longer grateful to Him for the beautiful world He has created for them. God decides He has to destroy them all, except for Noah. Noah is the only man who lives a good life and respects God, so he is spared. God separates Noah and his family from the rest of the people by shutting them safely inside an ark. Everyone outside perishes in the flood.

Flood stories
There are stories of great floods in many cultures all over the world. In a Babylonian tale called *The Epic of Gilgamesh* the gods are angry because noisy people are keeping them awake, so they plan a great flood. They instruct Gilgamesh's ancestor to build a boat and take his family and animals on board. Like Noah, only those inside the ark survive.
This 8th century Assyrian carving shows Gilgamesh with a lion.

Ship building
Noah and his sons would have built the ark using three layers of logs laid over each other, all coated with a sticky liquid called bitumen to make it watertight.

watched black storm clouds gather, blotting out the skies and sending dark shadows which covered the Earth. And after the seventh day, it began to rain.

> *All the fountains of the great deep burst forth, and the windows of the heavens were opened.*

It was as if fountains had burst up from the depths of the sea, while at the same time waterfalls poured down from heaven. Ponds at once became lakes; trickling streams gushed into raging torrents; swollen rivers burst their banks, swamping towns then submerging cities – and still the rain came down. People, animals and birds all fled together, higher and higher into the hills, desperately trying to find dry land on which to rest. But the waters caught them, waves tossed them, and swirling currents sucked them down. As the oceans rose, giant tidal waves crashed across whole countries, sweeping away every living thing until the Earth became a silent, underwater world. And still the rain came down. Day after day it fell, thundering down on top of the Ark. Day after long day all that Noah and his family could hear was the rain. All that they ever saw were the dark clouds and the steadily rising waters. Eventually, only the mountain tops were visible, and soon even they were hidden in the deeps.

Then there was nothing to be seen from the windows of the ark except water in every direction, stretching away as far as the eye could see, until it met the sky.

Noah's ark
The word 'ark' means 'box' or 'chest' in Hebrew. It is used here to represent a safe place provided by God. This detail from a wall painting in Saint-Savin Abbey in France shows the different decks of the ark. Noah's family and the animals are safe inside.

The Epic of Gilgamesh myth is very similar to the story of Noah. As both could be drawn from memories of an actual event in the same general area, this is not at all surprising.

Wood from the trees
The Bible says that the ark is made out of gopher wood. It is not known exactly from which tree this came. This is because people studying the original texts cannot agree on how the wood named in the Bible should be translated, but it is believed it could be the cypress tree, like this one. Whichever wood was used, a huge amount was needed to make a boat the size of Noah's ark.

God's Covenant to Noah

FOR 40 days and 40 nights, it kept raining. But just when Noah and his family thought it would go on forever, it stopped. Trapped inside the ark, the people and animals fell silent and listened. The constant hammering of rain on the roof had died away.

The ark drifted helplessly on the ocean. Then they heard the noise of a great wind blowing up. It howled and wailed, gusting around the ark as God began to dry up the waters. For five months the seas very slowly sank back, until one day everyone inside the ark felt a jolt. The bottom of the ship had scraped against dry land. The ark finally grated to a halt. "At last!" thought Noah, and he peeped excitedly out of the window. But still there was nothing to see except water all around. It was many more days before he saw land. Suddenly Noah realized that the craggy points were mountains! And the ark had come to settle at the top of the very highest, Mount Ararat. But he didn't dare to open the door.

Weeks went by and everyone grew more and more impatient to leave the ark. But was it safe yet? Exactly how much land was out there? He took one of the ravens they had brought with them and released it. It flew up into the clear sky, enjoying its new freedom, but it did not return, and Noah feared it had not found land.

Noah waited until everyone could bear it no longer, and then he sent out a dove. Later the same day, it came flying wearily back to the ark. Their faces fell. The dove had not found anywhere to settle. Noah reached out his hand and gently drew the bird back into the safety of the ark.

THE DOVE HAS BECOME A SYMBOL OF PEACE THROUGHOUT THE WORLD. THIS IS WHY PEOPE RELEASE DOVES INTO THE AIR AT INTERNATIONAL EVENTS, SUCH AS THE START OF THE OLYMPIC GAMES. ❧

Forty days and nights
This picture shows the return of the dove. The Bible says the rains lasted 40 days and nights. Some take this literally, but some now feel that the writer just meant 'a long time.'

❧ ABOUT THE STORY ❧

By sending the flood, God took the world back to the state of chaos it was in before the Creation. When the water subsides, there is a new beginning. Noah gives thanks to God and sacrifices some of the animals to Him. God blesses Noah and promises that He will never again destroy people in another such flood. This promise is often called God's Covenant to Noah.

Another seven days passed with everyone in the ark. Then Noah again released the dove. All day long they watched the skies. As evening drew in, they caught sight of a tiny speck approaching. Closer and closer flapped the bird, until everyone could see it carried a green olive leaf in its beak. How they celebrated!

But Noah still did not let anyone go outside. He waited for another week and then set the dove free once more. This time the bird did not come back. Noah opened the door and peered into the distance. Dry ground lay wherever he looked and he heard God calling. "Noah, it's time for you and your family to leave the ark. Let all the animals go and leave them to run free across the earth."

Noah did just as he was told. After all the days of darkness on the water, everyone was so glad to feel solid ground under their feet. He built an altar and offered thanks to God. And in turn God blessed Noah, his sons and their wives, telling them to live happily together.

> 66 *'I establish my covenant with you, that never again shall all flesh be cut off by a flood.'* 99

"I shall never again wreak such a terrible destruction on my people and creatures - no matter how wicked the world becomes," said the Lord. "To show I will keep my word, I will set a sign in the sky. Whenever you see a band of bright colours break through the clouds, you will know that I remain true to what I have said." And God put the rainbow in the sky, to remind everyone of His promise.

Mount Ararat
This map shows one of the possible locations of Mount Ararat, near the Black Sea in what is today the country of Armenia. No one can be sure exactly where Mount Ararat is. The Bible says that 'the ark came to rest on the mountains of Ararat'. We do not know whether the Bible means on Mount Ararat itself, or in that area. People have been looking for the remains of the ark for a long time. It caused great excitement when an archaelogist claimed to have found wooden remains in Lake Kop, actually on Mount Ararat, but no one has yet been able to prove whether this is Noah's ark or not.

Tower of Babel

NOAH died at the age of 950 years old, 350 years after the flood. He lived long enough to see the birth of several generations of his family and watch them spread out into different countries all over the world.

Over time, some of Noah's thousands of descendants travelled far to the east and settled on a plain in the land of Shinar. After the families had travelled for so long, facing many hardships and dangers on the way, they were anxious to establish a proper home for themselves. They were fed up with tents and moving from place to place. Individual houses would not do; they were too easy for enemies to attack. Now that they had come so far, they weren't about to risk the chance of having to flee from their homes. Instead, the men and women decided to build a whole city where they would be protected. They could then live, work and bring up their children in comfort and safety. "And besides," they said to each other, "if we build our own city, we won't just have a wonderful home, everyone will think we're really important, too." "Yes, people are sure to come from all around to see it," they gossiped, "and won't they be jealous!"

Everyone set about the massive task of making enough bricks to build, not only the city walls, but also all the houses, shops and streets. Day after day, month after month, they baked mud into hard blocks and used tar to cement them together. Gradually, the city took shape.

Because it was all going so well, the men and women began to get carried away with their achievements. They grew proud and suggested ever grander schemes.

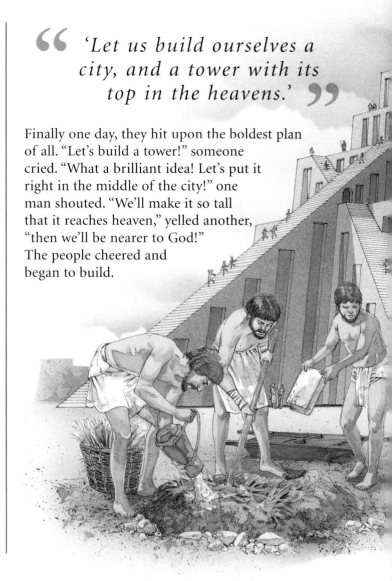

> ❝ *'Let us build ourselves a city, and a tower with its top in the heavens.'* ❞

Finally one day, they hit upon the boldest plan of all. "Let's build a tower!" someone cried. "What a brilliant idea! Let's put it right in the middle of the city!" one man shouted. "We'll make it so tall that it reaches heaven," yelled another, "then we'll be nearer to God!" The people cheered and began to build.

Building the Tower of Babel
This picture shows a 17th century artist's view of how the tower would have looked in Biblical times. It shows what it would have been like building the tower in the 17th century. Here the tower is being built out of stone, when at the time the story takes place it would actually have been made of mud bricks.

The Tower of Babel
The Tower of Babel is most likely to have been a ziggurat, constructed by people in this area and also in South America as religious buildings. Remains of ziggurats have been found not only at Babel, but also Ur, Nippur, and several other places in this area.

Brick by brick, higher and higher, upwards and ever upwards, the tower rose towards the sky. Several times, the workers thought they had built it tall enough and came down to admire it. But as they stood back, craning their necks in an effort to see the top, they were always dissatisfied. "We can build higher than that," one would scoff. "Yes, I bet we could make it a little taller still," another would encourage. "I suppose the higher it is, the more everyone will admire us," another would sigh. And they'd start work all over again.

When God looked down and saw what the people were doing, He was very worried. "They are becoming so vain!" He said to Himself. "They are accomplishing a great deal, but they don't know when to stop. Soon there will be no limit to what they want. I have to do something to halt them. They could get themselves and others into terrible trouble with their foolish desires."

With one stroke, God shattered the people's over-confidence. He changed the words coming out of their mouths so that no one could communicate. Everyone found themselves listening to their friends speaking nonsense, while they each spoke a gibberish that no one else could understand. To add to everyone's annoyance, no building could be done. It was impossible for the architects to give instructions, the builders couldn't call to their workmates, and they were forced to down tools.

Eventually, the people gave up trying to talk to each other in frustration. They drifted away from the unfinished city and went off on their own to new places. And from that time onwards, people in different parts of the world have spoken different languages.

❧ ABOUT THE STORY ❧

This story shows that pride comes before a fall – God is not happy with the way the people are acting, so he changes the words they speak. This is how the Bible explains why people in different places speak different languages. This is linked to the word 'babble' which means to talk in a way that is hard to understand. We can see the link because, after God changed their words, the people could not understand each other.

Medieval scene
This detail from a medieval painting shows the building of the Tower of Babel. The men on the right are passing stones to the masons who are standing on the top of the tower, gradually adding the layers of bricks to build the tower as high as they can.

God's Promise to Abram

ONE of the descendants of Noah's son Shem was a man called Abram. Abram had grown up in Ur in Mesopotamia and married a woman called Sarai, before moving to the city of Haran with his elderly father, Terah, and his nephew, Lot. Not long after they had set up home Terah died, leaving Abram and Lot to build their lives alone.

The men worked hard, raising large numbers of sheep and cattle, and they became wealthy. Their houses were filled with beautiful possessions. They had servants to wait on them and friends for company. But Abram and Sarai did not have the one thing they wanted most – a child.

> ❝ *'Go to the land that I will show you and I will make you a great nation.'* ❞

Nevertheless, Abram and Lot were settled, and had no plans to move elsewhere. But one day, God spoke to Abram. "Abram, I want you to leave this place and everyone you know. Take your family, your servants, and all you own, and go where I tell you. Do as I say and you will be blessed. I will make you known as a great man, and your family will become a great people." So Abram instructed his household to pack up everything, told Lot to do the same, and they all wandered into the wilderness.

For many months the people lived in tents, moving their animals wherever the grazing seemed good. God guided them just as He had said, and brought them eventually to the country of Canaan. "Look at this land," the Lord commanded Abram. "One

day, all this will belong to your descendants." Abram built an altar and gave thanks to God. How relieved everyone was to stop travelling! The tents went up and the animals were put out to grass. At last God had shown them the place that was to be their new home.

But it wasn't long before trouble arose. Abram and Lot had so many animals that their herdsmen found the grazing areas were overcrowded. They started to quarrel over the pasture. No matter how Abram and Lot tried to solve things, there just didn't seem to be enough nearby pasture. "There's nothing for it. We'll have to split up," decided Abram. "There's ample land here for us both if we spread out. But which way will you go?"

Lot looked around him. His eyes fell on the Jordan valley, looking like the Garden of Eden. "I'll go east," he said.

It was strange after Lot and his household had gone. In the quietness, Abram again heard God calling him. "Lift up your eyes, Abram, and look all around you in every direction. All the land you see will be owned by your family forever, and you will have as many descendants as there are specks of dust on the face of the Earth. Go out and explore the countryside. I am giving it all to you."

In the days that followed, Abram grew more and more bothered about what the Lord had said. He and Sarai were still childless, and rapidly getting too old to start a family. How could God's words come true? The Lord told Abram to look up at the sky. "Do you see how many stars there are?" He asked. "Too many to count - just as it will be with your descendants. Bring me some animals and birds for sacrifice and I will show you that I mean what I say."

The following day, Abram killed some creatures for sacrifice. He cut the animals into two and placed the halves opposite each other, together with the birds, as was the custom. Then he kept watch over the offering and waited to see what would happen. As the Sun set, Abram fell into a deep sleep. He dreamt he was alone and he was terrified. Then he heard the voice of God, saying, "For 400 years your descendants will be slaves in a strange land. But

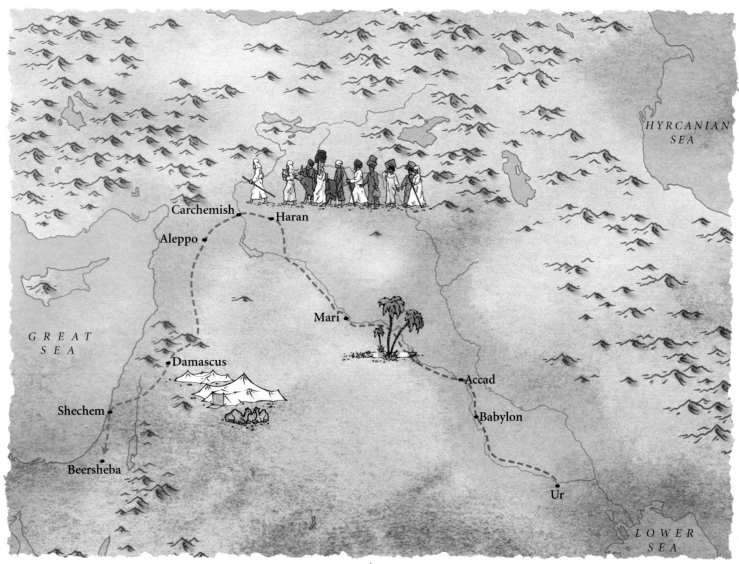

I will punish their captors and they will escape, returning to your promised land. You yourself will live for many years and will die in peace." In the pitch black of the night, Abram saw a blazing torch and a flaming fire pot pass between the sacrificed animals, and he knew that God had made a promise with him that could not be broken.

The Journey of Abram
Abram's journey started in Ur with his father, Terah. Their whole family moved to Haran, hundreds of miles to the north. Then God told Abram to move, so he set out from Haran without knowing where he was going to stop. God guided Abram to Beersheba, in Canaan. Here Abram settled, in the land that the Israelites would return to claim centuries later.

Sacrifices
The picture here shows a procession of people carrying animals to be sacrificed. In ancient times, the practice of sacrificing animals to God was commonplace. Sometimes this was done to honour God, or give thanks. At other times, it was to make amends for some wrong-doing.

⊷ **ABOUT THE STORY** ⊷

God tells Abram that his descendants will become a great people and that the land of Canaan will belong to them. Abram is unsure as he has no children, but he sees a sign from God, he hears God's voice and no longer has any doubts.

Promise of a Son

AFTER God had made His covenant with Abram, he and his wife couldn't wait for the time when they would have a child. But the days passed into months, the months turned into years, the years stretched into decades, and there was no sign that Sarai would have a baby. As the couple grew older, their hope turned into impatience and frustration. "Take my maid Hagar as a second wife," Sarai told Abram, at her wits' end. "God might let her have children for you."

As soon as Hagar realized that she was pregnant, she began to put on airs and graces and look down on Sarai. "I have succeeded where you failed," she told her former mistress, "so I must be better than you." She started to order Sarai about, becoming more and more rude to her, until one day Sarai had had enough. She punished Hagar so severely that she ran into the desert.

An angel found Hagar weeping by a spring. "What are you doing here?" he asked. "God wants you to return to your mistress and behave yourself better. You will soon give birth to Abram's son and he will grow up to be a mighty ruler. The Lord wants you to call him Ishmael." And Hagar did just as the angel told her.

Years went by and Abram turned 99 years old. Just as he and Sarai had given up hope of ever having children together, the Lord spoke to him once more. "I am God Almighty and I will keep my covenant to you. I tell you again, your descendants will be kings who will rule over Canaan. I want you to change your name to Abraham, and I want Sarai to become Sarah."

> ❝ *'Behold, you are with child, and shall bear a son; you shall call his name Ishmael.'* ❞

"How can a child be born to a man who is nearly 100 years old and a woman who is 90?" the cowering Abraham protested. "And what about my son, Ishmael?"

❧ ABOUT THE STORY ❧

Because of his faith, Abraham is prepared to wait patiently until God gives him the child He promised. Sarah, on the other hand, grows more desperate the older she gets. Unable to wait any longer and doubtful as to whether God will ever fulfil His promise, she suggests that Abraham has a child with Hagar. But Ishmael is not the son God promised to Abraham, and Sarah is not happy until she has a son of her own.

Old oak tree
People used to like sitting under oak trees because of the shade of its leaves. Big oak trees standing alone were also often used as landmarks for travellers.

Annunciation
When the angel appeared to Hagar in the desert, this was an annunciation. The word 'annunciation' means proclamation, or announcement.

God thundered, "Ishmael will be the leader of a great nation. But this time next year, Sarah will have a son of her own, whom you must call Isaac."

Some weeks later, Abraham was sitting and wondering about the Lord's words, when he saw three strangers approaching. Abraham knew they were messengers from God and he rushed to his nearby tent for food and drink while the men cooled off under a broad oak tree.

"God will visit you next spring and Sarah will have a son," the men told Abraham, as they refreshed themselves. Abraham didn't realize that Sarah was listening at the tent door and could hear everything. "How can we have a baby now?" she scoffed out loud. "We're both far too old!"

"Nothing is too difficult for the Lord," the strangers insisted, and they went on their way, leaving the couple quite bewildered.

At last the time came when God fulfilled His vow. On a beautiful spring day Sarah gave birth to a son whom they called Isaac – all just as the Lord had said.

"God has made me so happy!" sang Sarah. "No one who hears of this can fail to be happy too!"

But despite the celebrations, Abraham was saddened. Now Sarah had had a child of her own, she wanted to get rid of Ishmael and his mother. Abraham loved each of the boys and hated the thought of losing Ishmael. God reassured him. "Don't worry, do as Sarah says," He told Abraham. "I will make both of your sons the founders of great peoples."

The next morning, before anyone else was awake, Abraham said a last and sad goodbye to Hagar and Ishmael and sent them off into the desert. They walked and walked through the heat and the dust until they were exhausted, and the supplies of food and water that they had brought with them were all gone. There was no sign of life in any direction and Hagar knew that they were going to die. She couldn't bear to watch Ishmael suffer, so she laid him down under a shady bush and wandered a little way off before collapsing with grief. But God heard Hagar weeping and He sent an angel to comfort her. "Have no fear," said the angel. "Ishmael will not die. God has promised that he will grow to be a great man. Now go and take care of him." Summoning all her remaining strength, Hagar picked herself up. To her surprise, she saw a spring a little way off and she dashed to get water to revive her son. Hagar and her son lived together in the wilderness for a long time and Ishmael grew up to be a brave warrior, the father of all the Arab peoples.

Living in tents
Today, some people live a nomadic lifestyle in the deserts of the Middle East, as Abraham did. They keep herds of animals and follow them around wherever there is good grazing. Abraham, though, was used to living in one place, so would not have been as used to this life as these Bedouin people.

Banished!
This shows Abraham banishing Hagar and Ishmael. Abraham does not want to lose Ishmael, and wishes that God would recognize both his sons. Abraham always accepts God's will, but his love for Ishmael causes him to question God on this occasion.

Arabs
Abraham's first son, Ishmael, grew up to be a great warrior. While Isaac was the father of the Israelite nation, Ishmael grew up to become the ancestor of all the Arab people.

Abraham and Isaac

AFTER the many years of waiting, Abraham and Sarah's happiness was complete. Isaac grew to be a lively, strong little boy. As his parents watched him run errands and play in the fields with the other children, it was hard for them to believe that their son was a part of the Lord's great plan.

Then one day, Abraham heard God calling him once again. "Abraham! Take your only son, Isaac – who I know you love dearly – and go to a mountain I will show you. There, I want you to offer him to me as a sacrifice."

Abraham was truly horrified. How could God be asking him to kill his own son? The Lord knew how long

Abraham and Sarah had been desperate for children, and how precious their son Isaac was! What could Abraham say to Sarah? And how on earth could he tell Isaac?

Abraham mentioned nothing to his family of God's terrible request. The next morning, he rose early and took his son and two servants to cut firewood, which they loaded on to a donkey. The awful secret Abraham carried was far heavier. They set off across the countryside, Abraham hanging his head in misery. After three days, Abraham knew they had reached God's chosen place.

⌁ ABOUT THE STORY ⌁

Although Abraham is horrified at the idea of killing his son, he puts his faith in God and obeys Him. He follows God's instructions until the point where he is about to make the sacrifice. When God is certain that Abraham's faith is strong, He spares the boy and repeats His promise, that Abraham's descendants will become a great people. By proving that he puts God above all, Abraham has passed the test God set for him.

Climbing the mountain
God would not usually ask anyone to make a child sacrifice. It seems clear, though, that God never actually intended Abraham to sacrifice his son.

Dome of the Rock
The Bible describes the sacrifice as taking place on a mountain in the land of Moriah. This is believed to be the hill in Jerusalem where King Solomon later built his magnificent temple. Later still, in the 7th century AD, the Muslims conquered Jerusalem and built a mosque where the temple had stood. This mosque, called the Dome of the Rock, still stands today.

"Stay here with the donkey and wait for us," he told the servants. "Isaac and I are going to go and make an offering to God." Then Abraham and Isaac began to climb the steep hillside.

After a while, Isaac grew a little puzzled. "Father," he asked. "I'm carrying the wood, you have a knife and some fire, but where is the lamb we're going to offer?"

Abraham tried hard to keep his voice steady. "My son," he replied with great anguish, "God will provide Himself with a lamb."

Side by side, the two went on until they reached the spot for the sacrifice. They gathered stones and built an altar. Then, Abraham arranged the firewood. The time had come. Tenderly, Abraham bound Isaac and lifted him on to the sacrificial pile. He stretched out his hand for the knife. Overcome by grief, Abraham steeled himself to obey God. He raised the blade up over the terrified boy.

All at once he heard someone calling his name. "Abraham! Abraham!"

Abraham stopped still. Slowly, he lowered the knife and listened. Then he fell to his knees. It was the voice of the Angel of the Lord.

"Here I am," Abraham replied.

"Abraham!" called the Angel of the Lord. "Do not harm the boy! Since you would have given God your only son, He knows now that you are true to Him."

Abraham could hardly believe his ears. Slowly, he raised his eyes to look at the trembling, terrified boy tied to the altar. His son had been spared! There was some movement in a thicket and Abraham caught sight of a ram, snared in the brambles and struggling to break free. Weeping with

> **'Because you have not withheld your son I will multiply your descendants'**

joy, Abraham lifted Isaac down from the firewood. He took the animal and offered it in Isaac's place, giving great thanks to God. And the Angel of the Lord called to Abraham for a second time from Heaven. "Abraham, the Lord says that because you have obeyed Him, both you and your son shall be blessed. You will have as many descendants as there are stars in the sky, as many descendants as there are grains of sand on the seashore, and they shall become a great people."

Abraham and Isaac
God knew where he planned to put Abraham's faith to the test, but it was not near Abraham's house. It took Abraham and Isaac three days to make the journey from their home in Beersheba to Mount Moriah, at the other end of the Salt Sea. It must have been a terrible journey for Abraham, giving him a long time to reflect on what he knew God had asked him to do. Even after this gruelling journey, Abraham was still faithful to God, and would have sacrificed his only son had God demanded it.

Isaac and Rebekah

THE years passed and Abraham outlived Sarah, reaching an extremely old age, just as God had told him he would. The most important thing to the elderly man was seeing their son, Isaac, settled with a wife before he died. Abraham had to be sure that Isaac would carry on the family, so God's promise that his descendants would become a great nation could be fulfilled. He called his most trusted servant to him and said, "Go back to my country of Mesopotamia, where I grew up all those years ago. Find Isaac a good woman from my own family to be his wife." Honoured to be entrusted with such an important task, the servant loaded up ten camels with lots of expensive gifts of jewellery, perfume and silks and set off on the difficult trek across the desert.

Abraham's servant was tired and dusty when he eventually reached the city of Nahor and he made straight for the waterhole. Dusk was falling and the women were coming to draw their water for the night. "Maybe I'll find one among them fit to be Isaac's wife," the servant thought to himself. "Oh God," he prayed silently, "please help me pick the right girl. Show me which one I should choose and give me a sign so that I can be sure. I'll ask the girl to give me a drink from her water jug, and if she says yes and offers to fetch me some water for the camels too, I'll know she's the one Isaac should marry."

> **❝** *Before he had done speaking, behold Rebekah came out with her water jar upon her shoulder.* **❞**

While Abraham's servant was still deep in prayer, a beautiful young girl made her way up to the well. She lowered her jug down into the depths and drew it up again, heavy with water. There was something about the girl that caught the servant's attention. "But surely the very first young woman couldn't be the one?" he wondered. Hurrying up to her, he asked, "May I have a little of your water to drink?"

"Of course," she answered with a smile, and poured him some straight away. She watched as the servant refreshed himself and then laughed, "Your camels look as if they could do with a drink, too." She went off to water the thirsty animals. Abraham's servant was so surprised that he nearly forgot why he was there. Luckily, he remembered in time and rushed to offer her some of the gold jewellery he had brought as presents.

He asked the girl who she was, and could hardly believe it when the girl replied, "I am Rebekah, daughter of Bethuel." Bethuel was Abraham's nephew! He thanked God for guiding him straight to his master's relatives.

The servant accompanied Rebekah back home and her brother, Laban, hurried to make his guest welcome, stabling the camels and setting out a feast. But the servant couldn't bring himself to eat anything until he knew whether or not Rebekah would agree to be Isaac's wife. After he'd explained everything, Laban and Bethuel, Rebekah's father, agreed it could only be God's work. "We must do as He wishes," they told Abraham's servant, "Rebekah shall go with you to marry Isaac." Before the celebrations began, the servant shared out Abraham's presents: more gold and silver jewellery for Rebekah, together with richly embroidered materials; valuable trinkets and ornaments for the rest of the family. They feasted until late into the night and the following morning, Rebekah left for the long trip to her new home.

It was late one evening when Isaac looked up and saw the tiny shapes of camels approaching in the distance. Suddenly nervous and not knowing quite what to expect, he slowly began to walk out to meet them.

"Who's that?" Rebekah asked the servant, as she caught sight of the broad-shouldered young man walking hesitantly towards them.

"He's your husband," came the reply, to Rebekah's delight. Abraham's servant explained to Isaac everything that had happened, how God had made sure that Isaac and Rebekah would be together, and Isaac welcomed Rebekah as his wife with love in his heart.

The Tribes of Israel

Isaac's grandsons were to become the fathers of the twelve tribes of Israel. When the Israelites reached the promised land, each tribe was promised an area that they could call their own, but they could only claim the areas that were allotted to them once they had defeated the people that were already there. The Israelite tribe of Dan, in the north, originally lived around the city of Beth-dagon, but they could not defeat the Philistines and force them to leave, so they had to move to a new area.

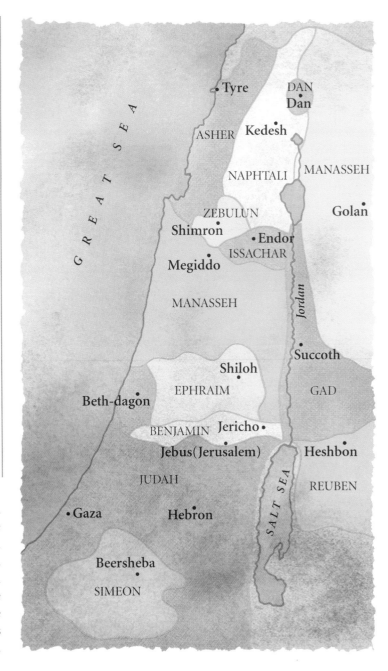

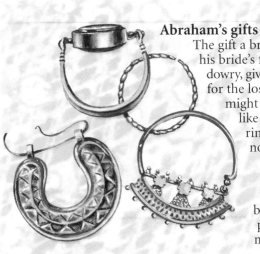

Abraham's gifts
The gift a bridegroom gives to his bride's family is called a dowry, given as compensation for the loss of a daughter. It might include jewellery like this, necklaces, rings, earrings and nose rings.

Water carrier
Rebekah may have been carrying a water pot like this when she met Abraham's servant.

❧ ABOUT THE STORY ❧

It is important that Isaac marries, so he can have children and fulfil God's promise. Abraham's servant prays to God to help him find the right girl. Rebekah appears, as if in answer to his prayer. Rebekah's family agree to the wedding, knowing it to be God's will.

Jacob and Esau

GOD blessed Isaac and Rebekah with twins. But when the babies were born, it was strange to see that they looked nothing like each other. Esau, the elder, was covered with red hair, and Jacob, the younger, was smooth-skinned. The parents loved both children, but as time went by and the boys grew up, each secretly grew to have a favourite. Isaac became particularly fond of Esau, because he proved to be good at hunting and Isaac's favourite meal was venison. Rebekah, though, grew to love Jacob best,

> **Then Jacob gave Esau bread and pottage of lentils and he ate and drank. Thus Esau despised his birthright.**

because he didn't like running about outdoors and preferred to stay quietly at home with her.

Because of their different characters, Esau and Jacob were often to be found arguing - especially over Esau's birthright. Even though Esau was only minutes older than Jacob, as the first-born, he was the heir to all Isaac's riches and would become head of the family when their aging father died. But one day, Jacob saw an opportunity to seize the precious birthright for himself. He was cooking some lentil soup when Esau returned home from a long hunting trip, faint with hunger. "Give me some of that, I'm famished!" his brother demanded.

Jacob was angry at his rudeness. "I'll swap you some soup for your birthright," he bargained.

Esau didn't even think about what he was doing. "All right. It won't be any good to me if I've died of starvation," he snapped, tormented by the good smell.

"Swear you mean it," said Jacob solemnly, holding the steaming bowl just out of Esau's reach.

"I swear on my life that I give you my birthright!" yelled Esau. "Now hand me the soup before I collapse!" In a few gulps, it was all gone.

Years went by and Isaac became old and blind. He knew that he didn't have long to live and he called Esau to him. "My best son," he said, tenderly. "Go and hunt a deer so I may taste the venison you cook for me just one more time. Hurry, so I can give you my blessing before I die."

But Rebekah had overheard. She was well aware that if a man on his deathbed blessed or cursed someone, it sealed their future either good or bad. She was determined that Isaac should bless Jacob instead of Esau, and dashed off to

Wild goats
Esau would have hunted animals such as the ibex, a type of wild goat. Ibexes are still found in rocky areas of the Middle East today. He would have used weapons similar to those that some hunters use today such as traps and nets, as well as a bow and arrows.

Old age
Isaac was already over a hundred when he blessed the wrong one of his sons, but he lived on until the age of 180. Many people in the Bible lived to extraordinary ages, for example Abraham lived to 175, Adam to 930 and Noah to 950. The oldest man in the Bible is Noah's grandfather, Methuselah, who lived until he was 969. Old people were held in great respect for their experience and wisdom.

The birthright
A father's special blessing to his oldest son, normally just before he died, was called the birthright. It gave the son leadership over his brothers, but it also placed on him the responsibility of taking care of the family after his father's death. While it most often went to the eldest son, a father could choose to give it to a younger son, or to someone else. A birthright could be sold, or given away before it was passed on by the blessing, but once the special blessing had been given, it could not be taken back. This is why fathers usually waited until they thought they were soon to die before passing on the birthright.
Esau would have known how important the birthright was, and the fact that he gave it away so easily shows that he did not deserve to receive his father's blessing.

clothes, covered his hands, face and neck with the hairy goat skins, and sent him in to see Isaac.

"Father, it's me, Esau," lied Jacob.

Isaac was surprised. "That was quick!" he said.

"God helped me in my hunting," Jacob replied. Isaac was suspicious, but feeling Jacob's hairy skin reassured him. He ate the food, kissed his son, and blessed him with every good wish. "God will make you rich and prosperous, a ruler of great men, and master over this family. May God reward everyone who blesses you and curse everyone who wishes you bad luck!"

Scarcely minutes after Jacob had left, Esau arrived. "Here we are, father," he said. "Enjoy the delicious meal I have brought you and then you can bless me."

Isaac began to tremble. "Who are you?" he asked.

"Don't you recognize your first-born son?" Esau laughed. "It's me, Esau."

Isaac was pierced with anguish. "But I've already blessed somebody else and I can't take it back!"

Esau was devastated. "Father, bless me too!" he begged.

"I can't, my son," the grief-stricken Isaac told him. "I've blessed your brother with everything. He will become rich, a ruler of men and master of the family."

The tears streamed down Esau's face and Isaac blessed him as best he could. "Your life will be difficult, but you will become a great warrior and a great leader, and you will break away from your brother's control."

From that day on, Esau hated Jacob bitterly and plotted how he might kill him. But just in time, Rebekah sent Jacob away to live with her brother in Haran, so he would be safe from harm.

find him. "Be quick," she instructed Jacob. "Go and get two young goats so I can cook them up into a tasty meal for you to take to your father. He'll think you're Esau and will give you his final blessing."

"But Esau is much more hairy than me," Jacob objected. "If father realizes that I'm trying to trick him, he will probably curse me instead of blessing me."

"Leave that to me," Rebekah replied, so Jacob did what he was told. Then his mother dressed him in Esau's best

❧ ABOUT THE STORY ❧

Part of the birthright Isaac will pass down to his son is God's promise to Abraham, that his descendants will be a great people and that the land of Canaan will one day be theirs.

Although Jacob deceives his father in order to receive the birthright, the blessing is still valid. Rebekah suffers for her role in the deception because her favourite son is forced to run away from home.

The Journey of Jacob
Jacob's journey from Beersheba to his mother's family in Haran is a long one. On the way to meet Laban, Jacob saw his vision of the angels travelling up and down a stairway to heaven. He renamed the place at which he saw this vision Bethel, which means 'house of God'. When he returns after 20 years away, he meets his brother Esau by the river Jabbok, at a place called Penuel.

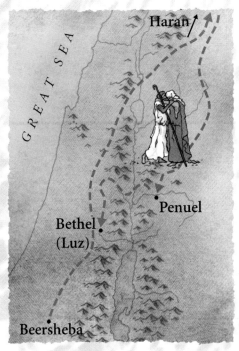

Jacob's Ladder

JACOB'S path to safety lay across the desert. The journey was so tough that at times he'd wonder if it wouldn't have been better to stay and face Esau's anger. By day he'd roast as the sun baked down, while at night he'd shiver out in the open under the stars. At least he didn't find it difficult to sleep – even though he had only rocks for pillows. At the end of each day, he'd gratefully collapse with exhaustion and fall asleep at once.

> *He dreamed that there was a ladder and the top of it reached to heaven.*

One night Jacob had a vivid dream that there was a huge staircase stretching all the way from the earth to heaven. Angels were going up and down between the two, and at the very top of the stairs stood God Himself. The Lord spoke to Jacob and repeated the promise He had made to Abraham. "Your descendants will become a great people," He said. "No matter where you go, I will keep you safe and bring you back home to this land."

As soon as Jacob woke, he took the large, flat stone that had been under his head and stood it upright in the ground to mark where he had been lying. He anointed it with oil in a sacred ritual and named the spot Bethel, or God's house. Then he prayed that God would keep His word and be with him on his journey, before continuing on his way.

Angels
The word 'angel' means messenger. In the Bible, angels are the messengers of God. They appear in front of people to tell them God's commands, or to inform them of something God wants them to know. The phrase 'the angel of the Lord' is used to describe how God came to people in human form, to give them a special message.

❧ ABOUT THE STORY ❧

While Jacob is dreaming, God appears to him, standing at the top of a huge staircase often called 'Jacob's ladder'. God repeats the promise He made to Abraham, which He renewed with Jacob's father Isaac – that Jacob's descendants will become a great people and will inherit the land of Canaan.
Jacob asks God to protect him on his journey across the desert and promises to serve Him if he does so.

Jacob and Rachel

As Jacob drew near to Haran, he came to a field where shepherds were watering their flocks at a well. He spoke to them, hoping they could give him directions, "My brothers, where do you come from?"

They said, "We are from Haran." Jacob knew that this was very close to where Laban lived.

"Do you know Laban of Nahor?" Jacob asked them.

"Yes, we know him well," they replied. One of the men pointed across the pasture at a shepherdess approaching with her sheep. "That's his daughter, Rachel," he said

Jacob waited patiently until his cousin had driven her flock up to the well. He watched as she began trying to roll away the heavy stone that covered the well mouth and leaped up to help. "I'm Jacob," he told her, to her great surprise. "I'm your Aunt Rebekah's son." And he greeted her properly with a kiss. With great excitement, Rachel ran off to tell her father that his nephew was here.

> " *Then Jacob kissed Rachel and wept aloud. And Jacob told Rachel that he was her father's kinsman.* "

Just as Laban had rushed to welcome Abraham's servant so many years before, he now hurried out to meet Abraham's grandson. Laban greeted Jacob as if he were his long-lost son and took him home, where Jacob explained everything to him.

Women in the Bible
Women in ancient times played an important part in daily life. Probably their most significant role was that of mother. A mother was honoured, feared and obeyed in her household. She was responsible for naming her children, and for their early education. They went to worship at religious gatherings and brought offerings for sacrifice. If there were no male heirs, a woman could inherit land and property from her parents.

As Abraham's servant had found his master's family, so Jacob immediately finds his mother's family and his future wife. God is always present, making sure that everything happens according to the way that God has planned it.

❧ ABOUT THE STORY ❧

This story tells of the beginning of Jacob's love for Rachel, one of the Bible's outstanding examples of human love. Rachel is described as a woman of great beauty and Jacob falls in love with her as soon as he lays eyes upon her. His love remains strong until the day Rachel dies. Rachel is important as her sons are the ancestors of three of the tribes of Israel: Benjamin, Ephraim and Manasseh.

The Wedding of Jacob

LABAN welcomed Jacob to live with him and the grateful young man tried to show his thanks by working in his uncle's fields, shepherding his flocks. After four weeks had gone by, Laban called Jacob to him. "It isn't fair that you should work for me for nothing," he said, generously. "What can I give you as payment?" Jacob didn't need to think about it. Over the past month he had fallen deeply in love with Rachel and wanted to marry her. Rachel was young and full of life, and her beauty made her elder sister, Leah, seem plain and dull in comparison.

> ❝ *'I will serve you seven years for your younger daughter Rachel.'* ❞

"I will work for you for nothing for seven years if you promise to let me marry Rachel," Jacob told his uncle. "I'd rather give her to you than anyone else," the delighted Laban replied. So Jacob remained working for his uncle and the seven years flew past as if they were only seven days. At last the wedding day arrived and Laban threw a great feast. He invited all his friends and neighbours from miles around and they celebrated well into the evening. Then Laban covered his daughter's face with her wedding veil and sent her to Jacob's tent.

Next morning, Jacob was horrified to find that it was Leah, not Rachel, who was lying by his side. He woke Laban in a fury. "You've tricked me into marrying the

Wearing a veil
Jacob could not tell which sister he was marrying because Leah's face was hidden by her veil. The tradition of brides wearing veils continues in many cultures today, though often the face is only partly covered. In some Middle Eastern countries the women wear veils all the time, not just at their weddings.

MOSES WOULD LATER FORBID A MAN FROM MARRYING HIS WIFE'S SISTER DURING HIS WIFE'S LIFETIME. THE TENSION BETWEEN JACOB AND HIS WIVES SHOWS THE WISDOM OF THE LAWS GOD GAVE TO MOSES ✎

Powerful plant
In ancient times, people believed that the root of the mandrake plant had the power to increase wealth and overcome infertility. Women who were unable to have children used to go in search of mandrakes. Although Jacob loved Rachel, it was Leah and the maids who gave him the children he wanted first.

wrong sister!" he yelled at the top of his voice. "I didn't work for you for seven years to have Leah for my wife!"

Quite calmly, his uncle replied, "In this country, it's not the done thing for the younger daughter to take a husband if her older sister is still single. Now that Leah is a married woman, I'm more than happy to give you Rachel too – in return for another seven years' work, of course. Also, you must wait until the week of Leah's wedding festivities is over before marrying her."

There was nothing Jacob could do and because he loved Rachel so much, he agreed to his uncle's demands. At the end of the week, he and Rachel were finally allowed to be together, and Jacob began seven years more work.

As soon as Jacob and Rachel were married, poor Leah found herself left out and ignored. God saw how rejected and miserable she felt and He took pity on her, blessing her with a baby boy. Leah went on to have three more of Jacob's sons while Rachel remained childless. "Jacob, I shall die if we can't have a baby!" she wept one day.

Her husband was just as frustrated. "What can I do about it? It's all up to God," Jacob yelled back.

"Then marry my maid, Bilhah," Rachel cried. "If she has children, they'll count as mine."

Bilhah gave birth to two sons. But, no matter how hard she tried, Rachel couldn't stop hoping for children of her own. God kept her waiting a long time before He granted her wish. Even after Leah's maid, Zilpah, bore Jacob two sons, and Leah herself had a further two boys and a daughter, Rachel remained childless. Finally, God took pity on her, and He sent Rachel a little boy. She was overjoyed and treasured her son, calling him Joseph.

Wine sets

At Jacob's wedding feast, wine would have been served with the food. Wealthy people had bronze wine sets made up of three pieces: a juglet to scoop the wine out of a storage jar, a strainer to filter out any impurities, and a shallow bowl to drink from.

> ❧ **ABOUT THE STORY** ❧
>
> *Jacob deceived his brother, Esau, out of his birthright. Now it is his turn to be deceived by his uncle. Although Jacob has already worked for Laban for seven years before the wedding, he is tricked into marrying the wrong sister, and forced to work another seven years in order to marry Rachel. Jacob has God's blessing, though, and he fathers twelve sons, who go on to be the forefathers of the twelve tribes of Israel.*

Jacob's Return

JACOB endured the further seven years' work he had agreed to do for Laban in return for Rachel's hand in marriage. But he planned to leave his cheating uncle as soon as the time was up. When that day arrived, Laban was horrified. "You're the only reason I've become so wealthy," he told Jacob. "God must truly be with you, because everything you turn your hand to is a success. What can I do to make you change your mind?" Jacob saw the chance to start building a flock of his own and told his uncle that he would only stay if Laban would let him have any sheep or goats that had spotted or black coats. Laban readily agreed, secretly thinking he would trick Jacob once again. He told his sons to sort out all the non-white animals and hide them in pastures far away. But God helped Jacob outwit his uncle. He blessed the remaining flocks so that some lambs and kids were born with spotted and black coats. Slowly, Jacob separated out a flock, and at the end of six years, he was a rich man.

As Laban and his sons grew more and more jealous at how well Jacob had done for himself, living with his uncle became increasingly unpleasant for Jacob. He prayed to God for guidance and decided that it would be best to return home. Jacob knew that Laban would be very angry at losing not only his daughters but also his best shepherd and would make it extremely difficult for him to leave. So he didn't tell his uncle he was going. He waited until sheep-shearing time, when Laban and his sons had to stay away in the fields, then he fled with his wives, children, servants, flocks and possessions.

When Laban found out, he dashed off in pursuit. After a week's hard riding, he caught up with Jacob and the two men had a bitter argument. Laban accused Jacob of stealing his daughters and his animals, while Jacob reminded Laban that he had deliberately deceived him more than once. No doubt things would have come to blows, but God had warned Laban in a dream not to harm Jacob in any way. Eventually, when neither man would apologize, they agreed to make up for the sake of Jacob's children, and they went their separate ways in peace.

Now Jacob's main worry was his brother. While he hoped that Esau had had a change of heart during the 20 years they had been separated, Jacob feared the worst. He remembered the deep hatred there had been between them, and Jacob suspected that Esau was still determined to kill him. In an effort to patch things up, Jacob sent messengers on ahead with gifts. But just in case his brother wasn't prepared to forgive him, Jacob split his household up into two groups. Then if Esau attacked the family group, Jacob could be sure that at least some of them stood a good chance of escaping.

Meeting place
When Jacob and Esau met again after 20 years the meeting took place where the river Jabbok flows into the river Jordan, above, to the north of the Dead Sea. Today, the Jabbok is known as the river Zerqa.

Sending gifts
It was common practice for two people to send gifts to each other before meeting. The gifts were usually related to the people's occupations, so Jacob, as a herdsman, sent livestock like sheep, goats and camels to Esau.

As they drew close to their journey's end Jacob became more and more troubled. One evening he took himself off to find a quiet place where he could think. Though Jacob was sure he was alone, a stranger appeared from out of the darkness and challenged him to wrestle. They struggled all night long, equally matched in strength and will, and neither grew any nearer to winning. When dawn began to break the two men broke apart, worn out. "What's your name?" asked the stranger.

"Jacob," came the weary reply.

"From now on you will be known as Israel," the stranger commanded, vanishing as suddenly as he had appeared. Jacob was left on his knees in awe. His new name meant 'he who has grappled with the Lord', and he realized he had been fighting with God Himself. After having cheated to become Isaac's heir and having been sent away from the land the Lord had especially chosen for Abraham, Jacob had proved his

> ❝ *So Jacob called the place Penuel, saying 'For I have seen God face to face.'* ❞

worth and God had blessed him with a new beginning.

Then Jacob went down to meet Esau, who had come with 400 men at the ready. Telling his family to stay back, Jacob nervously walked to his brother. Jacob left God to decide his fate and bowed down before his brother. To his complete amazement, Esau ran to meet him. "Welcome home!" he cried, throwing his arms around Jacob, and the brothers both wept with happiness.

Dreams from God
Dreams are used in the Bible as a means by which God can send messages to the sleeper. God's warning to Laban is an example of such a dream.

Jacob's prayer
Jacob prays to God that Esau will not harm him or his family, and trusts in God to keep them all safe.

❧ ABOUT THE STORY ❧

When Jacob is near Canaan, just before he is reunited with his brother, he wrestles with a stranger, who turns out to be God Himself. This is the culmination of a lifetime's struggle for Jacob. He is unlike Abraham and Isaac, in that his faith did not come easily to him. In the end, though, he has proved his worth and God blesses him with a new name and a new beginning.

Joseph and his Brothers

JACOB settled in the land of Canaan with his large family: his four wives had had many children between them. Just like his father, Isaac, Jacob had a favourite child – Joseph, the son of his beloved wife Rachel. When the boy reached 17 years old, Jacob gave him a special present: a beautiful long-sleeved coat, elaborately woven in many different colours and patterns. His 11 brothers knew that the expensive gift showed Jacob thought of Joseph as his heir – despite the fact that he wasn't the eldest – and they were extremely jealous. Their resentment and hatred grew when Joseph described two dreams he had had. "First I saw us all working in the fields, tying up sheaves of corn," he told them. "But all of a sudden, your sheaves turned to mine and bowed to it! And my second dream was even more peculiar. This time it was the Sun, the Moon and 11 stars that all bowed down to me!"

His brothers were immensely annoyed. "So are you saying that you're going to rule over us?" they mocked, sarcastically. Even his father was irritated.

"Do you really want us and your mother to come and grovel at your feet?" Jacob snapped. But all the same, he couldn't put his son's words out of his mind.

It was usual for the brothers to ignore Joseph as far as they could and they often sneaked off together, taking their flocks over the fields without him. Jacob would send Joseph after them to report back on what they were up to – which only made the brothers dislike him even more. One day the 11 boys had travelled to the very furthest pastures, thinking they had left Joseph behind as usual, when they noticed a bright-coated figure in the distance, heading their way. "It's the dreamer," groaned one.

"Coming to spy on us again," sneered another.

"Wait a minute," interrupted a third. "This could be the chance we've been waiting for. We're a long way from home and there's no one around. Why don't we do away with him?" The others soon took up the idea.

"We could kill him and hide the body where no one will find it," said one. "And we could tell Father that a wild animal attacked him," suggested another. They were enjoying laying their plans but Reuben, the eldest, was shocked. Thinking quickly, he

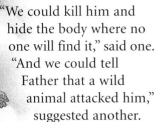

❝ *They said, 'Here comes this dreamer. Come now, let us kill him.'* **❞**

came up with a way to stop them. "I say we don't kill Joseph," he urged. "Do any of you really want to be responsible for his death? Why don't we dump him in a pit?" The brothers reluctantly agreed. Little did they know that Reuben intended to come back and rescue Joseph.

When the boy reached his brothers they suddenly turned on him and attacked him, kicking him to the ground. Enraged by the sight of the coat, they ripped it off and stamped on it in the dirt, before throwing their bruised and bleeding brother into a disused well. All except Reuben were well satisfied with their work and while the upset Reuben wandered off, out of earshot of Joseph's cries for help, the others sat down to eat.

Halfway through the meal the brothers were startled to hear people approaching. Nervously, they looked up and saw a band of Ishmaelite traders coming towards them, their camels loaded down with exotic spices. Judah's eyes lit up. "Here's a way to make ourselves some money and solve the problem of what to do with Joseph at the same time," he told his brothers, cunningly. "These merchants are on their way to Egypt. I'm sure they'd be glad to have a slave to sell when they get there." And the boys took 20 pieces of silver in exchange for their brother.

When Reuben returned, he was totally horrified to find the pit empty. "What have you done!" he screamed. "Whatever am I going to do now?" He wept bitterly while his brothers got on with the business of making up an excuse for their father. They killed a young kid, took the

remaining tatters of Joseph's coat and smeared them with blood, then went to give Jacob the evidence that his favourite son had been killed by wild animals.

At the sight of the savaged coat, Jacob wept uncontrollably, beside himself with grief. He mourned Joseph day after day, and no one could comfort him.

Joseph sold into slavery

Joseph leaves his home in Hebron to go and join his brothers in the normal pastures at Shechem, but they are trying to avoid their brother so they have moved on to other meadows. Someone tells Joseph where they have gone, so he follows them to Dothan. When he is sold he is taken hundreds of miles away, down into Egypt where he works for Potiphar.

Slave traders

This illustration shows Joseph's brothers selling him to the Ishmaelite traders, also called Midianites. They are the same group of people that Gideon, one of the Judges, fought against in the Old Testament Book of Judges.

Sold!

These coins are shekels, and they are the sort of coins that Joseph's brothers were given when they sold him.

❧ ABOUT THE STORY ❧

Joseph's brothers are irritated by his strange dreams, and jealous of Jacob's favouritism. They plan to kill him, but God is on Joseph's side and his life is spared. Instead, he is sold and taken to Egypt, where the meaning of his dreams will eventually become clear.

Joseph in Egypt

JOSEPH had been betrayed by his brothers and felt lost and terrified. He spent every minute of his uncomfortable journey wondering what would become of him and worrying about what his brothers would have told their father. When they reached Egypt, Joseph realized it was unlikely he'd ever see home again. The Ishmaelites sold Joseph as a slave to Potiphar, the captain of the Egyptian royal guard, and he found himself working in the house of Pharaoh.

Even though it felt to Joseph as though he'd been abandoned, God watched over him, keeping him safe and blessing everything he did. People soon noticed that Joseph seemed to be unusually lucky; even Potiphar realized that everything worked out well when Joseph was around, so he put him in charge of his household.

But Joseph also attracted unwelcome attention. Potiphar's wife began to fancy the young man she saw taking control of everything so well. She took great pleasure in spending her day tracking Joseph down and finding new ways to flirt with him. Joseph didn't want to have anything to do with her. "My master has been good to me. There's no way I'd go behind his back," Joseph would tell the woman firmly. "Anyway, loving another man's wife is a sin against God." But Potiphar's wife wouldn't give up. Each time Joseph said no to her, it simply made her more determined. "If sweet talk isn't working, I'll have to try something a bit more obvious," she thought to herself in the end. She waited for a quiet moment and then flung herself at Joseph, grabbing him and pulling him close to her. Struggling frantically, Joseph

wriggled free, leaving Potiphar's wife grasping a torn handful of tunic. "No one rejects me like this and gets away with it," she thought to herself in a rage. She waited until her husband came home and then began to create a terrible fuss. "Your slave broke into my room and tried to attack me," she wailed. "It was so frightening! I screamed as loud as I could and he ran off, catching his tunic on the door." Potiphar was angry and hurt. Without giving Joseph a chance to explain, he had him flung into prison.

Even locked up inside a deep, dark dungeon, God didn't desert Joseph. The prison warden knew how successful Joseph had been as Pharaoh's housekeeper, and he made

Pyramids
Ancient Egypt is probably most famous for its pyramids. These massive constructions took around 20 years to complete. Each one housed the tomb of a pharaoh, buried deep inside. The sphinx is a lion's body with a human head. This one was carved about 4000 years ago for the Pharaoh Khafre.

Royal signature
The kings of Egypt are referred to in the Bible as the Pharaohs. 'Pharaoh' originally meant the royal palace, and was only later used to mean the ruler himself. The picture signs, or hieroglyphs, shown here are the Egyptians' writing, and spell out the name of Rameses II on a tablet called a cartouche.

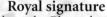

him responsible for taking care of the prison, giving him special rights and privileges. Two of the prisoners in Joseph's charge were also members of Pharaoh's household: his baker and his butler. One morning, Joseph found them both deep in thought, looking very puzzled. "We've each had a strange dream," they told him, "and we haven't a clue what they mean."

"Dreams come from God," Joseph said. "Tell me about them and I'll see if I can interpret them for you."

The butler went first. "I dreamt that I was looking at three bunches of grapes on a vine and I pressed them into wine for Pharaoh."

> *But the Lord was with Joseph, and gave him steadfast love.*

"Your dream means that in three days' time you will be released and will go back to your job," Joseph assured the delighted man. "I beg you, don't forget me. If it's possible for you to ask Pharaoh to pardon me, I'd be so grateful."

Then it was the baker's turn. "I dreamt that I was carrying three baskets of cakes on my head, but birds flew down and pecked away every crumb."

Joseph was troubled. "I fear your dream means that in three days Pharaoh will hang you," he said, and for three days, the men waited in agony to see what would happen.

Everything that Joseph had predicted came true. The baker was put to death, but Pharaoh restored the butler to his former job. The butler was so overjoyed that he tried to wipe all memories of the dungeon from his mind. He threw himself back into his old job and forgot about Joseph, who continued to spend his days locked up in Pharaoh's dark and damp prison.

❖ ABOUT THE STORY ❖

Throughout Joseph's time in Egypt, God watches over him and he soon does well. He rejects the love of Potiphar's wife, for he knows that it is a sin to love another man's wife. The woman's lies cause him to be thrown into prison but, even there, God stays with him and Joseph is well treated. Using the gift given to him by God, Joseph interprets the dreams of the butler and the baker, and his predictions come true.

Cupbearers
Not all slaves were forced to work as builders or farmers - some were given an important role in the household, and were greatly trusted by their masters. Joseph soon rose to such a position of responsibility. We do not know what his title was, but one of the highest officials was the cupbearer. His duty was to taste food and drink before serving it to the royal family, to ensure it did not contain poison. This painting shows a cupbearer serving an Egyptian prince and princess.

Pharaoh's Dream

Two years after the butler had been released from prison, Pharaoh was troubled by vivid dreams that he couldn't understand. All of his wise men offered opinions on what they meant, but Pharaoh knew they were only guessing. There seemed to be no one in the whole of his kingdom who could interpret them correctly.

It was only then that the butler remembered Joseph, and Pharaoh rushed to have him brought up from the dungeon. "I was standing by the River Nile," Pharaoh told him, "and seven fat cows came to graze at the grassy riverbank. As I watched, seven thin cows came and ate them – but the thin cows didn't get any bigger. In my second dream, I saw seven plump ears of corn being swallowed up by seven thin, shrivelled ears of corn."

The whole court waited anxiously to hear what Joseph would say. "God is warning you that there will be excellent harvests throughout Egypt for seven years, followed by seven years of devastating famine," he announced. "You should put somone in charge of stockpiling grain over the next seven seasons, otherwise your people will starve." Pharaoh knew exactly who he wanted for such a responsible task – the man before him. So Joseph went from being a captive in Pharaoh's prison to his right-hand man, dressed in the finest robes and wearing Pharaoh's ring, and he went through the country, making sure the peoples' stores were filling with grain.

After seven years, just as Joseph had predicted, the crops suddenly failed – not just in Egypt but in the lands beyond, too. Families found themselves and their animals without food and unable to grow anything in the dry ground. Joseph opened the storehouses and starving people came from far and wide for corn. Imagine Joseph's shock when one day, among the desperate people, he recognized ten of his own brothers. His only sadness was that his favourite brother, Benjamin, wasn't with them.

> ❝ *And Pharaoh said to Joseph, 'Behold, I have set you over all the land of Egypt.'* ❞

Storing grain
Joseph was responsible for storing-up grain for the famine. Severe famines have been recorded in Egypt at this time, caused by the Nile's annual floodwaters either being too low, or flooding too high. Either situation was very bad for farming.

Signet rings
This ancient Egyptian signet ring is probably like the one Pharaoh gave Joseph. Handing over the ring was a sign that Pharaoh was giving Joseph great power. Signet rings were also used to sign documents. By pressing it into clay or wax, the writing made a signature.

❧ ABOUT THE STORY ❧

Joseph is the only person who can interpret Pharaoh's dreams. So Pharaoh appoints him to a position of authority. Joseph's predictions come true and it is only because of his gift of interpretation that the Egyptians survive the famine. Joseph is reunited with his brothers, but the roles have been reversed. Joseph forgives them for the past and treats them with love, and Jacob is reunited with his favourite son.

In the 20 years since the men had sold their brother into slavery, Joseph had changed a great deal and they had no idea who he really was. Joseph resisted the urge to hug them and instead treated the foreigners severely. He spoke to them in Egyptian, using an interpreter. "You are spies come to search out our storehouses," he accused the famished, exhausted men.

"No, we're from a starving family in Canaan," they explained. "Our youngest brother is at home with our father." Joseph pretended not to believe them and threw them in prison. After three nights, he saw them again.

"Prove that you are telling the truth," demanded Joseph. "You can go back with your corn, but one of you must stay until you bring me this youngest brother of yours."

"This is our punishment for killing Joseph," whispered Reuben, not realizing that Joseph could understand. When he saw the guilt on his brothers' faces he turned away and wept. Then he gave orders for Simeon to be bound and had every sack filled with corn, replacing their money, too.

The brothers were deeply shaken when they arrived home and found that their silver had mysteriously appeared back in their sacks. Their father was even more upset. "I lost Joseph and now I've lost Simeon," Jacob wept. "I won't let you take Benjamin or he might not come back either." But the famine lasted longer than the corn, and the family soon faced starvation again. Jacob was still determined not to let his sons return to Egypt, but when Judah promised to guard Benjamin with his life, Jacob reluctantly changed his mind. He loaded them up with gifts of exotic spices, making sure they had enough money to pay back the silver they owed.

When Joseph saw Benjamin, he wept with joy. He left the room and sent in the finest food and drink to the men. Also Joseph told his steward to fill the sacks and replace their money again, this time hiding his own silver drinking goblet in Benjamin's sack.

The brothers hadn't got very far on their return journey when Joseph sent his steward chasing after them, on the pretence of looking for the precious goblet. They were bewildered and horrified when it was found in Benjamin's sack. Back at Joseph's house they threw themselves at his mercy. "You're all free to leave," Joseph told them, "except the man in whose sack the goblet was found."

'I am your brother Joseph, who you sold into Egypt.'

Judah knew this would break Jacob's heart. "Please let Benjamin go, or my father will die of grief," he pleaded. "Allow me to stay here in his place."

Joseph could bear it no longer. "I am your brother, Joseph, who you sold into slavery in Egypt," he told the astonished men, "and I forgive you for everything. It was all God's work. Spend the remaining years of the famine here, where I can look after everyone."

Jacob wouldn't believe that Joseph was not only alive, but lord of all Egypt under Pharaoh. But when the two men met and Jacob looked into Joseph's eyes, he knew that God had given back the son he thought was dead. "Now that I've seen you again, I can die happy," he said, thanking God. And Jacob lived out the rest of his days in Egypt.

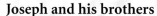
Joseph and his brothers
When Joseph meets his brothers again for the first time in 20 years they have no idea that the grand Egyptian official in front of them is the boy they sold as a slave, and Joseph does not immediately reveal his true identity to them. The picture on the right, from a 6th-century manuscript, shows the brothers filling their sacks with grain. Joseph wears a long cloak, while his brothers are dressed in short tunics. These are not, in fact, the clothes that would have been worn in Egypt at the time of Joseph, but it is common for artists to show people wearing the clothes of the artist's time.

Moses in the Bulrushes

WHEN Joseph reached the age of 110 years old, he realized he was going to die. He called his brothers to him and promised them that God would one day return their families to Canaan - the land that the Lord had given to Abraham's descendants. But for now, the descendants of Joseph and his brothers would remain in Egypt.

Over hundreds of years their families grew and spread through the country, and they became a strong, successful people. There came a time when the Pharaoh grew worried about the huge number of powerful Israelites living in Egypt. 'Surely there are now more of these Hebrew foreigners living in our country than there are Egyptians!' he thought to himself.

'What happens if there is a war? They might join with the enemy against us and try to take Egypt for themselves.' Pharaoh came to the conclusion that the only way to protect his people was to crush the Israelites completely. He commanded that they should all be taken as slaves and set to hard labour. It was no use anyone trying to resist Pharaoh's soldiers. Soon, groups of Israelites were to be seen digging dusty roads, ploughing up rocky fields, and being flogged when they collapsed in the baking sun. But Pharaoh wasn't satisfied. Even though he could control the Israelites' activities, he couldn't control their spirit. The more harshly they were treated, the more bitter and defiant they became. And worst of all, the number of Israelites in Egypt continued to grow! Pharaoh decided to be totally ruthless and wipe them out. He gave the order that all newborn Israelite boys should be put to death.

> ❝ *Pharaoh commanded, 'Every son born to the Hebrews you shall cast into the Nile.'* ❞

The terrified Israelites did everything they could to save their newborn sons. Anguished parents all over Egypt tried to hide their baby boys away or smuggle them out of the country to relatives or friends. They'd do anything to save their sons from the swords of Pharaoh's soldiers. One woman from the tribe of Levi managed to hide her baby boy in her house for three months. Every minute, she was afraid that an Egyptian would hear him crying. But as the baby grew bigger, she knew it would be impossible to keep

Finding Moses
This illustration shows Pharaoh's daughter standing on the riverbank, surrounded by her maids. In the story, the basket is covered, but here it is shown to be open, with the baby clearly visible. When illustrating a story, artists will often change details like this, to make their pictures more interesting or dramatic.

Adoption
Adoption is not common in the Old Testament. Families had other ways of dealing with the problem if parents could not have children, for example by the practice of polygamy, where a man has more than one wife. When an adoption did take place, it was more likely to be within the family.

him safe at home forever. She wove a basket out of bulrushes from the river Nile and made it watertight. Then the grief-stricken mother laid her baby in it, covered it over, and set the cradle floating among the reeds at the river's edge. The poor woman couldn't bear to leave her son without knowing what happened to him, yet she knew she was in danger if she was found nearby. So she told her daughter to stay close and watch what happened.

It wasn't long before the little girl saw a young woman coming down to the river to bathe, accompanied by many maids. "It's Pharaoh's daughter herself!" the girl realized, and watched, trembling, as the princess caught sight of the basket. Pharaoh's daughter sent a maid to fetch it, and the women all crowded round, excited to see what was inside. Gingerly, the princess began to remove the cover. Whatever could it be? Maybe someone had hidden precious jewellery, or rich spices? She was amazed to lift out of the basket a wriggling baby boy! As the baby looked up at her and began to cry, the princess's heart melted. 'This must be a Hebrew child,' she thought.

As soon as the baby's sister saw that the princess had taken pity on the baby, she plucked up her courage and approached the royal party. The little girl curtseyed and took a deep breath. "Maybe I could find an Israelite nurse to help you look after him?" she suggested. The princess thought it was an excellent idea.

The woman couldn't believe it when Pharaoh's daughter employed her to look after her own child. "I am calling him Moses," the princess said, "because it means 'to draw out' and I drew him out of the water." The princess loved Moses as if he were her own child.

❧ ABOUT THE STORY ❧

Pharaoh is troubled by the growing number of Israelites in Egypt, fearing they will rebel against him. He forces them all into slavery, and even gives an order that all Israelite baby boys must be killed. However, it is God's will that the Israelites will return to Canaan and will inherit the land He promised them, so Moses is spared. He is brought up in the royal household, as the son of Pharaoh's daughter.

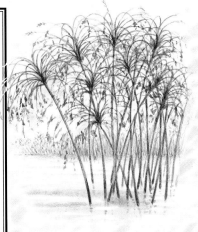

Farming in Egypt
Most Israelites in Egypt were farmers. They depended on the river Nile, which flooded every year and spilt fertile soil over its banks and watered the ground.

The name of the plant
Although it is said that Moses was found among the rushes, these are more likely to have been papyrus plants, which grew in abundance beside the Nile. 'Rushes' was a word that was used as a general word for plants that grew in water.

The Burning Bush

EVEN though Moses grew up in the heart of the Egyptian royal family, he could never forget that he was an Israelite. It pained him to see that while he lived a life of luxury, all around his people suffered terribly at the hands of the Egyptians. It had become so usual to see Egyptians beating Israelite slaves that nobody took any notice. But once, Moses came across an Israelite being kicked to the ground, and suddenly he found himself rushing at the Egyptian attacker. He hit him until he was dead. Nobody was about, so Moses took the body and buried it. But next day, as he tried to split up an argument between two Israelites, one of them angrily said, "Who gave you the right to judge us? Are you going to kill us like you killed the Egyptian?" Somehow, Moses had been found out. He knew he would be in trouble if Pharaoh heard of his crime, so he fled Egypt to the land of Midian.

Moses would have been homeless if he hadn't stopped to help seven sisters trying to water their sheep. In return for his kindness, their father, Jethro, invited Moses to stay with them and also gave him work as a shepherd. Moses lived happily with Jethro's family, eventually falling in love and marrying one of Jethro's daughters, Zipporah.

Shepherding was a quiet life in comparison to the Egyptian royal household. Moses would take his flock out onto the mountain pastures with nothing but the sun and the animals for company. One day, he was deep in thought when a nearby thornbush suddenly burst into flames. After recovering from the shock, Moses went to have a closer look. He was amazed to see that although the bush was on fire, it wasn't burning up. He was even more amazed when a voice called from the flames.

> ❝ *'I will send you to Pharaoh, that you may bring forth my people out of Egypt.'* ❞

"Moses! Moses!" Moses was terrified. "You are standing on holy ground," came the voice, "and I am the God of Abraham, Isaac and Jacob. I have seen how my people suffer in Egypt and I have heard their cries for help. I want you to go to Pharaoh

The fire of God
Usually when a bush or plant burns, the flames spread over the field, as here, and the grass catches fire, burns up and is destroyed. However, the bush Moses saw was burning in a different way. Although it was on fire, the flames did not destroy it. Moses was amazed by this unusual sight. God's presence is often symbolized by fire, which serves as a reminder of his power and holiness.

Moses's sandals
In ancient times, most poor people went barefoot, as sandals were a luxury. They were mainly worn when travelling long distances. Moses would probably have worn sandals woven from papyrus, palm leaves and grass, like the Egyptian ones here.

and rescue them. Then take them to the land I promised would be given to Abraham's descendants."

"Who am I, to be able to do all that?" he said, anxiously.

"I will be with you," replied God.

"But the people will ask me who you are," said Moses. "What shall I say?"

"I am who I am," thundered the voice. "Tell them that the God of their fathers has sent you."

"What if they don't believe me?" Moses protested.

"Throw your shepherd's crook to the ground," the voice commanded. Moses did as he was told and watched as the crook became a hissing snake. "Take hold of the snake's tail," the voice ordered. Moses forced himself to reach out his hand and the snake became his crook again.

"Now put your hand inside your shirt," it instructed. Once again, Moses did as he was told. When he pulled his hand out, he was horrified to see that his skin was covered with sores. Quickly, he thrust his hand back inside his shirt, and on drawing it out found the skin healed.

While Moses was still marvelling at these miracles, the voice spoke again. "If the people don't believe these signs, take some water from the river Nile and sprinkle it on the ground. The drops will turn into blood."

Yet Moses still had one worry – he hated speaking in public. "Take Aaron, your brother," He commanded. "He can act as your spokesperson while you show the people the signs I have sent you. Now go, and remember that I will be with you."

With a heart full of fear, Moses came down from the mountain to prepare himself for the seemingly impossible task that lay ahead.

Holy ground

This detail from a mosaic in San Vitale Church in Italy shows Moses removing his sandals. God asked him to do so as a sign of respect, because he was walking on holy ground. In the Middle East at this time it was customary to perform religious ceremonies barefoot. This helped to keep holy places free from dirt. Moses's meeting with God took place on Mount Sinai, also called Mount Horeb. This is believed to be the mountain known today as Jebel Musa, which means Mountain of Moses.

❖ ABOUT THE STORY ❖

Although Moses was brought up at the Egyptian court, he is concerned about his people, the Israelites. He kills an Egyptian man when he sees him attacking an Israelite slave. Because of this, he has to flee from Egypt. After living as a shepherd, Moses is visited by God, who calls upon him to go to Pharaoh and rescue the Israelites from slavery. At first, Moses hesitates, but he is persuaded by God's miracles.

Moses warns Pharaoh

WHEN Moses told his father-in-law what God had instructed him to do, Jethro gave him his blessing, saying that he shouldn't delay in doing the Lord's work but leave at once. So Moses, his wife Zipporah and their sons packed up all their belongings, said goodbye to the comfort and safety of their home, and headed off towards the possible dangers lying in wait in Egypt.

God had already tried to reassure Moses by telling him that the Egyptians who wanted to kill him were now dead. But Moses was still very anxious about God's command. He grew more nervous when the Lord again appeared to him during the journey. He warned Moses that even if he performed all the miracles, Pharaoh still might not believe that he was sent by God. "Tell Pharaoh that the people of Israel are as dear to me as a first-born child," He commanded Moses. "You must warn Pharaoh that if he doesn't free my people, I will wreak a terrible vengeance."

God had told Moses' brother, Aaron, to meet Moses along the way, and the two men carefully discussed every detail of all they had to say and do. How important it was that they convinced Pharaoh! The freedom of the whole Hebrew race was resting on their shoulders, and if they failed, the Egyptian people would suffer too.

The first thing they did on reaching Egypt was to gather together the leaders of all the Israelite communities. Aaron gave a rousing speech, inspiring them with great hope and courage. And when they saw that Moses had the power to perform miracles they gasped and fell on their knees, praising God. The people realized that the Lord was truly

" But Pharaoh said 'Who is the Lord that I should heed his voice and let Israel go?' "

SEVERAL TIMES GOD IS SAID TO HAVE HARDENED PHARAOH'S HEART AND MADE HIM OBSTINATE, BUT THIS WAS NOT DONE AGAINST PHARAOH'S WILL. GOD JUST LET PHARAOH HAVE WHAT HE WANTED. ❧

The slaves suffer
Moses and Aaron had hoped to improve the lives of the Israelite slaves. However, Pharaoh was so angry at their request for freedom that he ordered the slave-masters to treat the slaves even more harshly than before. He did not care that it was the will of God that they be freed.

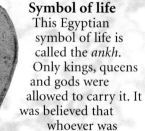

Symbol of life
This Egyptian symbol of life is called the *ankh*. Only kings, queens and gods were allowed to carry it. It was believed that whoever was holding the ankh had the power to give life, or take it away from others. This ankh is decorated with a dog-headed sceptre, which symbolizes power.

with them; He had answered their prayers and sent Moses to deliver them out of the cruel hands of the Egyptians. They were eager to follow him and do whatever he said.

After this success, Moses and Aaron felt more confident. But the most difficult task was yet to come. They had to get an audience with Pharaoh, and then tell the king of Egypt that what he was doing to the Israelites was wrong.

As they had expected, Pharaoh was outraged when the two Hebrew men dared to criticize him. "Who is this God of yours that you say has sent you?" he roared. "And even if he exists, why should I listen to him?"

"Our God has commanded all the Israelite people to travel into the desert and make a sacrifice of thanks to Him," Moses and Aaron protested. "If we don't obey, He'll strike out at everyone with His anger."

"I know nothing about your God," spat Pharaoh in a rage, "and I certainly will not set the Israelites free!" He turned to his royal guard. "Get these two out of here," he yelled. "Since they put these ridiculous ideas into the Israelites' heads, it's all the slaves can think about. Their work is getting slower and slower." As the soldiers dragged Moses and Aaron away, Pharaoh furiously commanded, "Tell all the slave-masters to stop giving the Hebrews straw to make their bricks. They'll have to go out into the fields and find straw for themselves. And if they make any fewer bricks than before, there'll be serious trouble!"

Of course, it was impossible for the Israelites to find their own straw and still make as many bricks as before. When Moses and Aaron saw how savagely the Egyptians beat them for failing at their work, they felt as if it was all their fault. "Why ever did you send me, Lord?" Moses

cried. "Ever since we spoke to Pharaoh, the people have suffered more, not less."

"Reassure the people that their God has not forgotten them," the Lord told Moses. "If I have to, I will force Pharaoh to let them go. Try once more to talk to him, and if he still refuses to obey me, wait and see what I will do. In the end, Pharaoh will be glad to see them go!"

Moses and Aaron did as God commanded. "I've told you before, I don't believe a word you say," Pharaoh scoffed. "If a god really had sent you, you'd be able to perform miracles." At this, Moses threw his crook on the ground and it became a snake. But Pharaoh wasn't impressed. He had many magicians in his court and they too threw down staffs which turned into snakes. Even though Moses' snake swallowed all the magicians' snakes, Pharaoh simply sneered. Moses was just as far away from rescuing the Israelites as ever.

A meeting with Pharaoh
This engraving shows Moses changing his staff to a snake. But Pharaoh has seen magicians do this, so he is not impressed, and has no faith in God.

❖ ABOUT THE STORY ❖

Moses is very aware that God has made him, and his brother Aaron, responsible for the freedom of the Israelite people. Pharaoh, though, remains arrogant and refuses to believe in God. Instead of freeing the Israelites as is God's will, he makes them suffer even more. The Israelites too suffer from a lack of faith, and turn against Moses. But God reassures Moses, and he approaches Pharaoh again, but to no avail.

Plagues of Egypt

GOD saw that even a miracle wouldn't convince Pharaoh to let the Israelites go, and He knew that Pharaoh's heart was as hard as stone. The Lord told Moses and Aaron to go to the river Nile the following morning and wait for Pharaoh. As soon as Pharaoh was near, Moses drew himself up. "We were sent to you by God and you have failed to recognize Him!" Aaron thundered. "You have disobeyed His commands and refused to let the Hebrew people go. Now prepare to see how powerful the God of the Israelites really is." Moses lashed his crook down on the waters. Instantly, the river began to run red with blood. Each drop of water in every pool, lake, canal, stream and river throughout Egypt turned to blood. As the fish choked and died, the stench of rotting was everywhere, and for seven days there was no fresh water.

But Pharaoh remained unmoved. His magicians showed him that they could make water turn red through trickery, and Pharaoh ignored what Moses and Aaron had done. So God commanded the two men to strike the Nile with the sacred crook again. Straight away the bloody waters began to bubble as frogs started to hop out onto the banks. First there were hundreds, then thousands. Soon every Egyptian house was filled with leaping, croaking creatures. The Egyptians couldn't cook, eat or sleep without frogs jumping on them. Even the royal palace was overrun with the slimy creatures. Pharaoh called Moses and Aaron to him. "Tell your God to take away the frogs and I will let the Israelites go." The rejoicing men prayed to the Lord and the frogs immediately began to die. But the cheating Pharaoh told Moses that he had changed his mind, and the Israelites had to stay where they were.

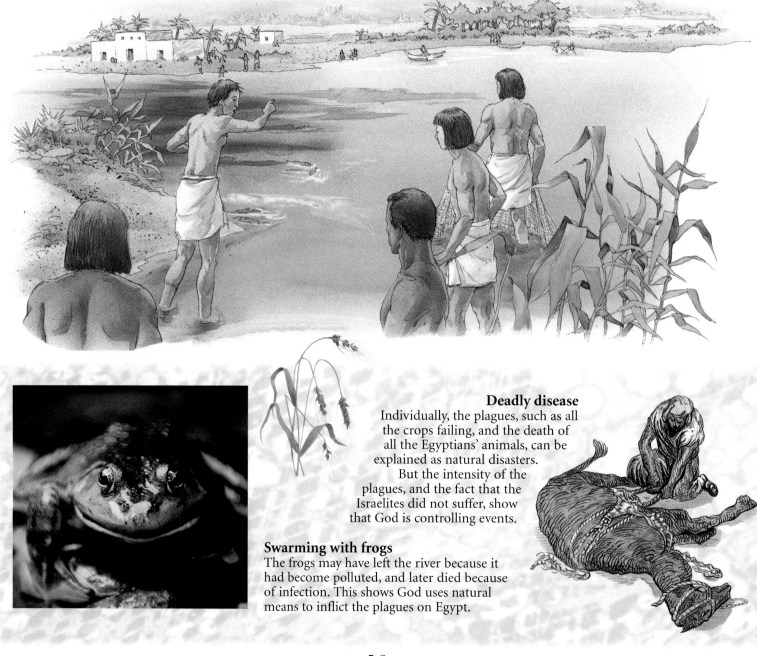

Deadly disease
Individually, the plagues, such as all the crops failing, and the death of all the Egyptians' animals, can be explained as natural disasters. But the intensity of the plagues, and the fact that the Israelites did not suffer, show that God is controlling events.

Swarming with frogs
The frogs may have left the river because it had become polluted, and later died because of infection. This shows God uses natural means to inflict the plagues on Egypt.

At this, God commanded the two men to hit the earth with Moses' crook. Each tiny speck of dust turned into a squirming maggot – it looked as if the whole of the ground was moving! Maggots wriggled over every man, woman and animal, and as fast as they brushed them off, they found more crawling over their skin.

Then God sent a plague of flies. "But you'll see that there will be no insects where the Israelites live," they told Pharaoh. Almost before they had finished speaking, huge humming clouds of flies came swarming through the air, settling in their millions on the Egyptian households without going anywhere near a single Israelite.

The very next day, the Egyptian farmers found all their animals struck down with a mysterious disease. They could do nothing but watch as every cow, sheep and camel died, while the animals belonging to the Israelites remained healthy. But this only infuriated Pharaoh, and made him determined not to give in to the Israelites.

God told Moses to take two handfuls of soot and scatter it into the wind. The breeze carried it far and wide, and people found their skin breaking out into hideous sores. Then the two men sent a hailstorm so fierce that anything caught outside would die. The Lord hurled down bolts of thunder and flashes of lightning, and pelted the Egyptians with piercing hailstones. Pharaoh said that the Israelites could leave, and the sun broke through the clouds.

But the sunshine did not last long. Pharaoh told Moses and Aaron that he had once more lied to them, and the skies darkened again the very same day. A strange rustling noise blew towards Egypt on the wind, and the people realized that it was the wings of swarms of locusts. Millions of the insects fell on the earth like a black carpet, stripping the soil bare by devouring every remaining leaf and shoot. Utter destruction faced the whole country and Pharaoh once again tried to compromise with Moses and Aaron. He promised to let all the male Israelites go free - but it wasn't enough. Moses raised his hand and Egypt

" *And the locusts came up over the whole land of Egypt* "

suddenly found itself in darkness. God had blotted out the Sun, leaving the Egyptians in inky blackness.

After three days, Pharaoh could take it no longer. "Go!" he ordered Moses and Aaron. "And take every last Israelite with you! But I say this on one condition – they have to leave all their flocks and herds behind."

"You know we cannot agree to that," Moses answered.

Pharaoh gripped the arms of his throne so hard that his knuckles turned white. "Then the Israelites will remain as slaves in Egypt forever," he hissed "and if you ever dare to enter my presence again, you will be put to death."

❖ ABOUT THE STORY ❖

God brings about the plagues to show His supreme power. The Egyptians worshipped many gods of their own. By destroying the symbols of the Egyptian gods, God shows He is more powerful. However, despite the plagues, Pharaoh refuses to obey God's will.

In the dark
Some people say that the darkness was caused by an eclipse, but this could not last three days. It is more likely that earth washed down by the storms dried into dust. This was whirled up into a dust-storm by a strong wind that stopped the sun getting through.

The Passover

How arrogant Pharaoh was! The Egyptians traditionally believed that their Pharaoh was a god, and he expected to be treated as one. He certainly wasn't used to people telling him his laws were wrong and defying his orders. No matter how much suffering was inflicted on his people, Pharaoh couldn't bring himself to acknowledge the existence of the Hebrew God - let alone admit that the Lord was far mightier than he was. Moses and Aaron had correctly predicted plagues nine times, and even Pharaoh's counsellors had been convinced. "Don't you understand that Egypt is ruined?" they had pleaded in frustration with Pharaoh. "You must let the Israelites go to worship their God!" But Pharaoh shut himself away in his palace, closing his eyes to his people's wretchedness and blocking his ears to their cries.

After Pharaoh's final threat, God again spoke to Moses. "I will bring one last plague upon Pharaoh and his country. It will be so terrible that he will end up begging the Israelites to leave Egypt. Tonight, all first-born children will die – from the family of Pharaoh himself to the very poorest household. I will even kill first-born animals. Through the whole of Egypt, only the Israelites will be spared from grief. This is what you are to tell them to do. Each Hebrew household must kill a male lamb at sunset and sprinkle some of its blood around the front door. The lamb is then to be roasted and eaten with bitter herbs and flat bread, and any left overs must be burnt. The people must hurry and go to bed early. Tell them to lock themselves inside their houses and, whatever happens, not

> ‘*For I will pass through the land of Egypt and I will smite all the first born.*’

Holy book
This is an illuminated page of a Jewish book called the Haggadah. Parts of the book are read or recited during the Passover feast. The Haggadah contains stories, poems and rituals that are significant to the Jewish religion, including sections of the Torah. The Torah is the name given to the first five books of the Old Testament in the Bible, the most important part of Jewish scriptures.

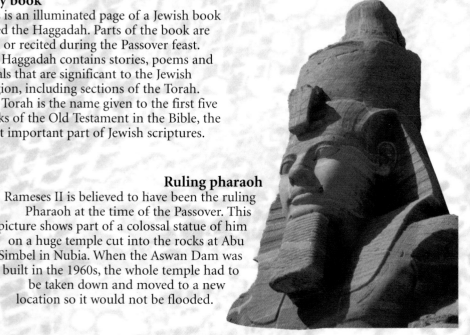

Ruling pharaoh
Rameses II is believed to have been the ruling Pharaoh at the time of the Passover. This picture shows part of a colossal statue of him on a huge temple cut into the rocks at Abu Simbel in Nubia. When the Aswan Dam was built in the 1960s, the whole temple had to be taken down and moved to a new location so it would not be flooded.

to go outside until morning. For at midnight I will pass over the whole land and slay the first-born child in every household that isn't marked with blood. This night will be known as the Passover and you must remember it each year as a holy festival." With dread and fear in his heart, Moses hastened to call the Israelite leaders together and give them God's instructions.

The next day, it wasn't the sun that woke the land of Egypt – it was the sound of screaming. As each family found their beloved first-born child lying dead in their bed, they sent up heartbroken cries that tore the air, until it seemed as if the whole of Egypt was wailing. Somebody had died in every household from the royal palace to the darkest prison – except for the homes of the Israelites.

Even before the dawn had fully broken, Moses and Aaron were summoned to see Pharaoh. They found the once-proud king completely broken by grief. His eyes were swollen with weeping, his face wrenched into haggard lines of pain, and his shoulders slumped with the heaviness of utter misery. "Leave my land," he groaned in agony, barely able to speak. "Take whatever you want and go." Moses and Aaron knew that, this time, Pharaoh's words came from the heart. Without further hesitation, they turned to go and spread the good news to the Israelites. But the thin crackle of Pharaoh's voice stopped them. "Ask the Lord to bless me, too," he whispered.

And so it was that, after 430 years of slavery, the Israelites finally left Egypt. The Egyptians hurried them away with presents of gold, silver, fine materials and other expensive gifts. And led by Moses, over six hundred thousand men, women and children set off on foot on their long journey into the wilderness.

Passover today
Today, Jewish families hold a feast to remember the Passover as God commanded. They gather together to eat specially prepared food that symbolizes the sufferings of the Israelites in Egypt. The meal begins after dark and before any food is eaten, the youngest child asks the oldest family member to retell the story of the Passover.

Hyssop
Hyssop, the name given to the leaves of the marjoram plant, was a common symbol of purity. Moses told the Israelites to use a bunch of hyssop to smear the lamb's blood around their doors on the night of the Passover.

❧ ABOUT THE STORY ❧
Although many people, even in Pharaoh's household, are convinced about the existence of God, Pharaoh remains arrogant. It is only when God sends the final plague that Pharaoh realises Moses is right. Pharaoh abandons his pride, releases the Israelites and asks for God's blessing. The Passover is so called because God 'passed over' the houses of the Israelites, meaning He spared them from the plague.

Crossing the Red Sea

THE minute the Israelites had gone, Pharaoh regretted his decision. The rate at which grand buildings and beautiful monuments were going up slowed right down as soon as the slave labour departed. Each time Pharaoh caught sight of a deserted building site he was reminded that he had lost some of his power. He imagined his former slaves travelling further out of his grasp, and he became more and more resentful. After several days of being tormented by his own thoughts, Pharaoh finally called a meeting of his counsellors. "We should never have let the Hebrews go!" he raged. "I want as many troops as possible sent after them. You must find the Israelites and bring them back!"

Meanwhile, the Israelites were making good progress through the desert, helped by God. By day a whirling column of cloud guided them and by night a blazing pillar of flame lit the way.

The Israelites were at first puzzled when they looked back and saw a cloud of dust coming towards them at top speed. Then, as they recognized the glints of golden armour in the sun, and heard the noise of thundering hooves, panic spread among them. "Did you bring us here to die!" they shrieked at Moses. "It would have been better to live in slavery under the Egyptians than die here!"

"Have faith in the Lord who brought you here," he said.

Moses fell silent, believing wholeheartedly that God would answer his prayer. He listened as the people's cries changed from terror to wonderment. The column of cloud had moved behind them, smothering the Egyptians in darkness so they could not see where they were going.

> " *The Lord drove the sea back and made the sea dry land and the waters were divided.* "

Then God told Moses to stretch out his hand towards the Red Sea ahead of them. At once, a mighty gale blew up from the east. Moses commanded the Israelites to press forward. Though no one dared protest to Moses a second time, each person knew that they were heading straight for the ocean. Surely they would all be drowned! But when they drew nearer, the Israelites could hardly believe their eyes. The wind had driven back the waters, leaving a path of dry land through the waves. They walked all night long, with walls of water towering over them on either side.

In the morning, when every last Israelite had crossed safely, Moses turned and looked back. The Egyptians had tried to follow them across the ocean floor, but the wheels of their chariots had sunk into the mud, along with their horses and the soldiers. In the chaos, they had become very afraid. "Run! Run! God must truly be with the Israelites!" some of them were yelling.

Moses stretched out his hand once more. Instantly, the walls of water came roaring down on the Egyptians. When the tide at last settled, it was as if the desperate men and all their equipment had never been there.

GREAT SEA

REED SEA

Rameses •

E G Y P T

Succoth

BITTER
LAKE

WILDERNESS

OF SHUR

• Heliopolis

Weeping with relief and overcome with gratitude, the Hebrew people threw themselves to the ground, giving thanks to God. Then Moses' sister Miriam took up her tambourine to sing God's praises – after over 400 years the Israelites were on their way to their Promised Land.

Crossing the Red Sea
No one knows exactly where Moses crossed the Red Sea. We know the Israelites went from Rameses to Succoth. After this, their route, in blue, may have crossed the Reed Sea. The red route shows they may have crossed the Bitter Lake. Finally, the mauve route shows a journey along the Great Sea.

Chariots
The Egyptians' horse-drawn chariots would have been very light, made mainly of wood and leather, with a few bronze or iron fittings. The chariots were mostly open at the back, and had hooks or racks on the outside to hold weapons.

⊹ **ABOUT THE STORY** ⊹

By parting the waters of the Red Sea for them, God shows the Israelites that He intends to free them from slavery. Under the watchful gaze of God's chosen leader Moses, He guides them safely out of Egypt and sets them on the long journey towards the Promised Land.

Poetry in the Old Testament

Poetry and song played an important part in people's lives at the time of the Old Testament. Poetry would have been recited aloud and would generally have been accompanied by music, so the difference between a poem and a song was not as marked as it is for us today. Songs were sung by all kinds of people, for all kinds of reasons and at many different times.

People who worked at particular occupations probably had special songs, for example, the 'Song of the Well' (Numbers 21:17–18) might have been sung by people drawing water from a well, or by people actually digging the well. Another mention of songs connected to occupations occurs in Isaiah 16:10, where there is a description of singing in the vineyards while making wine.

Songs were also used on special occasions, such as when people arrived or departed. When Jacob tries to steal away from Laban's house without his uncle's knowledge, Laban is angry that he was not given the opportunity to send his nephew away with songs and music, as was the custom (Genesis 31:27). Songs of celebration were sung at weddings, and laments were sung for the dead.

Songs were not usually heard as voices alone; they were nearly always accompanied by instruments. The main purpose of

instruments in the Old Testament appears to be to accompany songs. The Hebrew language is very rhythmic so even passages of the Old Testament which are not really poetry can sound like poems, especially if they are part of someone's speech.

The poetry in the Old Testament does not rhyme, but it does use other devices common to all poetry, such as similes (where something is likened to something else, such as 'they went down into the depths like a stone'), metaphors (where something is described as if it were something else, 'the earth swallowed them')

Miriam's song

After the Israelites have crossed the Red Sea, Moses' sister Miriam raises a tambourine and begins to dance. All the other women join her in the dance, and Miriam sings a song of praise to God. The words of her song (on the opposite page) tell of the Israelites' escape from Egypt and the crossing of the Red Sea.

THIS SHOWS AN ILLUMINATED, OR ORNATELY DECORATED, SONG. THIS OFTEN HAPPENED WITH RELIGIOUS SONGS.

and alliteration (where several words close to each other begin with the same letter, like 'your people pass' where the 'p' is repeated).

The use of imagery (visually descriptive language) is abundant in the poetry of the Old Testament. It draws on the universe, including the stars, the Moon and the Sun, on nature, including the seasons, the weather and the sea, and on the activities of the countryside, such as shepherding, harvest time and wine making. However, the inspiration behind all the songs and poetry in the Old Testament is the love and worship of God.

❧ THE SONG OF MIRIAM ❧

I will sing to the Lord for He has triumphed
gloriously;
the horse and his rider He has thrown into the sea.
The Lord is my strength and my song,
and He has become my salvation;
this is my God, and I will praise Him,
my father's God and I will exalt Him.
The Lord is a man of war;
the Lord is His name.

Pharaoh's chariots and his host He cast into the sea;
and his picked officers are sunk in the Red Sea.
The floods covered them;
they went down into the depths like a stone.
Thy right hand, O Lord, glorious in power,
thy right hand, O Lord, shatters the enemy.
In the greatness of thy majesty thou overthrowest
thy adversaries;
thou sendest forth thy fury, it consumes
them like stubble.
At the blast of thy nostrils the waters piled up,
the floods stood up in a heap;
the deeps congealed in the heart of the sea.
The enemy said, "I will pursue, I will overtake,
I will divide the spoil; my desire shall have its
fill of them.
I will draw my sword, my hand shall destroy them."
Thou didst blow with thy wind, the sea covered them;
they sank as lead in the mighty waters.

Who is like thee, O Lord, among the gods?
Who is like thee – majestic in holiness, terrible in
glorious deeds, doing wonders?
Thou didst stretch out your right hand, the earth
swallowed them.

Thou hast led in thy steadfast love the people
whom thou hast redeemed,
thou hast guided them by thy strength to
thy holy abode.
The peoples have heard, they tremble;
pangs have seized on the inhabitants of Philistia.
The chiefs of Edom will be terrified,
the leaders of Moab will be seized with trembling,
the people of Canaan will melt away;
terror and dread will fall upon them.
By the power of your arm they will be as
still as a stone,
until your people pass by, O Lord,
until the people you bought pass by.
You will bring them in and plant them
on the mountain of your inheritance,
the place, O Lord, you made for your dwelling,
the sanctuary, O Lord, your hands established.
The Lord will reign for ever and ever.

Judaism and the Old Testament

The books of the Old Testament form the Scriptures, or sacred writings, of the Jewish people. They tell the story of their ancestors, the Israelites, or Hebrews. To Jews, the most important part of the Old Testament is the first five books: Genesis, Exodus, Leviticus, Numbers and Deuteronomy. These five books are called the Torah, which means 'teaching'. The Torah contains stories, poetry, prayers and laws which teach people about God, and how they can live their lives according to His will. Of particular importance are God's covenant with Abraham, and the laws God reveals to His people through Moses.

Jewish people go to worship in the synagogue on the Sabbath, which, for them, is Saturday. Parts of the Torah are read aloud each Sabbath, by a rabbi or by another member of the congregation. After a year, the whole Torah has been read and a celebration called Simcha Torah takes place. People hold the scrolls on which the Torah is written high above their heads, and dance in a procession around the synagogue. At the next reading, the Torah is begun all over again.

Many Jewish festivals commemorate events from the Bible. For example, the Festival of the Passover, which is celebrated with a special meal, reminds Jews of how God sent a plague to kill all first-born babies, except those in the homes of the Israelites, which He 'passed over'. The festival Yom Kippur is a solemn day of fasting and prayer. In the Bible, a goat was sent into the wilderness as a sacrifice. During the festival of Succoth, also known as the Feast of Tabernacles, people camp in tents to remember the Israelites' years of wandering in the wilderness.

ABRAHAM   SARAH

ISAAC   REBEKAH

ESAU   JACOB   LEAH   RACHEL   ZILPAH   BILHAH

REUBEN SIMEON LEVI JUDAH ISAACHAR ZEBULUN DINAH JOSEPH BENJAMIN GAD ASHER DAN NAPHTALI

The Star of David
This is used as a Jewish and Israeli symbol. David was an Israelite king who captured Jerusalem and made it his capital city.

Patriarch's family tree
In the Bible, Abraham is the first great leader of the Israelites. At his death, the leadership passes to his son, Isaac, to Isaac's son, Jacob and finally to Joseph. Abraham, Isaac, Jacob and Joseph are known as the Patriarchs, meaning the male heads of a family. Jacob's other sons were also thought of as Patriarchs, and were the forefathers of the twelve tribes of Israel.

TIMELINE 2200BC TO 1400BC

Abraham, who was to become the first father of the Israelites, was born.

ANIMALS PREPARED FOR SACRIFICE

2200BC

ISAAC MEETS REBEKAH

Abraham's sons, Ishmael and Isaac, are born.

2100BC

Jacob, father of the twelve tribes of Israel, is born.

On his way to Haran Jacob sees a vision, sent by God, of a stairway to heaven, and God's covenant is renewed with Jacob.

Jacob gets married and his sons, including Joseph, are born.

Joseph is sold to traders and taken to Egypt, where he finds favour with Pharaoh.

2000BC

Jacob and his family move to Egypt to live with Joseph.

Over the years the Israelites increase in number. Later pharaohs make them slaves to protect their power.

JACOB AND ESAU ARE REUNITED

1900BC   1800

The Origins of the Bible

The words of the earliest books of the Old Testament were passed down by word of mouth before they were written down in Hebrew. The first five books may have been written as early as 1400bc, and the latest books not until around 450BC. It took almost a thousand years for the whole Old Testament to be written down.

The books of the Bible were written by many different authors, but not all can be identified. Some may have had several authors, or may have been altered by other people. The first five books of the Bible are traditionally believed to have been written by Moses and are sometimes called The Five Books of Moses. There are passages which he could not have written, such as the account of his death.

The Old Testament in most Christian Bibles is divided into four sections: the Pentateuch (the first five books); the Historical Books (the following 12); Poetry and Wisdom (the next five) and Prophets (the last 17). The books in the Jewish Bible are arranged differently, putting the five books of the Pentateuch, what the Jews call the law, or Torah, first. This is followed by the books of Joshua and Judges, both books of Samuel and Kings, Isaiah, Jeremiah and Ezekiel with the minor prophets. The Jewish people call this section the Naviim. Finally come the Writings, the Kethubim, which includes the remainder of the books, including Psalms, Proverbs, and the books of Ruth and Daniel.

The Jewish Talmud
This contains the Mishnah, the oral law of the Jews.

❖ NAMES AND THEIR MEANINGS ❖

Many names given to people and places in the Bible are specially chosen because of their meaning.

Noah   This means 'comfort'; through Noah, God brings comfort to an otherwise evil world.

Isaac   This means 'laughter', because his elderly parents laughed in disbelief when God told them they would have a son, and they laughed with happiness when he was born.

Esau   This means 'red and shaggy'. It describes Esau's appearance.

Jacob   This means 'supplanter' or 'usurper'. It refers to Jacob stealing Esau's birthright.

Israel   Jacob's name was changed to Israel, which means 'he who has grappled with the Lord'.

Rachel   This means 'ewe'. Names like this were popular amongst herdspeople because they symbolized wealth.

Moses   This means 'drawn out'. As a baby, Moses was drawn out of the Nile by an Egyptian princess.

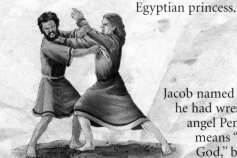

Jacob named the place where he had wrestled with the angel Penuel, which means "the face of God," because he saw God face to face there.

THE PYRAMIDS WOULD HAVE LOOMED OVER THE ISRAELITES AS THEY WORKED FOR PHARAOH

THE EGYPTIANS MAKE LIFE VERY HARD FOR THE ISRAELITES

1700BC

Moses is born, and is rescued from the Nile by an Egyptian princess.

Moses kills an Egyptian, and flees to exile in a distant land called Midian.

Moses sees the burning bush, and hears God's command to return to Egypt and free the Israelites.

1600BC

After over 400 years as slaves, Moses leads the Israelites out of Egypt to the Promised Land.

1500BC

MOSES COMMANDS THE RED SEA

1400BC

LOOK OVER JORDAN

How the Israelites found their Promised Land and their Judges ruled

Look over Jordan

THIS chapter covers the part of the Old Testament from halfway through Exodus to the end of Ruth. At the beginning of this section, the Israelites are a group of homeless wanderers in the desert, and by the end they have settled in the Promised Land. This section tells of their struggles along the way and charts the rises and falls of their faith in God.

The first story, "Manna from Heaven", describes the early years in the wilderness, when God provides manna and quails to feed his starving people. In "The First Battle", the Israelites experience their first victory in their campaign to take over the Promised Land. When they arrive at Mount Sinai, God tells Moses the laws by which he wants his people to live their lives, including the most important laws known as the Ten Commandments. According to God's instructions, a holy tent called a tabernacle is built. This is to be God's home on earth, a visible sign that He is living among His people. The Israelites carry it with them until they settle in Canaan and set it up permanently.

On leaving Mount Sinai, another period of wandering begins and the Israelites grow weary of the months of hardship. When they finally reach the borders of Canaan, they are too afraid to obey God's order to attack the local people. God is so angry at their disobedience, he punishes them by sentencing them to a further 40 years of wandering. As the years go by, the Israelites who had fled from Egypt grow older and die, and a new generation grows up. These young people have never known anything but the struggles of the travelling life and are better adapted than their parents were. They fight battle after battle with the local people, trying to drive them from their homes and take over their lands.

A long journey
The Exodus began in the fertile Nile valley, which must have made the hardships of the wilderness even harder to take.

Calm before the storm
Before the Israelites invaded the Promised Land, they camped here, at the Oasis of Jericho, near Gilgal, to rest.

The story "Death of Moses" tells of the great leader's last days. Although Moses does not enter the Promised Land, he climbs to the top of Mount Nebo to see with his own eyes the land his people will inherit. Before he dies, he hands over the leadership to his successor, Joshua. The following stories describe Joshua's impressive achievements as leader, from crossing the mighty river Jordan to storming the great city of Jericho. He goes on to capture the town of Ai, and he is tricked into making a treaty with the people of Gibeon. In the story "The Longest Day", he manages to overcome five of the region's kings in one long battle. At last, after many victories and much bloodshed, the Israelites finally take over the land of Canaan. The Promised Land is divided between the tribes, and the Israelites settle down to a life of farming and home-making.

After the death of Joshua, no single leader takes over. Instead, the Israelites are ruled by a succession of Judges, including Deborah, Gideon, Jephthah and Samson. Before the Judges begin to rule, there has been peace for many years. But as time goes by, people start to forget the struggles of the past and the hard-won victories. Instead of continuing to wage war on their enemies, as God had ordered, they begin to live alongside them as neighbours. Despite the Judges' warnings, they even start to worship the Canaanite gods. Time after time, God punishes his people by letting them fall into the hands of foreign rulers. After a period of suffering, they beg for forgiveness, and God appoints a Judge to save them. But as soon as the Judge dies, they slip back into their sinful ways.

Pilgrims to Jerusalem
A trip to the holy city of Jerusalem, first colonized by the Israelites at the time of Joshua, has been a goal for religious pilgrims like these for hundreds of years.

In contrast to all the discord in the stories of the Judges, the book ends with the story of Ruth – a gentle tale that deals with family life and everyday issues. Although it relates to the same period as the Judges, its subject matter is very different. The story ends with the birth of Ruth's baby, who will grow up to become the grandfather of the greatest King of Israel, David.

Throughout this section, the Israelites' faith in God ebbs and flows. After the Exodus from Egypt, their faith is strong and they look forward with excitement to reaching the Promised Land. When thirst and hunger take over, though, their faith weakens until God provides food and water. They go on to win their first victory. God is well aware of the weaknesses of His people, and accepts a great deal of wrongdoing from them. The story of the Golden Calf is another low point, when the people turn from God and start to worship an idol. Their faith is re-established with the building of the tabernacle. Once back on their travels, the Israelites become impatient again and begin to have doubts about Moses as their leader. When they disobey God's instruction to invade Canaan, their punishment is another 40 years of wandering. While a period of strong faith follows the crossing of the Jordan, it ebbs away after Joshua's death. *Look over Jordan* shows the remarkable faith and leadership of Moses, who continually defends his erring people against the wrath of God.

❖ **LOOK OVER JORDAN** ❖

This section covers the Israelites' time in the wilderness after the Exodus, their entry into the Promised Land and settling down in their new country.

IN THE WILDERNESS
Exodus, Ch. 16 to 18.
Numbers, Ch. 11 to 22.
THE TEN COMMANDMENTS
Exodus, Ch. 19 & 20.
THE DEATH OF MOSES
Deuteronomy, Ch. 31 to 34.
ENTERING THE PROMISED LAND
Joshua, Ch. 1 to 4.
JOSHUA IN CANAAN
Joshua, Ch. 6 to 24.
THE TIME OF THE JUDGES
Judges, Ch. 1 to 17.
RUTH
Ruth, Ch. 1 to 4.

Holy mountain
Mount Sinai, which at the time of the Bible was called Mount Horeb, was already a holy place before God gave Moses the Ten Commandments there. It was where Moses was first spoken to by God from the burning bush, when he was told he was to lead the Israelites from slavery in Egypt. He was told by God to remove his sandals, a common sign of respect still followed in many places of worship today.

Egypt to the Promised Land

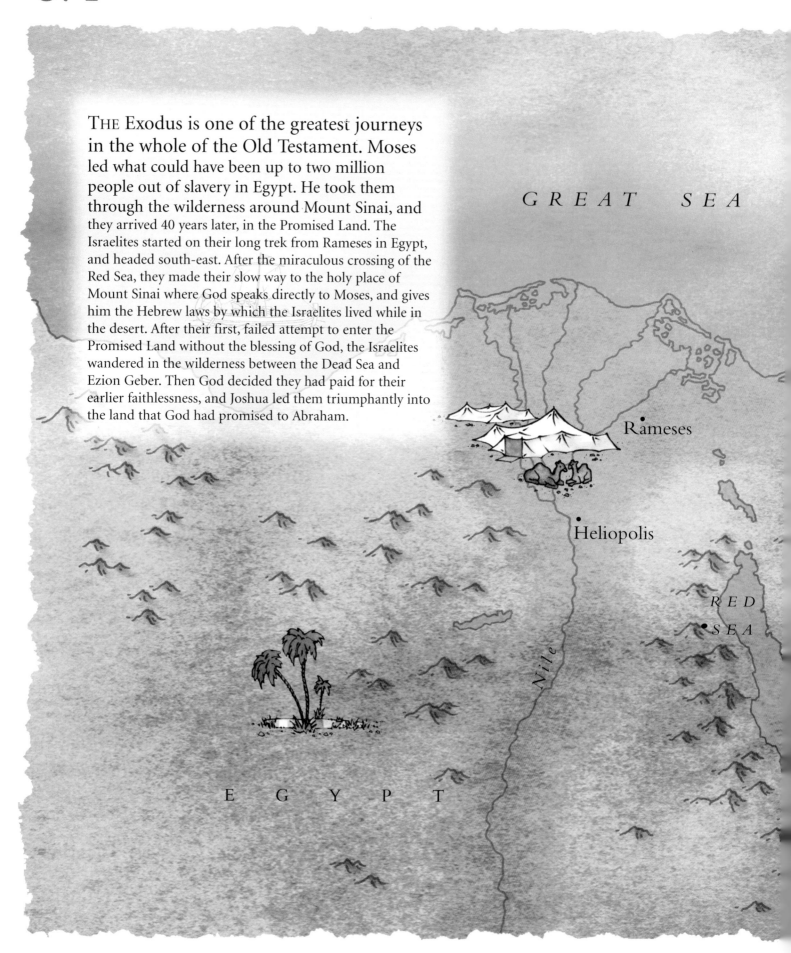

THE Exodus is one of the greatest journeys in the whole of the Old Testament. Moses led what could have been up to two million people out of slavery in Egypt. He took them through the wilderness around Mount Sinai, and they arrived 40 years later, in the Promised Land. The Israelites started on their long trek from Rameses in Egypt, and headed south-east. After the miraculous crossing of the Red Sea, they made their slow way to the holy place of Mount Sinai where God speaks directly to Moses, and gives him the Hebrew laws by which the Israelites lived while in the desert. After their first, failed attempt to enter the Promised Land without the blessing of God, the Israelites wandered in the wilderness between the Dead Sea and Ezion Geber. Then God decided they had paid for their earlier faithlessness, and Joshua led them triumphantly into the land that God had promised to Abraham.

GREAT   SEA

Rameses

Heliopolis

RED
SEA

Nile

E G Y P T

Hazor•

Shechem•

Bethel•
Jericho•

• Gaza

• Beersheba

• Ezion Geber

Mt. Sinai

M I D I A N

Manna from Heaven

JUST as God had promised centuries earlier, Abraham's descendants had now become a great people – the Israelite nation. The mighty Egyptian Pharaoh had done everything in his power to crush them but had been defeated, all thanks to the work of the Lord. For the first time in over four centuries, the Israelites were free, but homeless.

Imagine how tough it must have been for the hundreds of thousands of people who found themselves wandering through the Sinai Desert, not knowing where they were going or when they might get there. Mothers nursing their babies, children wailing with tiredness and men weighed down by their family's belongings. Day after day they plodded on together with only the cold, uncomfortable nights and the occasional rest days of the Sabbath to mark out time passing. The weeks seemed to melt together into an endless nightmare of heat, dust and walking . . . heat, dust and walking, and gradually their food began to run out. "We can't keep going like this!" some people moaned.

"We'd rather be back in Egypt," agreed others, feeling terribly hungry. "At least there we weren't starving."

God heard the suffering Israelites and called to Moses. "Reassure the people that I am with them," He said. "I shall make sure they don't go hungry."

Moses and Aaron gathered the famished people in a huge crowd. Aaron lifted his voice so his words of hope could be heard over the constant sound of crying, and the glory of the Lord suddenly came blazing through the clouds. Once again, Moses heard God speaking to him. Aaron announced the message. "Know that the Lord is

with you," he thundered, as the crowd tried to shield themselves from the blinding light. "Today, He will give you meat to eat, and tomorrow, He shall bring you bread!"

In the evening, as dusk fell, flocks of quails appeared in the sky and fluttered down to land around the camp. The starving Israelites dashed eagerly back and forth catching the little birds, then settled down to a feast of roasted

> **" Then the Lord said to Moses, 'Behold, I will rain bread from Heaven for you.' "**

❧ **ABOUT THE STORY** ❧

After weeks of wandering in the desert, the Israelites begin to lose faith in God. God sees their suffering and sends them quails and manna to eat. Although He promises to provide enough food every day, some people doubt Him and stockpile manna. God is disappointed, but He forgives them and continues to provide for them. When the people complain of thirst, God provides water, despite their lack of faith.

The manna appeared for six days and on the morning before the Sabbath, Moses told the people to gather twice as much. "There will be no manna tomorrow," Moses explained, "so we can spend the day worshipping God and resting, as is proper." When the Sabbath dawned, they found that the manna they had kept overnight was just as delicious as before. But once again, there were some who disobeyed. They went out looking for more. When the Lord saw these groups of greedy people, He was very disappointed. "How long will the people ignore my wishes?" He said to Moses. Yet He kept sending the manna day after day, to feed the hungry Israelites.

It wasn't long, however, before the Israelites were again complaining. When they reached Rephidim, they made camp, but there was no water to be found round about.

"If we keep following Moses and Aaron through this wilderness, we'll surely die of thirst," the people gasped angrily. "Tell God to send us water – or else!" they croaked through cracked lips at Moses and Aaron.

When the Lord heard the people's challenge, He was again deeply saddened. But even so, He still didn't desert them. He instructed Moses to strike a rock with his crook. As the rock split apart with an almighty crack, a jet of icy water came gushing through, creating a waterfall from which everyone could quench their thirst.

quail meat. That night, for the first time in weeks and weeks, they slept without the nagging ache of hunger interrupting their dreams.

Next morning, the Hebrews awoke to find strange, round, white flakes covering the ground. At first, they thought it was frost. But on closer inspection, they were amazed to discover that it was a type of bread that tasted of honey. "We'll call it manna," they cried excitedly, "which means bread from the Lord!" They rushed to gather as much as they could, but a stern order from Moses stopped them. "The bread is a gift from God. Take only as much as you need for today," he warned. Some people didn't listen and secretly hoarded manna in their tents. But they soon came to regret it when next day they found that the manna had turned mouldy. They also realized that there was no need to have saved it, for once again, there was fresh manna everywhere.

A flock of quails
A quail is a small, brown, short-tailed bird, like a tiny pheasant. Quails cross the Sinai Peninsula on their migrations between Europe and Africa. They can fly quickly for short periods of time but get tired on longer journeys. When this happens, they fly very slowly and very low making them easy to catch.

Daily bread
During their 40 years in the wilderness, the Israelites relied on the manna for food. The only time it would last overnight was the day before the Sabbath, the only time that God said they should collect more than they could eat in a day. This shows how in control God was, and how reliant the Israelites were on Him.

What is manna?
The word "manna" means "What is it?" in Hebrew. In the Bible, manna is described as white, like coriander seeds, and tasting like wafers made with honey. It is not known exactly what this substance is. Some people believe it is a sweet, white substance produced by some desert plants, such as the hammada shrub (see right). However, the regular appearance of the manna on six days out of seven, and the amount of it, point to God carrying out His will by controlling natural events.

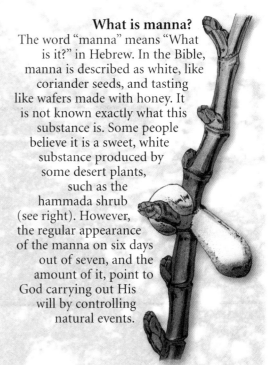

The First Battle

IN every area the Israelites travelled through, they made the local people very nervous. Imagine how intimidating it would be if you lived in a small desert community, and suddenly over 600,000 people looking for a home arrived on your doorstep – people you knew had defeated the mighty Egyptian army! The Israelites must have expected trouble to brew up sooner or later, and it first happened while they were camped at Rephidim. The leader of a local tribe, a man called Amalek, came to meet Moses, challenging the Israelites and declaring war.

Even though there were a lot of Israelites, they weren't at all ready to go out and fight. They had been travelling through the desert for many months and had little remaining strength to attack an enemy. But, unfortunately, they also had no choice. Moses searched through the people and entrusted the courageous young Joshua with the job of somehow turning the weary Israelites into fierce soldiers. "I want you to choose men for our troops and lead them in the battle against Amalek tomorrow," Moses told him. "Don't be afraid! God will be with us."

> " Joshua mowed down Amalek and his people with the edge of the sword. "

Next day, Aaron and Hur accompanied Moses to the top of a nearby hill. With beating hearts they watched as Joshua and the Israelites raced out to meet the savage Amalekites and clashed into a seething tangle of blood and determination. Praying to the Lord, Moses took his crook and lifted up his arms to Heaven. Almost straightaway, Aaron and Hur noticed that the Israelites began to have the upper hand. In the midst of all the slashing and stabbing, they could see Amalekites dropping on every side. But it wasn't to last. Moses gradually grew tired, and when he could hold his shaking arms up no longer, the tide suddenly

turned. At once it seemed as if there were Amalekites everywhere, killing Israelites whichever way Aaron and Hur looked. In desperation, the two men moved a rock so Moses could sit on it and then took up position on either side, each holding up one of Moses's hands. All day, Aaron and Hur supported Moses without wavering. No matter how cold or weary their muscles became, they kept his arms aloft. And when the Sun finally set, they heard cheering. The Israelites had won their first battle!

Now rumours had already spread of how God had brought the Israelites out of slavery and defeated the Egyptian army. And when news of this most recent victory reached Jethro, Moses's father-in-law, he rushed to be with Moses and join in the celebrations. Jethro knew that his son-in-law had become a great leader, but even so, he was surprised to see how the people relied on Moses to decide everything for them. Jethro found Moses surrounded by huge crowds, each of whom wanted private guidance from God and a solution to their individual problems. The people thought nothing of waiting around all day in the hope of talking to Moses. Jethro was shocked. "This is no good!" he told his son-in-law. "You'll soon be exhausted and the people will never get anything done. The nation has grown too big for you to manage on your own. Divide the people into groups, appointing a good man at the head of each one. Choose leaders you can trust to make their own decisions on everyday matters, while you deal with the more important issues, making sure that God's will is being done." So Moses set wise judges as governors over the people and arranged the Israelites into a strong nation under his command and the leadership of the Lord.

Joshua
This story contains the first mention of Joshua, when Moses chooses him as his assistant. Joshua achieves victory in this first battle. Later, when the Israelites reach the border of Canaan, he and another man called Caleb are the only ones who trust God's judgement and are prepared to invade when God tells them to. Because of this, only Joshua and Caleb of the original Israelites actually enter Canaan. Joshua, like Moses, has patience and humility, and he goes on to succeed Moses as leader of the Israelites, and to fight many successful campaigns in Canaan.

The Ten Commandments

THREE months after they had left Egypt, the Israelites reached a mountain called Mount Sinai and made camp there. This peak, which thrust up towards Heaven itself and towered over the wilderness all around, was believed to be a holy place, and Moses climbed to the top to talk to the Lord alone.

"The people have seen what I did to the Egyptians for their sake, they have seen how I lifted them out of slavery and have been with them ever since, looking after them on their wanderings," said the Lord. "All the Earth is mine – and if the Israelites are true to me and my wishes, I shall make them a holy nation. Tell the people to prepare themselves," God ordered Moses, "for in three days' time, I shall come down to Mount Sinai myself to give you my sacred laws. All the people will be able to see me descend from Heaven, but you must put up barriers around the foot of the mountain so no one sets foot on this holy ground. If anyone disobeys, they will die."

> *And Moses went up to God, and the Lord called to him out of the mountain.*

On the morning of the third day, spears of lightning suddenly started to stab through the clouds and giant drumrolls of thunder came rumbling over the people's heads, threatening to bring the heavens tumbling down on top of them. While the Israelites stood gazing upwards like fearful statues, the skies split open with a mighty blast of trumpets and flames came bursting through, consuming the peak in fire. The ground began to tremble and quake as Mount Sinai was turned into a blazing torch, and the people tried to shield themselves from the searing light and burning heat. Above them, the smoke gathered in a heavy cloud, which spread a shadow all around and darkened their faces. And when the thick fog had completely wrapped the mountain top from their view, all eyes turned to the small figures of Moses and Aaron making their way up the slopes. Closer and closer the two men drew to the dense, smouldering cloud, then – without hesitating – they walked straight into it.

God spoke to Moses on the mountain top, telling him all the laws for His people to obey, but ten were the most important:

You must not have any other God except me.

You must not make and worship statues or pictures of anything in the skies, on Earth or in the sea.

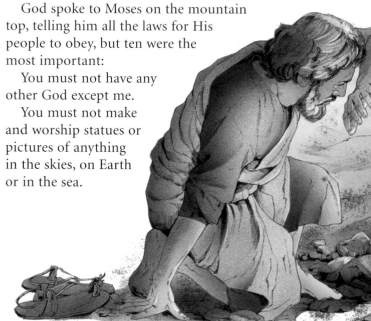

Mount Sinai
It is not known exactly where Mount Sinai is, but it is usually identified as a mountain called Jebel Musa (above). God appeared to Moses on Mount Sinai, also known as Mount Horeb, and gave him the Ten Commandments.

Forbidden idols
An idol is an image of a god used as an object of worship. Other tribes and nations commonly made images of their gods and worshipped these. God made it clear to the Israelites that He could never be represented by an object, and that they must never make idols to worship.

God's contract
The laws God gave to Moses would be carved onto two stone tablets as a contract between God and His people.

You must use the Lord's name only in a respectful way.

You must keep the Sabbath, the seventh day of the week, as a holy day of rest and worship.

You must love your father and mother.

You must not kill anyone.

You must not love anyone else's husband or wife.

You must not steal.

You must not lie.

You must not envy other people's possessions.

Meanwhile, at the foot of the mountain, the Israelites were terrified. The smoke pouring out above them was thicker than ever, lightning was whipcracking across the clouds, and above the raging of the thunderstorm could be heard the blaring of almighty trumpets. How relieved the people were when they saw Moses and Aaron coming down from the mountain, and even more amazing, they saw that they were completely unharmed! But they were no less terrified by God's power.

"Don't be so afraid," Moses told them. "God has chosen to appear to you like this so you'll never forget who He is and what He wants of you."

"We'll do everything the Lord says," everyone agreed, and that night Moses wrote down every word God had spoken in a book of laws, which the Israelites would keep, to make sure they remembered God's commands.

Early next morning, Moses set about building a huge altar at the foot of the mountain. All the people gathered in front of it, impatient to find out what God had said. Then the whole crowd listened in silence as Moses read his book of laws aloud. When he had finished, the nation solemnly swore to obey the Lord's words.

YOU SHALL HAVE NO OTHER GODS BEFORE ME.

❁

YOU SHALL NOT MAKE FOR YOURSELF A GRAVEN IMAGE, OR ANY LIKENESS OF ANYTHING THAT IS IN HEAVEN ABOVE OR THAT IS IN THE EARTH BENEATH OR THAT IS IN THE WATER UNDER THE EARTH.

❁

YOU SHALL NOT TAKE THE NAME OF THE LORD YOUR GOD IN VAIN.

❁

REMEMBER THE SABBATH DAY, TO KEEP IT HOLY.

HONOUR YOUR FATHER AND YOUR MOTHER.

❁

YOU SHALL NOT KILL.

❁

YOU SHALL NOT COMMIT ADULTERY.

❁

YOU SHALL NOT STEAL.

❁

YOU SHALL NOT BEAR FALSE WITNESS.

❁

YOU SHALL NOT COVET YOUR NEIGHBOUR'S HOUSE.

❁

❖ ABOUT THE STORY ❖

In this story, God comes down from Heaven to reveal His sacred laws. The people watch in amazement as Moses and Aaron disappear up the mountain to hear the laws. The most important laws are the Ten Commandments – the ten basic rules by which God wants His people to live their lives from now on. The Ten Commandments and the other laws form God's covenant with His people.

The Golden Calf

GOD summoned Moses again to the top of Mount Sinai, this time without Aaron. The Israelites watched nervously as Moses ventured into the darkness of the low, hovering cloud all on his own and disappeared from view. The people were eager for God to talk to them once more, and they kept a vigil at the foot of the mountain. But days passed into weeks without any sign of Moses, and the Israelites started to get impatient. "Where is Moses?" they wondered, tired with waiting. "Whatever is he doing?"

"He can't be talking to God all this time!" some said.

"He's abandoned us!" cried others, angrily.

"Tell us what to do!" the people shouted, surging forwards. "Give us a new god to follow!"

Aaron could see he had a riot on his hands and he was very worried. Thinking quickly, he ordered everyone to take off their gold jewellery and bring it to him. Soon a heap of glittering treasure was piled at his feet, and after melting it down, Aaron made the gold into the likeness of a calf. All the time Aaron was working he could hear the people growing out of control, and he hurried to build an altar too. "Here is your new god," he roared, taking the dull-eyed monster to show them. To his relief the people were delighted, and he declared a feast day to the new god.

At the top of the mountain, God looked down at the Israelite camp and was beside Himself with wrath. "I am furious with these unfaithful people," He thundered. "I will destroy them all!" But Moses begged the Lord to be merciful and managed to convince the Lord to leave punishing the people to him. Moses hurried off down the mountain, carefully carrying two stone tablets on which the Lord had written the laws by His very own hand.

Long before he reached the camp, the angry Moses could hear the wild noise of celebrating. When he finally caught sight of the Israelites he was enraged and slammed the stone tablets to the ground, where they shattered into a million pieces. He seized the idol and burnt it, before grinding it down into razor-sharp grains which he threw into the Israelites' water and made them drink.

"Don't blame me!" cried Aaron. "You know how sinful the people can be! I just collected their gold jewellery, threw it into the fire, and out came this golden calf all by itself!" he lied, daringly.

Apis the Bull
This picture shows the Egyptian god, Apis the Bull. The golden calf made by Aaron may have been modelled on Apis; as the Israelites had lived in Egypt, they knew about bull worship. In Egypt, the bull or calf was a symbol of fertility and strength.

The Levites
The Levites in the story were members of the tribe of Levi, which was Moses's own tribe. They were God's faithful followers, who helped Moses to punish the sinful Israelites. The Levites later became the assistants of the priests of the tabernacle. The picture shows the Levites slaying the Israelites.

When Moses realized that even his own brother's heart had become evil, he stood in the gateway of the camp, blocking anyone from leaving. "Who is on the side of the Lord?" he demanded of the whole nation. "If anyone remains faithful to God, come and stand by me." Straight away, members of Moses's own tribe of Levi pushed their way through to Moses. His eyes were cold, and his voice was stern and unforgiving. "Now put on your swords and slay all the unbelievers," he instructed the Levites. Moses didn't speak again until nearly 3,000 people lay dead. "You have sinned a great sin," he admonished the grief-stricken Israelites. "I will speak to the Lord, to see if I can somehow make up for it."

> *Moses's anger burned hot, and he threw down the tablets and broke them.*

Once more God forgave the Israelites their faithlessness and renewed His covenant with them. He also again wrote the laws by hand on to two stone tablets. "Now go and lead my people to the Promised Land," He told Moses. "I will send my angel to lead the way. But the people have today sinned greatly against me and I shall not forget it."

Swords
The Levites used swords to kill the unfaithful Israelites. The sword is the most frequently mentioned weapon in the Bible. The earliest swords were usually like daggers – straight, double edged and mainly used for stabbing. By the time of this story the Philistines, the Sea People, had introduced swords with longer blades. These swords were kept in a sheath attached to a belt when they were not is use, and they became more and more popular. Swords have been found all over the Middle East, and many of the sword hilts were very richly decorated, often with symbols of strength, like lions, to help the wearer in battle.

Gold
Some of the Israelites would have learned metalworking while in Egypt, so they could have helped Aaron make the golden calf. They could also have made the sort of gold and jewellery shown here– rings, bracelets and nose-rings– that were worn by women at the time.

∾ ABOUT THE STORY ∾
Impatient for Moses to reappear, the Israelites begin to lose faith in God, begging Aaron to find them another god. Aaron makes the golden calf, which he presents to them as their new god. God is furious and ready to destroy them. However, Moses intervenes. Only the faithful Levites stand by Moses and carry out God's punishment. God then forgives his people and renews his covenant with them.

The tabernacle

MOSES gathered all the people of Israel together and said, "The time is close at hand when we must leave Mount Sinai. However, before we move on to the Promised Land of Canaan, there is one very important thing God has asked of us that we must do. We must build Him a tabernacle – a holy tent where we can meet and pray – and a sacred chest called an ark to keep safe the stone tablets of His law. Anyone who would like to contribute towards these things is welcome to give materials, and any offers of help to do the building will be gratefully received."

The people went back to their tents very excited. What an honour it was to have the responsibility of making these things for the Lord Himself! Everyone began searching through their belongings, all eager to provide their most prized possessions, to make the tabernacle and ark as splendid as possible.

Soon people all over the camp were flooding towards Moses's tent to offer their treasures. They gave their jewellery, ornaments and dishes of silver and bronze; sweet-smelling acacia wood; rich materials, and the very best linen and animal skins. The leaders of the tribes offered precious gem stones and exotic spices and oils. Everyone was so happy to be able to offer things to God!

Moses soon had more treasure than could be used and had to order the Israelites to stop coming with their gifts. Then he appointed expert craftsmen to take charge of the building and the work started. Bit by bit, with great care, the Israelites constructed everything according to the design that God Himself had given Moses on Mount

Sinai. There was to be an outer enclosure with the tabernacle inside, housing the ark itself. They also needed holy robes for Aaron, whom God had chosen as the High Priest, and for his sons, the priests who would serve the Lord inside the tabernacle. Everyone did their absolute best, for each person knew that only perfection would do.

Finally, the time came when everything was ready. Moses waited until the first day of the first month, just as God had ordered, and then painstakingly assembled everything. First, Moses set up the tabernacle itself. It had wooden walls, but looked from the outside like a grand tent because it was covered over on three sides from roof to floor. On the outside was strong weatherproof leather.

❧ ABOUT THE STORY ❧

The word "tabernacle" comes from the Latin "tabernaculum", meaning "tent". The significance of the tabernacle is that it shows God coming to live with His people. He sets up His tent amongst their tents.

The tabernacle is a confirmation that God has forgiven His people for their past sins. The Israelites carry it with them on their journey and are reassured to know that God is travelling with them.

Sacred lamps
The type of seven-armed lamp-stand that Moses set up in the Holy Place is called a "menorah". It had a main stem, with three branches protruding from either side of this. The main stem supported a lampholder, and each branch ended in a flower-shaped lampholder. The whole lamp-stand was made of gold.

Trees in the desert
The ark was made from acacia wood, as the acacia was one of the few trees that would have grown in the desert. Acacia trees still grow in dry parts of the world today.

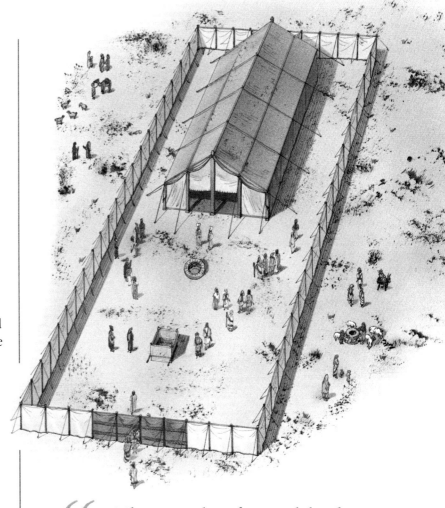

Moses set the entrance to the tabernacle at the eastern end, through a curtain hanging from five pillars. Then he prepared the inside. All around the ceiling and walls, Moses hung linen curtains in a wonderful blaze of violet, purple and scarlet. Then, just as God had instructed, Moses hung up a curtain called the Veil to divide the tabernacle into two rooms. The innermost room was called the Holy of Holies, and it was here that Moses positioned the Ark of the Covenant. Inside the sacred chest he laid the holy stone tablets on which God had written the Law. Then Moses sealed the lid. Returning back outside the Holy of Holies, Moses then set an altar in front of the Veil. He ordered the priests to keep incense burning there day and night, so that beautiful-smelling smoke would waft up, accompanying their prayers to Heaven. Then Moses set up the second room inside the tabernacle, the Holy Place, with a seven-armed lamp-stand and a table holding 12 sacred loaves, each representing one of the 12 tribes. Going outside the tabernacle, Moses positioned the priests' wash basin, and filled it with water before Aaron and his sons purified themselves with cleansing rituals. Next Moses set up the Altar of Burnt Offering and made the very first of the daily sacrifices that were to take place there. Finally, Moses put up the enclosure wall, to screen everything from view.

When Moses's work was finished, everyone saw a cloud descend over the tabernacle and a light enter the Holy of Holies – so bright that not even Moses could enter there. From that moment onwards, the Israelites only moved off on their travels when God gave the sign by lifting the cloud from the tabernacle.

> *The people of Israel had done all the work and Moses blessed them.*

The Ark of the Covenant
The word "ark" comes from the Latin word *arca* which means "chest". The ark was a rectangular wooden box, decorated with gold. On the lid were two cherubs with outspread wings, between which God was supposed to live when on Earth. The ark could be carried by inserting poles through gold rings attached to its sides. It was known by various names, including "The Ark of the Covenant" and "The Ark of the Lord". The two tablets inscribed with the Ten Commandments were kept inside the ark.

Holy robes
This picture shows the clothes that Aaron wore as the high priest of the tabernacle. Bells and pomegranates hung in a fringe from the hem of his long robe, and the shorter tunic over the top was tied with a girdle. His breastplate was decorated with 12 precious stones, one for each of the 12 tribes of Israel.

In the Wilderness

AT God's command, the Israelites left Mount Sinai and set out on the final stages of their journey towards Canaan. The Lord had sent so many signs to prove He was with them that the people should have forged ahead with confidence. But as the months of hardship went on, their faith wavered once again. Eventually, even Aaron and Miriam, Moses's own family, became discontented. "Who does Moses think he is? After all, he's not the only one God has appeared to!" The Lord was furious and summoned them to the tabernacle. "How dare you!" He roared. "I may sometimes talk to people in a dream, but Moses sees me as I am and talks to me face to face!" Miriam hung her head in shame and was horrified to see that her hands were covered with the sores of leprosy! She was cast out of the camp at once and left to suffer in the wilderness. Aaron knew that Miriam's only hope was for Moses to ask the Lord for mercy. Aaron begged Moses for help, and a week later Miriam found herself healed.

The miserable rabble eventually reached Canaan. However, several tribes were already settled in the country, people who would fight to defend their homes. So God instructed Moses to send 12 men to spy out the land. After 40 days they returned with wonderful reports of how beautiful and fertile the countryside was. But they also warned that the local tribes would be hard to conquer, and spread fear with stories of giant men and earthquakes. Only Joshua and Caleb trusted that it was the time to attack. But the scared Israelites would not follow them.

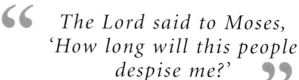

> ❝ *The Lord said to Moses, 'How long will this people despise me?'* ❞

The Lord was furious. "How long will you people go on refusing to believe what I say?" He thundered in the tabernacle. "Because you have turned your backs on the country I promised you, I shall give Canaan to your children instead. You will be condemned to wander for 40 years. You will die homeless, and your bodies will rot here in this wilderness, all except Joshua and Caleb!" At this threat, the Israelites grew desperate. Many of them rushed out early next morning to begin an attack. But without God's blessing the raiders were all killed. And in the camp, all the spies that told lies about Canaan were found dead of a mysterious disease.

With hope of entering the Promised Land now gone, the Israelites felt they had nothing left to lose. They thought Moses had lured them away from their homes for nothing but an empty promise. They no longer cared for his leadership and began to rise up against him. When three ringleaders called Korah, Dathan and Abiram demanded that they and 247 other men should be allowed to be priests, Moses decided he'd had enough. "Do what you like with them, Lord!" he cried. Next day, in front of all those gathered to worship, Moses announced, "These men want to be priests. It is against God's wishes, but I am powerless to stop them." As he finished speaking, there was a resounding crack and the ground swallowed up the would-be-priests, their families and all their belongings.

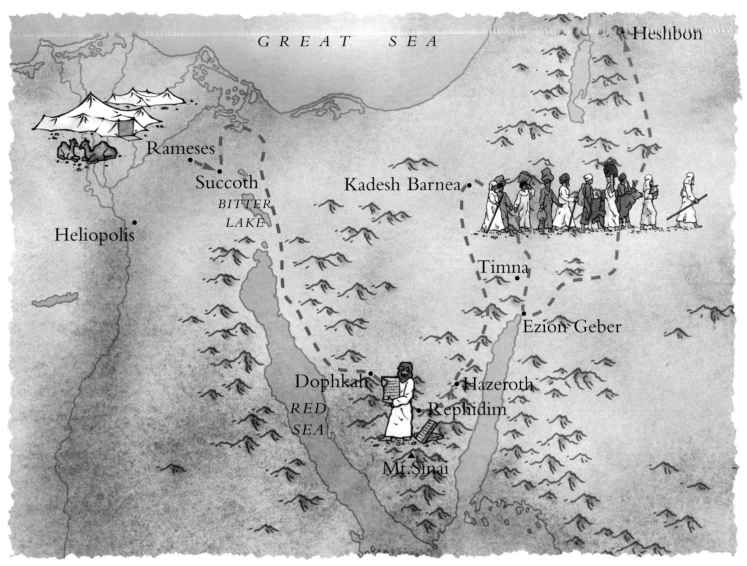

To end the people's uprisings once and for all, the Lord told Moses to instruct each tribe to bring him a rod with their leader's name written on it. When Moses put all the rods in the tabernacle, everyone was amazed to see that Aaron's blossomed with flowers and budded into almonds. Everyone was warned by this sign that Aaron was God's chosen High Priest, and Moses kept the rod as a reminder to everyone not to question God's will again.

The Exodus from Egypt

After the miraculous crossing of the Red Sea, the Israelites still had a long way to go to reach the Promised Land. They first made their way through the wilderness by the Bitter Lake. At Rephidim Moses performed the miracle of getting water from the rock for the Israelites. Then the Israelites camped at Sinai, and Moses received the Ten Commandments from God. At Kadesh Barnea Moses sent out the spies whose false report condemned the Israelites to 40 years wandering in the desert.

A great leader

Despite the Israelites' lack of faith, Moses remains loyal to his people, constantly appealing to God for mercy on their behalf. God himself pays tribute to Moses, telling Miriam and Aaron that He singles out Moses by appearing to him face to face, rather than in a dream or vision (Numbers 12: 6-8). Moses never seeks power for himself, and he is happy to spend his life carrying out God's will.

A sign from God

To try and end the problems of the Israelites, God sent a sign, a blossoming almond branch, to show them all that Aaron was His chosen priest.

❧ ABOUT THE STORY ❧

Once again, the Israelites begin to doubt Moses's word. God is furious at their contempt for Moses. When the people refuse to obey Him and invade the cities of Canaan, God's punishment is severe – He sentences them to another 40 years in the wilderness.

Balak and Balaam

THE years of wandering continued and the Israelites who had disobeyed God began to age and die – Miriam and Aaron among them – just as the Lord had vowed they would. A new generation began to grow up to take their place: tough young people who had never known anything but the hardships of the travelling life, and who were well-trained in fighting skills. As the nation moved around the borders of Canaan, the local tribes came out to defend their homes, and though sometimes the Israelites were forced back by the sheer number of warriors facing them, on many occasions they engaged in fierce battles. With the help of the Lord they began to win victory after victory, slaying the Amorite kings, Sihon of Heshbon and Og of Bashan, and taking their lands. Then they moved on into the plains of Moab.

The Moabites had heard of the destruction of the Amorite peoples, and when they saw the Israelites heading in their own direction, they were very frightened. Balak, the son of the king, decided there was nothing for it but to ask a great prophet called Balaam for help. Hastily, he sent several courtiers off to Balaam with money and an urgent message: "These Israelites we face won their way out of slavery in Egypt. How can we take on such a mighty people and win? Please come to Moab and put a curse on them, so we'll be able to drive them out of our lands."

Balaam listened to the courtiers and told them that he would answer their request for help the following morning, once he'd given it careful consideration. But that night, God appeared to him in his dreams. "Do not grant these people what they ask," He instructed Balaam, "for I have blessed the Israelite nation." Next day, the courtiers' faces fell as Balaam told them of his decision, and their hearts were heavy as they hurried back.

When Balak heard the disappointing news he began to panic, and instantly despatched some of his most highly

regarded nobles – laden down with even more riches – to Balaam. "Balak will give you whatever you want," they begged the wise man. "Only please, we beg you, return with us to Moab and put a curse on the Israelites." Balaam felt very sorry for the desperate nobles. However, he still refused to help. "Even if Balak gave me his whole treasure-house, I couldn't go against the word of God," he explained. But during the night God spoke to him once again. "I shall allow you to go with the Moabites after all," He told Balaam, "but do only what I tell you to do."

On rising next morning, the nobles were overjoyed to see Balaam saddling up his donkey. "There's no time to lose!" they cried, full of renewed hope, and hurried him

> ❝ *'The word that God puts in my mouth, that must I speak.'* ❞

❧ ABOUT THE STORY ❧

Balaam has the power to bless or curse people. Balak wants Balaam to help the Moabites by putting a curse on the Israelites. However, the Israelites have God's blessing, and Balaam will not go against God's will. Balaam blesses the Israelites instead of cursing them.

Telling the future
Balaam was a diviner, someone who tries to tell the future by magic. Several different forms of divination are mentioned in the Bible. One of these is astrology. Astrologers use the position of the Sun, Moon, planets and some of the star constellations to predict the future. Unlike other forms of divination, astrology was not actually forbidden by Moses's law, but people did look down on it. They did not see it as a proper science in the same way that they did astronomy, which involves studying the movements of the stars and planets.

off at once on the road back to Moab. Unfortunately, before they had gone very far, Balaam's donkey started to play up. She suddenly veered off the road and charged into a field, with the prophet clinging on for dear life. After heaving on the donkey's harness with all his strength, Balaam finally managed to bring her to a halt. As soon as he'd got his breath back, the cross prophet struck the animal with his staff.

After carrying on a little way the donkey suddenly shied again, this time crushing Balaam up against a wall and bruising his leg. The prophet was amazed that his usually peaceful animal was behaving in this way, and once again dismounted to give the donkey a beating.

Imagine Balaam's dismay when, before they had got much further down the road, he felt the donkey's legs begin to buckle beneath him. He managed to jump off just in time before the animal rolled over and lay down. "That's it!" yelled Balaam in anger, and he began to hit the donkey even more savagely than before.

Unbeknown to Balaam and the others, the donkey had taken fright three times because on each occasion the Angel of the Lord had suddenly appeared in front of her, blocking the way. Now, the poor animal was startled once again to find that she could talk! "What have I done?" she brayed at Balaam. "Why are you punishing me? I've never let you down before!"

Balaam was stunned, but he still managed to stutter a reply. "You made a fool of me, you stupid animal!" As soon as the words had left his lips, God lifted the veil that had been clouding the prophet's eyes and he saw the Angel of the Lord standing in front of him, brandishing his sword of flame. Balaam at once fell on his knees before the terrifying angel and prayed to God.

"I have sinned! But I didn't know the donkey was swerving to avoid you," he cried. "Have you come to tell me that I shouldn't be going to Moab? If so, I'll turn back straight away."

"You may go and meet Balak, but be careful to say only what I tell you to say," the angel warned, sternly. Then he vanished, and the baffled men continued on their way.

Balak couldn't wait for the prophet to arrive at his palace, but rushed out to meet him instead. Wasting no time he took Balaam up into the mountains, from where they could see all the tribes of Israel camped below. Three times, on three different peaks, Balak made a sacrifice to the Lord. And each time, on each peak, Balaam heard God telling him not to curse the Israelites, but to bless them. "Israel shall crush the people of Moab," Balaam prophesied. "The descendants of Jacob shall invade your cities and destroy them!" Needless to say, Balak was furious. He banished Balaam straight back home without delay. But everything came to pass just as Balaam had foretold, and the Israelites crushed the peoples of the plains of Moab.

Throwing arrows
Another way that people like Balaam may have tried to tell the future was through the practice of rhabdomancy. To do this, they would have taken a group of sticks or arrows, like those shown here, and thrown them into the air. Depending on how they landed they believed they could tell the future. Divination was widely practised, but it was forbidden by God through Moses.

Balaam's donkey
In ancient times, donkeys were very important especially to poorer people. They were the main form of transport and could travel up to 30km a day.

Death of Moses

WHEN Moses reached the age of 120 years old, the Lord told him it was his time to die. It must have been bitterly disappointing for Moses, after all he had done to free the Israelites from slavery and guide them safely through the wilderness, that he would not live to enter the Promised Land. Yet over and above his sadness, he longed to take his place in Heaven and be with God forever.

Summoning up his dwindling strength, Moses called the nation to gather together so he could speak to them for the last time. Moses looked out over the sea of faces, all anxiously looking up at him, to hear what he had to say. "The Lord has told me that I will not be going over the River Jordan with you," Moses told them.

The massive crowd gasped with one voice. They were deeply shocked. How would they manage to invade Canaan without Moses to tell them how? And whoever would be able to replace God's right-hand man?

Moses motioned for the worried people to calm down, and, when the noise from the worried crowd had died away, he raised his voice once again. "When the time comes to enter the Promised Land, the Lord Himself will go before you, destroying the peoples in your path. He will not let you down or abandon you, but will be with you always, leading you to victory."

Then Moses summoned Joshua to come and stand beside him, where all the people could see him. "Here is your new leader," Moses announced. "God has commanded that you shall follow Joshua!" A cheer rose up from the

❧ ABOUT THE STORY ❧

Moses was already 80 years old when he left Egypt. He has spent the last 40 years of his life wandering in the wilderness. The length of time taken to reach the Promised Land was God's punishment to the Israelites for their lack of faith. Moses's faith has remained strong, despite the fact that he is not to enter the land that was promised to his ancestors. The people's mourning is a tribute to Moses's greatness.

Mourning a death
When Israelites were in mourning, they had certain rituals to perform. They might remove their sandals, leave their hair unbrushed, or cover their head with a hand. At funerals, some people would hire mourners, like the Egyptian ones shown here, to make a better show at the burial.

Burial place
No one knows exactly where Moses was buried. Some people believe that the church on Mount Nebo, shown below, was built where his grave is situated.

front of the crowd and rippled backwards through the people like a wave, and Moses turned to rest his trembling hands on the young man's broad shoulders. "Be strong and courageous, Joshua," he bade him. "For the day will come when you will lead these people triumphantly into the land that the Lord promised their fathers. Trust in God, and He will be with you in whatever you do."

> ❝ *'The Lord will be with you, He will not fail you, do not be afraid.'* ❞

Moses was worried that, once he had gone, the people would forget everything he'd told them and turn to wickedness. So he wrote down each word of all the laws that God had given him and entrusted them to the safe keeping of the priests of the ark, so they could make sure that all the Israelites knew and understood them. Next, he went with Joshua to the tabernacle, to present the new leader of the people to the Lord. Finally, Moses called the elders of all the tribes together and gave them his blessing.

When all Moses's preparations were at last done, he went on his own to the top of Mount Pisgah.

"Look all around you," said the Lord, showing Moses the beautiful countryside of Canaan stretching away into the distance. "This is the land I promised to Abraham, Isaac and Jacob. Although you will not enter it yourself, I vow that it will belong to your descendants."

Moses died content that he had seen Canaan with his own eyes and with faith that it would indeed one day be his people's home. The whole Israelite nation had witnessed Moses's mighty power and great deeds, and they mourned his passing bitterly for 30 days.

MOSES WAS A GREAT MAN. ALTHOUGH HE WAS 120 YEARS OLD WHEN HE DIED, ACCORDING TO THE BIBLE, "HIS EYES NOT DIM, NOR HIS NATURAL FORCE ABATED".

Hebrew laws
The first five books of the Old Testament contain the Hebrew laws, also known as the Law of Moses. These are God's instructions to His people as to how they must live their lives. The most important laws are the Ten Commandments, but others cover a wide range of subjects, like laws on how to keep healthy, and punishments for lots of different crimes.

Moses's punishment
Many years earlier, Moses had once disobeyed God. His punishment was that he would not enter the Promised Land but only look upon it. This view shows Canaan over the sea of Galilee as Moses may have looked on it before his death.

Rahab and the Spies

Now Moses was gone, the responsibility of rousing the Israelites to take the Promised Land rested squarely on Joshua's shoulders. But even though this was a hugely daunting task, Joshua was not afraid. God spoke to him, inspiring him with confidence and courage. "It is time for you to lead the Israelites across the River Jordan, into the country I have promised will be yours. I never failed Moses and I will not fail you either, so be strong and brave-hearted! As long as you keep my laws, you will have nothing to fear. I will be with you always and you will have victory!" Standing tall and steadfast, Joshua commanded his officers to prepare the people for the invasion without delay.

Excitement rippled through the camp as the news spread to make ready. After 40 years, the moment that the travellers had been waiting for had finally arrived! The Israelites were about to see for themselves the wonderful countryside that their parents and grandparents had struggled for so long to reach. And God had promised them success. The Promised Land would at last be theirs! Everyone was so eager that even though there were hundreds of thousands of people to mobilize, the preparations took only three days.

Meanwhile, Joshua sent two men on a dangerous secret mission. "Go and investigate the city of Jericho," he told them. "I want you to find out as much as you can about its defences and its army." And the two spies slipped away.

Under cover, the men managed to dodge inside Jericho's gates and walk through the city, mingling with the enemy. After they had found out all they could, they went to the house of a woman called Rahab, who had promised to keep them safe for the night. But in the narrow streets of Jericho nothing went unseen. It didn't take long for neighbourhood gossip and rumours to reach the ears of the king, who immediately sent soldiers to Rahab's house. "Open up by royal command!" they yelled, battering at the door. "Open up or we'll force the door down!"

Rahab remained perfectly calm. "Whatever are you making all this fuss about?" she smiled sweetly, welcoming the soldiers into her house.

"Where are they?" the soldiers snarled, upturning tables and dragging curtains aside . "Come on. We know you've got them – you're hiding two Israelites, foreign spies and enemies in here somewhere!"

Rahab's faith
Rahab was a prostitute who lived in a house that formed part of the town wall of Jericho. She knew that the Israelites planned to capture the town, and she feared for her own life and for the lives of her family. Rahab had heard how God had helped the Israelites on their journey from Egypt, and she believed in His power. She declared her faith in God and begged the spies to save her family, in return for her helping them. When the Israelites destroyed Jericho, Rahab and her family were the only people who were spared.

Spies
A spy secretly collects information on the activities, movements and plans of an enemy, and then reports this to someone else. This story illustrates the use of spies in Bible times, and they are still used all over the world today. Spies are also known as secret agents. The rope that Rahab used to help the spies escape from Jericho could have been made of twisted hair or strips of animal skin.

"Israelites? No!" Rahab gasped, pretending to be shocked. "You don't mean they were spies! It's true that two men came to stay with me, but I had no idea they were Israelites!" She paused, and then said, "In that case, I'm afraid you've missed them. They waited until darkness fell and then they went out somewhere." Rahab's voice grew urgent. "You'll have to hurry – it's nearly dark and the city gates are about to shut! They can't have got very far. If you go quickly, you might just catch them." The soldiers rushed out of the house in a terrible hurry and dashed off down the street.

The minute the soldiers were out of sight, Rahab rushed up to the roof, where she had hidden the Israelites under a heap of reeds that she had laid out to dry in the sun. The two men were highly relieved when they saw that the fingers uncovering them were Rahab's – not those belonging to the King of Jericho's soldiers!

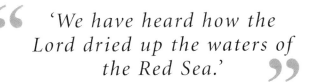

> ## 'We have heard how the Lord dried up the waters of the Red Sea.'

"It's too risky for you to stay here any longer," Rahab warned them in a whisper. "You must go and hide in the hills, where the soldiers can't find you. But before you go, please promise me one thing. Everyone here is terrified of your people. We know how the Red Sea turned aside and let you pass out of Egypt; we've heard how you crushed King Sihon and King Og and took their lands. Nearly everyone believes that God is on your side and that anyone who faces you is doomed. In return for the help I have given you,

promise me that you will spare me and my family when the Israelites come marching into Jericho."

The men took her hands. "When we attack, make sure everyone is locked inside your house and tie a scarlet cord at the window. We will then spare everyone inside, for the sake of the kindness you have shown us."

Rahab's house was built into the city wall itself. Opening up a window, she peered out nervously to see if anyone was around. Then she tied a rope firmly on to the ledge and flung the other end out into the darkness, listening to it tumble down a long way below. After a moment's anxious goodbye, the two Israelites climbed silently down, quite unseen, and escaped into the night.

Tribes of Canaan

When the Israelites arrived in the land of Canaan, there were already many tribes of people living there. The Bible tells us that the Canaanites were descended from Noah's son Ham, and the Israelites were descended from one of Noah's other sons, Shem. Noah said that the descendants of Shem would one day rule over Ham's descendants, which comes true at this point in the Bible. God tells the Israelites that they have to kill all the Canaanites, and that they are not allowed to live alongside them. This is because God knows that His people might be tempted to worship the gods of Canaan, like Baal. The tribes that the Israelites do not utterly defeat, such as the Midianites and the Philistines, appear as enemies of the Israelites later in the Bible. You can see here the spies escaping out of Rahab's window in the wall of Jericho.

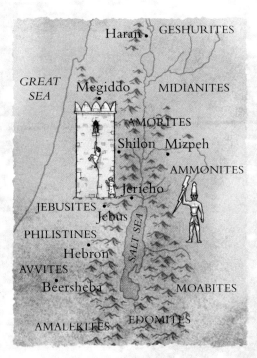

⟡ ABOUT THE STORY ⟡

Joshua takes over Moses's role as God's servant. The Israelites are filled with excitement as the day of reaching the Promised Land draws near. However, all is nearly lost when soldiers begin searching for Joshua's spies. If Rahab had not hidden them, the invasion might have failed. The scarlet cord that Rahab ties outside her house to save her family is symbolic of the blood smeared outside doorways during the Passover.

Crossing the Jordan

THE Israelites had faith in the Lord's promise that they would successfully storm Jericho, and when they heard the reports from Joshua's spies, they were elated. Now they knew that even their enemies believed that God was with them, and shook with fear in anticipation of their coming. However, in order to attack the great city itself, the Israelites had to first find a way to cross the flood of the mighty River Jordan.

The morning came when Joshua gave the order to advance over the river bank, and the mass of Israelites camped all over the plain prepared to march. First to move off were the priests, who carried high the Ark of the Covenant for all to see. Following behind, a safe distance from the holiness of the ark, came 40,000 soldiers, armed

> *The priests who bore the ark stood on dry ground in the midst of the Jordan.*

❧ ABOUT THE STORY ❧

God tells Joshua that He is with him, just as He was with Moses before. And just as God held back the waters of the Red Sea, He now holds back the mighty Jordan so that the Israelites can cross the river and step on to the land God promised their ancestors so long ago. At last, their years of wandering in the desert are over. They build a memorial with 12 rocks from the river bed, to mark the site of the amazing miracle.

Bethel
Jebus
Gibeon •   • Ai
        Jericho
            Abel Shittim

Bethlehem •

• Hebron

SALT SEA

Entering the Promised Land

After 40 long years in the wilderness, and many trials and lapses of faith, the Israelites enter the Promised Land. Led by Joshua, they make their way up the east side of the Salt Sea from the wilderness around Mount Sinai. They briefly make camp at Abel Shittim, before God leads them into Canaan, and the Israelite nation witnesses the miraculous crossing of the River Jordan.

Altar by the Jordan

At Joshua's command the Israelites build an altar by the river. This is to remind the people of the miracle that God performed for them.

and ready for war. Closer and closer came the great crowd of people to the fast-flowing waters of the Jordan, with the city of Jericho looming ever larger on the opposite side. When the priests had reached the edge of the river, Joshua gave them God's command. "As soon as your feet are in the water, go no further." One by one the holy men stepped down into the Jordan, and as they stood still in the midst of the channel, with the ark raised aloft, they found that the water level began to lower. The Lord was holding back the river at a spot higher up the valley, preventing it from sweeping the Israelites away. As Joshua watched, the waters started to drain from around the priests' feet and a dry path emerged across to the far bank. He wasted no time in giving the order for the army to advance, and rank by rank the troops marched past the sacred ark across the exposed river bed.

When the very last soldier was safely on the opposite side of the Jordan, the Lord told Joshua to send a man from each Israelite tribe to fetch a rock from around the priests' feet. When this was done, the priests themselves moved off over the dried-up river bed, step by step, carefully bringing the ark into the Promised Land. The moment the priests' feet had reached the Jericho side, the Israelites heard a distant rumbling, like the sound of far-off thunder. The noise rapidly turned into a roar, then a deafening boom, and suddenly they saw the waters of the Jordan come crashing down the river bed once more, spraying over the channel and overflowing the banks, soaking the Israelites who were standing, watching in awe as immense waves plunged onwards, rushing down to the sea.

"Take these 12 rocks and build a memorial to mark the site of this miracle forever," Joshua commanded the stunned soldiers. Then the Israelites began to cheer.

The Israelites' trust in their new leader had been rewarded, and each soldier stood with awe and respect in his heart for Joshua, just as they had done for Moses. "We will follow you wherever you take us and do whatever you command," the people cried to Joshua. And they knew that God Himself was among them as they turned to face the army of the powerful city of Jericho.

A nation on the move
Some people have tried to work out how many Israelites entered Canaan. The word *lp* is used in some Bible accounts, and people do not know what it means. Some think it means a thousand people and others "armed men". Depending on which meaning they use, the number varies between two million and 500,000 people.

THE PRIESTS CARRY THE ARK OF THE COVENANT INTO THE RIVER AHEAD OF THE PEOPLE. AS GOD'S HOME ON EARTH WAS BELIEVED TO BE BETWEEN THE WINGS OF THE ANGELS ON THE LID OF THE ARK, THIS WAS A SIGN TO THE PEOPLE THAT GOD WAS LEADING THEM TO THE PROMISED LAND.

The river runs dry
In 1927, an earthquake caused mud to block the River Jordan for 21 hours. God may have used natural forces to perform the miracle described in the story.

Fall of Jericho

JOSHUA and his 40,000 soldiers stood on the plain facing the great city of Jericho. Its towering stone walls stared blankly back at them – too high to climb, too thick to batter down – and the huge, sturdy city gates had been bolted and barred. Not even the smallest mouse would have found a chink in the defences to creep in or out. There were no weak points for the Israelites to attack, and Joshua decided that there was nothing for it but to sit and wait for the citizens to run short of food and water. But God had quite a different war plan and sent a messenger to tell Joshua what to do.

Following the Lord's commands, the next day the Israelite leader gave the soldiers the order to march. "Put on your armour and pick up your weapons," Joshua told them. "I want you to parade right round the outside of the city, in full view of the enemy. The priests will go with you at the centre of the march carrying trumpets and holding high the Ark of the Covenant. Everyone is to be very careful not to utter a single word until I give the signal. I won't give the signal today, but you must all be ready for when I do. Then I want you to shout until your lungs are fit to burst." The soldiers were more than a little puzzled by this strange battle strategy, but they all had faith in their commander, so they set off round the city.

WHEN THE ISRAELITES HAD KILLED EVERYONE, THEY DESTROYED THE CITY. THE FIRST FRUITS OF THEIR CONQUEST OF CANAAN – THE CITY, WITH EVERYONE AND EVERYTHING IN IT – WERE OFFERED TO GOD

Ancient Jericho
The place generally identified with Old Testament Jericho is the site of Tell es-Sultan (shown to the left). The first settlements grew up around an oasis. From about 8000BC, town after town was built and destroyed on the site. The first town had walls around it, and Jericho is the oldest walled city in the world.

Trumpet call
The trumpets used by the priests in the story were called *shophars*. They were made of rams' horns, and were used to call people to battle and also to worship. The shophar is still used by rabbis today in some Jewish religious ceremonies.

The terrified inhabitants of Jericho watched and waited, listening to the fanfare of trumpets outside their walls. The full might of the Israelite army was on display, and the icy silence of the warriors made their blood run cold. The sight of the ark filled them with dread. They knew it was the sacred chest of the all-powerful Israelite God – the God who had helped them defeat the Egyptians and the Amorites. When would the attack come on their own city?

Every morning for six days the Israelites tramped their way round the city. Each time the people of Jericho saw the army, they prepared themselves to face an invasion; and each time the Israelites withdrew, they grew more and more anxious. Whatever were the Israelites up to?

When dawn broke on the seventh day, Joshua gave the army a new command: today they were to circle the city seven times. Imagine the panic that rose among the inhabitants of Jericho when they realized something was at last about to happen. The soldiers must have been able to hear the people's frightened cries. "Why aren't they stopping? They're not going back to their camp! Any minute now, they'll turn and head straight for us . . . The ark will strike us down! The Israelites are coming!"

But the expected attack still didn't arrive. As soon as the ark had passed around the city seven times, Joshua gave the sign. The 40,000 soldiers opened their mouths and bellowed with all their strength, adding their voices to the blasts of the priests' trumpets.

The din was ear-splitting. Inside Jericho, no one could hear themselves speak. The unearthly noise circled the entire city like the howling of souls in torment, pressing in on all sides and seeming to grow louder at every second.

> **" The people raised a great shout and the wall fell down flat. "**

Outside the city, the almighty noise echoed and re-echoed around the hills and the Israelites felt the very ground beneath their feet begin to vibrate.

As the air throbbed, the earth trembled and then quaked, until with one great shudder the massive walls of Jericho came tumbling down. Immediately the soldiers rushed on the city, scrambling their way in over the heaps of crumbled stone. Only Rahab and her family were spared, just as the spies had promised. The fame of another Israelite victory spread far and wide across Canaan, and Joshua's name was spoken with fear throughout the land.

Fighting with bronze

Joshua's invasion of Jericho took place in about 1400BC, during a period known as the Late Bronze Age. Most weapons at this time were made of bronze. These pictures show some of the weapons the Israelites might have been carrying when they stormed into the city. They include battleaxes, a spearhead, a dagger and an arrowhead.

❖ ABOUT THE STORY ❖

This story shows that God is with the Israelites. He tells Joshua about the unusual way in which he must take the city of Jericho. Jericho is the first Canaanite city to be taken, and the Israelites honour God by devoting it to Him. The only citizens to be spared are Rahab and her family. She helped the Israelite spies and this is God's recognition of that faithful act. After the defeat of Jericho, Joshua's fame spreads.

Battle of Ai

SPURRED on by the victory at Jericho, Joshua immediately sent scouts further into the land of Canaan to spy out the Israelites' next target, the city of Ai. The news they brought back was encouraging. They felt that an army of two or three thousand soldiers should be able to defeat the city. But the ease with which Jericho had fallen had made the scouts over-confident. They had severely under-estimated how fiercely the small population of Ai would fight to protect their city. The determined citizens forced back the warriors sent by Joshua, leaving many Israelites dead, and chasing the rest away into the desert.

Joshua was deeply shocked. "Why, Lord?" the Israelite commander cried, striding up and down his tent. "Why have you let this happen?"

"What did you expect?" came the Lord's thunderous reply. "Israel has sinned against me!"

Joshua was baffled. "How? What do you mean?"

"There is one among you who has disobeyed my commands," roared the Lord. "Until he is found and punished, the Israelite nation must stand on its own!"

Next morning, Joshua gathered all the Israelites before him. Guided by God, his eyes slowly scanned the massive crowd, and came to rest on the tribe of Judah. In a steely voice, Joshua called for the households of the tribe to pass in front of him. As soon as Joshua saw the Zerahites, something made him shout, "Stop!" As the family stood trembling, Joshua slowly lifted an accusing finger. "You!" he breathed, pointing at a man called Achan. "You're the sinner who has brought God's wrath upon us!"

Achan immediately fell on his knees in front of the enraged Israelite leader and confessed. At the conquest of Jericho, Joshua had given strict orders that all precious booty was the property of the Lord, to be placed in the treasury for safekeeping. Yet Achan had stolen a beautiful mantle, along with some gold and silver, and hidden them.

Digging for history

Most of the discoveries that have been made about this time have come from archaeologists, people who learn about the past by digging up old buildings and objects. The archaeologists in the picture have found a place where they think ancient people lived and they are trying to find objects, or artefacts, that have been left behind. For example, finding cooking pots may tell them what people ate at the time. There are specialists who only study the area around the Salt Sea, now called the Dead Sea, trying to find out about the people and places mentioned in the Bible. A lot of objects, such as things made of leather or wood, seldom survive, but enough has been found to give us a good idea of what life may have been like.

Luxury robe

This picture shows the type of robe that Achan might have stolen from Jericho. It would have been worn by a nobleman, and would have been made of expensive fabrics, richly embroidered and decorated.

The Lord told Joshua to try a second attack on the city of Ai and instructed him to set a clever trap. At night, 30,000 soldiers crept into the hills behind the city. Next day, while these troops lay in wait out of sight, the rest of the Israelite army attacked the city from the front. However, the soldiers of Ai were well-prepared and their king was delighted to find that, just as before, his fighters soon got the upper hand. Bit by bit, the Israelites were beaten back. Even when the order came for the Israelite army to retreat, the warriors of Ai didn't give up. They chased the retreating Israelites into the wilderness.

But, unbeknown to the King of Ai, everything had happened exactly according to plan. The Israelites had only pretended to be overcome in order to lure the fighters away from the city. Now the Israelite ambush rushed into Ai and began the destruction of the city.

> ❝ *Joshua burned Ai and made it for ever a heap of ruins.* ❞

Out in the countryside, Joshua saw smoke start to rise as Ai was set on fire, and he gave the signal for his fleeing troops to turn and face their pursuers. With utter horror, the King of Ai realized they had been trapped. The invaders were closing in on his army from the front and from the city at the rear and there was no hope of escape.

By sunset, the King of Ai's dead body hung from a tree. His army lay slain in the wilderness and his people lay dead in the streets. All the kings of the lands beyond the Jordan swore to join forces to take revenge on the Israelites.

While the miserable man begged for mercy at Joshua's feet, messengers were sent to search his tent. They quickly returned with the stolen treasures. "God punished us for your wrongdoing by taking the lives of our soldiers," Joshua coldly told Achan. "Now, you must be punished, and pay the same price that they did." And then the people stoned Achan to death.

Shekels
The Bible tells us that Achan stole "two hundred shekels of silver, and a wedge of gold of 50 shekels' weight". The shekel was not a coin, but a weight. Most of the people at this time measured amounts of silver and gold in terms of how much they weighed, rather than how much they were worth.

Achan's death
This picture shows Achan being punished for his sin. In the Bible, we are told that after the stoning, Achan was burned, together with his oxen, his sheep and goats, his tent and all that he had. He had committed a sin against God that all the Israelites had suffered for, so according to the law God gave to Moses on Mount Sinai he had to be punished.

❖ ABOUT THE STORY ❖

God brings about the Israelites' defeat at Ai because He knows Achan has disobeyed Him. He punishes all the people for one man's sin. This can be compared to the way in which Adam's sin affected the whole of humanity. Once Achan has been punished, the Israelites have God's blessing again, and their second attack is a success. This story shows that God will always find those who disobey Him, and will punish them.

Tricked by the Gibeonites

NOT far to the south-west of Ai lay the mighty city of Gibeon. The Gibeonites were a strong and powerful people, but news of how Joshua had razed the great city of Jericho to the ground and slaughtered the people of Ai had struck fear into their hearts. The Israelites weren't far off, and the Gibeonites knew that if they waited for the Israelites to arrive they might suffer the same fate as the people who were once their neighbours. Instead, the Gibeonites made a cunning plan . . .

Joshua was resting in his tent where the Israelites had camped at Gilgal when a messenger suddenly dashed in. "The scouts have reported that strangers are approaching, sir," he panted, all out of breath.

Joshua sat up, immediately alert and ready for action. "Send soldiers out to meet them and escort them to me," he commanded. He was always suspicious when anyone was seen heading for their huge army camp.

When the strangers were brought to his tent, Joshua was amazed. These weren't royal messengers sent from any Canaanite king, they were just a ragbag rabble of peasants! Joshua found himself facing a dirty, stinking group of exhausted people, whose patched clothes were in tatters and whose worn-out shoes were falling off their feet. "At last we have found you!" they cried, falling on their knees

with gratitude in front of Joshua. "We have been travelling for many weeks to get here. Even though we live far away, news of your wonderful God has reached our tribe. You are obviously a blessed people, and we would like to join you. Our elders have sent us as ambassadors to ask you to make a treaty with us."

Joshua was not convinced by the flattery. "How can I be sure that you are who you say you are?" he queried. "The tribes of Canaan know well that we have sworn never to make peace with them. You might therefore be people from the very cities we plan to attack, come in disguise to try to trick us into making peace."

Wine
There are frequent references to both drinking and making wine in the Bible as the land was well suited to growing vines.

Baking bread
The Gibeonites in the story carry bread in their packs. Bread was the most important food in this area at the time. The picture shows an Egyptian model of two servants baking bread. One is sitting down and tending the fire, while the other servant is kneading the dough. The model dates from around 1900 BC.

It took the Israelite army only three days to reach the city of Gibeon, and Joshua realized his dreadful blunder at once. His first guess had been completely right – the Gibeonites were local people who had dressed up to trick him, to try and escape death at the hands of a huge army led by God Himself. Joshua was furious that he'd allowed himself to be persuaded by their story, but it was now too late. Even though the army were eager to attack and take their revenge, Joshua knew that to break his solemn vow to let them live would bring God's wrath upon them, even though they would have killed them all had they not made the peace. The Gibeonites were therefore spared, but to punish them for their lies they were taken as slaves to spend the rest of their days working for the great Israelite army and the tabernacle of their God.

> 66 *Now you are cursed, and you shall always be slaves for the house of my God.* 99

The dejected travellers reached inside their packs and produced hunks of stale, mouldy bread and battered, torn wineskins. "When we set off from our homes, this bread was still warm from the oven and the wineskins were brand new," they said, earnestly. "Please make our long, hard journey worthwhile. We beg you to make a peace treaty with our people."

Joshua granted the travellers their precious peace treaty, and all the Israelite elders swore to let their people live. The tattered group were eager to be off with their wonderful news, and they hurried away from the Israelite camp at once. After all, they had many weeks of travelling ahead before they would reach home . . .

Carved in stone
This Egyptian stone contains the first mention of the nation of Israel outside the Bible. It dates from around 1230BC, when Pharaoh Mereneptah was ruling. The inscription on the stone describes his military campaign in Canaan, and says that he defeated the Israelites.

Canaanite man
The picture on this Egyptian glazed brick shows what a nobleman from Canaan might have looked like at around the time the Israelites settled in the area.

❧ ABOUT THE STORY ❧

Joshua makes a treaty of peace with the Gibeonites, and the Israelites swear a solemn oath not to harm them. Oaths were regularly used in treaties, as a way of enforcing the terms. Once Joshua realizes that he has been tricked, it is too late. He has to honour the treaty.

The Longest Day

KING Adonizedek of Jerusalem was among the Canaanite rulers who had sworn to join forces to drive the Israelites out of Canaan. He knew that presenting a strong, united front was their only hope against the massive Israelite army. The fall of the mighty city of Jericho had spelt out disaster for any city that tried to stand alone. Now the Gibeonites had weakened their number by betraying the Amorite kings' pact. In saving themselves from destruction, they had abandoned everyone else to a more certain doom, and Adonizedek was enraged. He immediately sent messengers to the four kings that neighboured his lands, saying, "The Gibeonites have made peace with the enemy. I say we should destroy the city of

> ❝ *The Sun stood still and the Moon stayed, until the nation took vengeance.* ❞

Gibeon ourselves. Send your armies straight away and together we'll take our revenge on these deserters." So King Hoham of Hebron, King Piram of Jarmuth, King Japhia of Lachish and King Debir of Eglon immediately mobilized their forces and declared war on their one-time ally.

Gibeon was soon under siege. The citizens had scarcely finished celebrating how they had tricked the fearsome Israelites, when the five savage armies of the hill kings surrounded them on all sides and the city found itself in the very position it had tried so hard to avoid! The

Defeated enemies
On the left is a decorative palette showing the first king of Egypt, King Narmer, holding a defeated enemy by the hair. On the right is a picture of an Israelite with his foot on the neck of an enemy. Both these images show typical gestures of subjection of enemies after battle. It was a sign that the enemy knew they had been defeated. In the Bible, we are told that Joshua's captains put their feet on the necks of the five defeated kings. As Joshua marched through Canaan, his army defeated many more cities along the way. These cities were called city-states, and were like small countries, as large as the city.

Gibeonite leaders now sent messengers to their former enemy to beg for help to get them out of trouble.

The news that the Amorite kings of the hills had gathered against Gibeon reached Joshua in the middle of the night, but he immediately gave the army the order to march. There would be no better chance to crush several important Canaanite tribes all in one go, and God reassured Joshua of victory. Without waiting for daybreak he made the army strike camp immediately, marching all night through the darkness.

The Israelite attack came as a complete surprise. While all the Amorite forces were facing Gibeon, half-asleep and half-awake, the full strength of the Israelite army fell on them from behind. The soldiers panicked. Some stayed to fight and were hacked down as the Israelites rushed upon them. Others turned and tried to flee. But even though they were out of reach of the Israelite swords, suddenly the Lord sent huge hailstones the size of rocks from above, stoning them to death as they ran.

Then Joshua gave a mighty shout. "Sun, stand still in the sky! Moon, hang where you are in the heavens! Let time itself be stopped until we have crushed these enemies completely!" To the horror of the Amorite armies, the Lord heard Joshua's plea. Hour after hour, the Israelites continued to hack down their enemies, yet, to the terrified Amorites, the day didn't get any shorter.

In the midst of the killing, a messenger came running up to Joshua excitedly. "Sir, the five kings tried to escape, but some of our troops found them," he told Joshua. "They were hiding in a cave at Makkedah, but we've now got them cornered. What shall we do with them?"

Joshua wanted to deal with the rebel kings himself, to make an example of them to any other Canaanite peoples that might dare go against the Israelites. "Block the cave mouth up with rocks," he instructed the messenger. "That will hold them fast until we've finished destroying everything they own!" And while the Amorite kings were locked up, the Israelites slaughtered their people.

At the end of the extraordinarily long day, the Israelites had crushed five of their strongest enemies. When not one Amorite soldier remained alive, Joshua gave the command for the five kings to be brought out of the cave. He threw them to the ground in front of the Israelite war leaders. "You should never be afraid, people of Israel!" Joshua cried. "For this is what the Lord has promised will happen to our enemies." In front of the Israelites, the kings were hanged, one by one, and their bodies thrown back into the cave from which they had just come.

❧ ABOUT THE STORY ❧

God reassures Joshua that He is with him and that the Israelites will win. When the battle begins, God sends hailstones which rain down on the enemy from above. Then He grants Joshua's request and makes the Sun stand still. The day does not end until the Israelites have defeated their enemies. In the Bible, we are told that there was no day like that before or after it. This is another great success for Joshua's leadership.

Light or darkness?
The Longest Day in this story is usually taken to mean that daylight lasted longer than usual. However, it could be that the story refers to an eclipse of the Sun, which would mean that the darkness of the night lasted longer than usual. There is no mention of it being daylight, so it could be that the darkness helped the Israelites win.

Dividing the Promised Land

NOT content with having slain the five Amorite kings and crushing their armies, Joshua next attacked and destroyed each of their cities, killing every person found there. News of the terrible bloodshed spread at once through Canaan and, with hearts full of dread, the Canaanite chiefs realized that no one stood a chance of being spared. Their choice was either to sit back and wait for their people to be slaughtered, or to come out and fight. So, under the leadership of King Jabin of Hazor, the rulers mobilized their armies. Hundreds of thousands of troops, horses and chariots gathered in a massive camp at Merom. The soldier were all in full battledress, and determined to stop the Israelites from taking their homeland.

Report after report reached Joshua's ears of the vast army preparing to attack. But God reassured him. "Have no fear," He told Joshua, "for I will deliver all these troops slain into your hands. Tomorrow, you will kill their horses and burn their chariots." Joshua trusted the Lord and immediately led the Israelites into an attack. The battle was more savage and bloody than any either army had suffered before. When the ruthless killing was eventually over, the bodies littering the battlefield were Canaanite. As God had vowed, they lay next to the corpses of their horses and the smoking wrecks of their once glorious chariots. The Israelites had won their mightiest victory yet.

For several more years, Joshua was to continue waging wars against the Canaanite tribes, conquering more and more of the Promised Land until at last most of the country was theirs. Then the fighting ceased. It was time to divide the land up between the 12 Israelite tribes.

The boldest Israelite elders made haste to lay claim to the areas they wanted for their families or that they thought were rightfully theirs. One of the first to get his allocation was Caleb, Moses's courageous scout and now an old man of 85, who finally received the reward the Lord had promised him. For having faith in God's order to invade Canaan when everyone else was faint-hearted, Joshua granted him the great city of Hebron and the surrounding hill country. However, not everyone was as sure about which part of the beautiful country they wanted to live in. Seven tribes simply couldn't decide! So after sending three men from each to survey the land, Joshua divided it up into seven parts and the tribe chiefs drew lots for their new homes.

The only tribe not to be given an entire area was the Levites, whom God had long ago chosen to be His priests. They were given 48 cities in different parts of the country, so they could lead the Israelites in worship. The tabernacle itself was set up permanently in the city of Shiloh, at the heart of the Promised Land.

Finally the Lord told Joshua to appoint six cities as Cities of Refuge. In these places, people accused of crimes would be protected against those wanting to take their revenge, and they would be assured a fair trial.

With the country organized, the Israelites began to move into their allocated areas. But it wasn't always easy. Handfuls of Canaanite people still stubbornly remained in some far-flung places, and the powerful Israelite families had to either drive them off their land or force them into slavery. The Reubenites and Gadites fell into particular trouble. Along with half the tribe of Manasseh, Joshua had given them some of the first lands the Israelites had conquered – the plains of Moab. However, these lay on the far side of the Jordan. The tribes were concerned that the river acted as a boundary dividing them from the rest of the Israelites.

As the other 10 tribes settled into their own areas, they were appalled to

hear that the Reubenites and Gadites were building a huge altar on the banks of the Jordan. Thinking that they were setting themselves up as priests or even turning to other gods, the Levite High Priest, Phineas, and the chiefs of the other tribes raced to stop them. The Reubenites and Gadites were astonished to find that such an important committee had travelled so far to see them. "Whatever are you doing?" the priest and chiefs asked the puzzled people. "Hasn't God's wrath in the past taught you a lesson? If you offend God's commands, He will strike down not only you, but all of us!"

'Let us build an altar to be a witness between us and you.'

With shock, the Reubenites and Gadites realized what the other Israelites thought they were up to. "The Lord knows we weren't building an altar to any other god!" they gasped in horror. "We are just worried because we are going over the river. We feared that your descendants might see our lands as outside Israel's borders and turn against our descendants. So we have built a copy of the Altar of the Lord, which now stands at Shiloh, to stand as proof that we follow the same God." The priests and elders were highly relieved and left the Reubenites and Gadites to settle into their lands in peace.

And so it happened that the Israelites at last took possession of the Promised Land, just as God had promised Abraham that they would.

The war for Canaan

The Israelites fought a long war over all of Canaan to take possession of the land that God had given them. With God's help they quickly spread out over the country. Here you can see, in red, the area that they had conquered, including the cities of Jericho and Bethlehem, as far south as Abraham's home town of Beersheba, and north as far as Shechem.

Altars built to God

An altar is a table or flat-topped block used as the focus for a religious ritual. In the Old Testament, altars were mainly used for making sacrifices or offerings to God. The Hebrew word for altar, *mizbeah*, means "place of sacrifice". Smaller altars were used for burning incense. In later times, events taking place at an altar were supervised by a priest, but in ancient times, people built their own altars and offered sacrifices on them. Noah, Abraham, Isaac, Jacob and Moses all built altars, usually to remember an event in which they had dealings with God, such as Jacob seeing his ladder to heaven, with God waiting at the top.

❧ ABOUT THE STORY ❧

The Israelites conquer most of the Promised Land. When each tribe is given its own area, the Reubenites and Gadites are concerned that their land is separated from the rest of Israel by the Jordan. They build an altar to bind themselves to the rest of Israel through their faith.

Death of Joshua

By the time Joshua had become a very elderly man, there had been peace in Israel for many years. The Israelites' enemies were overcome, the land was fairly divided, and the 12 tribes were settled contentedly throughout the country. The mighty war leader's work was done.

At the age of 110 years and knowing death was near, Joshua summoned all the Israelites together one last time so he could address them. Joshua's tone was serious and stern, and as the Israelites listened to his stirring words, their blood tingled in their veins. "Remember where you have come from and all the great things God has done for your sake," the aged warrior urged his people. "Your fathers of old lived far off in the lands beyond the River Euphrates and they served other gods. But the Lord chose Abraham and guided him away to a new life, showing him this very country you now own. The descendants of his son, Jacob, fell into slavery in Egypt, but God sent Moses and Aaron to set our ancestors free, striking the whole of that land with terrible plagues. God Himself led our fathers out of Egypt. When the Egyptians gave pursuit with chariots and horsemen, the Lord heard our fathers' cries. He smothered the Egyptian army in darkness and drowned their troops and horses in the Red Sea, every last one of them. Then the Lord

brought your families safely through the wilderness to the lands bordering the Jordan. He delivered the mighty Amorite kings into your hands and gave you their royal cities. Then He helped you across the River Jordan and crushed each Canaanite tribe for you.

"Do not forget that it is the Lord who has done all these things for you. It was He who drove your enemies out of the Promised Land; they didn't go because of your swords and bows and arrows. It was He who gave you a land you hadn't toiled to cultivate; today you enjoy eating the fruits of vineyards and olive groves that you didn't plant. And it was He who gave you cities that you hadn't sweated to build; you live in homes constructed by the sweat and work of other people's hands.

"But mind this – in order to serve the Lord, you must fear Him and follow His commands sincerely and faithfully. If you are not prepared to keep to His law, then so be it: worship other gods. But you must choose."

The Israelites listened carefully to Joshua's words and thought long and hard about the seriousness of what he was saying. Then voices began to cry out from the crowd. "We won't abandon the Lord!" they shouted. "Not after He

> **" The people said, 'The Lord our God we will serve.' "**

delivered us from slavery in Egypt and worked miracles for us and gave us the Promised Land! We will serve the Lord truly! He is our only God!"

With trembling hands, the elderly war chief motioned for the huge throng of Israelites to be calm. "If you do wrong and turn to sin, you will not be forgiven," he warned the waiting crowd. "If you forsake the Lord and turn to worshipping idols and false gods, you will bring the full force of His wrath down upon you."

Undeterred, the Israelites replied as if with one voice, "We will serve the Lord our God! We will obey Him and do whatever He tells us."

Joshua was content that the people were speaking from their hearts and that they really meant what they were promising. Finally, he felt that he could die in peace. Taking the holy book of God's laws, he wrote in it that the Israelites had renewed their covenant. Then, slowly but steadily, the great leader took a large stone from nearby and set it up in the sanctuary of the Lord. "This rock has heard everything that has passed between us and God today," he told the committed people. "If you disobey the Lord, it will bear witness that you have broken your word, and you will be punished for your sins."

Not long afterwards, the battle-scarred warrior passed away. Amid great grief and mourning, the Israelites carried his body to the part of the Promised Land where he had made his home, the high hill country of Ephraim, and there they laid him to rest.

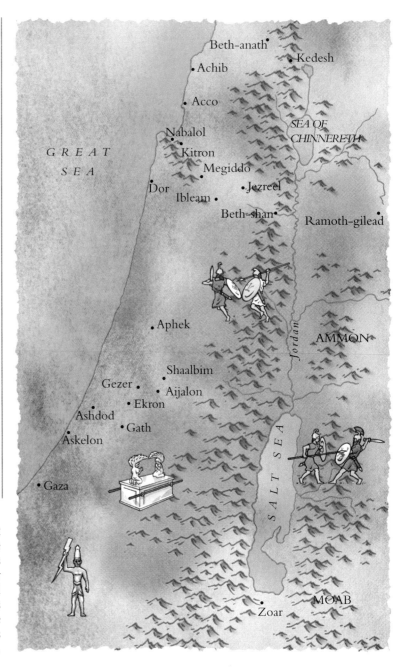

The battle still to be fought

Joshua was a great warrior and a mighty leader, but when he died he had not conquered all Israel. This map shows the cities he had not conquered. The Philistines were particularly difficult to defeat, and their fortified towns, such as Gaza and Gath, remained undefeated until the reign of King David. This meant that all around the Israelites there were people worshipping idolatrous gods, like Baal and Ashtoreth, and this proved to be too much of a temptation after Joshua's death.

Ancient city

One of the cities captured by Joshua in his long battle to gain complete control of the Promised Land was called Megiddo. King Solomon later chose Megiddo as one of his main fortified cities outside Jerusalem. The site where ancient Megiddo stood is believed to be Tell el-Mutesellim, in north-west Israel. Archaeologists who have dug there have found evidence of a large town that, at different times, contained stables, storehouses, palaces, office-type buildings and a gateway.

❧ ABOUT THE STORY ❧

Joshua is soon to die, and no single person will take over his role as leader. He reminds the Israelites of their history and how God has helped them at every step, from their escape from Egypt to their new lives in Israel. The Israelites choose to renew their covenant with God.

Israelites Disobey the Judges

FOR a long time after Joshua's death, the Israelites were careful to keep their promise to obey God's commands and live according to His laws. Without a war chief or king at the nation's head, it was up to the wise officials called Judges to bind the people together in their single faith. However, as the years went by, the brave men and women who had invaded Canaan grew old and passed away. There were no longer eyewitnesses to tell of all the wonderful things that God had done for the Israelites, so many people began to wonder whether they had ever happened at all. Perhaps the miracles of crossing the River Jordan dry-footed, and the miraculous collapse

of the walls of Jericho, and the day that the Sun stood still for Joshua and his warriors, were just the stuff of legends.

One of Joshua's last orders had been to drive out all the inhabitants of Canaan. Even though the Israelite war parties continued to have great success in taking new territories, they sometimes allowed the local people to remain as slaves. Other times, the Israelites simply moved into areas and settled down among the tribes. The Judges often repeated Joshua's warning about what would happen if the Israelites mixed with the Canaanites: the temptation to follow the pagan gods would prove too much, and the Lord would turn away from them in anger, resulting in the fall of the nation. And the time indeed came when an angel came down from Heaven with a final caution that God was losing patience. "It's thanks only to the Lord that you were brought safely out of Egypt and into the land He swore to give your ancestors," the angel said, sternly. "He made a special covenant with the Israelite nation; your part of the bargain was to drive out the pagan peoples from this land and break down their altars to false gods. Now God finds you have disobeyed His commands and are living among these unbelievers. The Lord will no longer fight these tribes for you and, if you aren't careful, your neighbours will become your enemies."

At this threat the despairing Israelites wept with remorse and prayed for forgiveness. But it wasn't long before they were carrying on just as before. God's anger grew as His chosen people turned their backs on Him, and in His turn He withdrew His protection.

Without God on their side, the Israelites soon found themselves in the hands of King Eglon of Moab. The

✦ ABOUT THE STORY ✦

Despite the angel's warning, the Israelites begin to forget God's laws. They live alongside the Canaanites, and start to worship their gods. The judges try to enforce God's laws but in vain. Finally, God loses patience and removes His protection. The Israelites fall under the control of their neighbours. It is only because of the bravery of Ehud that the Israelites win back God's favour, and their freedom.

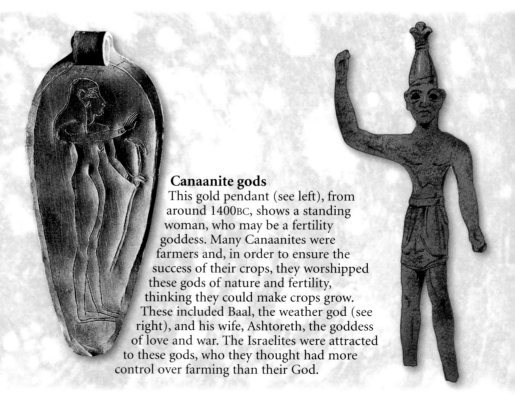

Canaanite gods
This gold pendant (see left), from around 1400BC, shows a standing woman, who may be a fertility goddess. Many Canaanites were farmers and, in order to ensure the success of their crops, they worshipped these gods of nature and fertility, thinking they could make crops grow. These included Baal, the weather god (see right), and his wife, Ashtoreth, the goddess of love and war. The Israelites were attracted to these gods, who they thought had more control over farming than their God.

106

> ## " *The people of Israel did what was evil in the sight of the Lord.* "

Israelites lived under Moabite control for 18 long years – plenty of time for them to think back on the ways they had offended God and to feel true repentance. Yet at last God chose to give His betrayers yet another chance and answered their cries for help.

A party of Israelites had gone one day to pay tribute at the Moabite court, and King Eglon had received their gifts and sent them on their way when he suddenly received word that one of them had returned – a man called Ehud, saying he had a secret message. Intrigued, Eglon agreed to give him another audience. However, Ehud insisted that his message was private and for the king's ears alone. Still more curious, Eglon hurried Ehud up to his roof chamber.

No sooner had Eglon closed the doors behind them than Ehud drew a two-edged sword and stabbed it into the king's stomach. In horror, as he lay dying, Eglon realized that Ehud was left-handed, and his soldiers must have checked for weapons only on the normal side of the body.

By the time King Eglon's servants had realized something was wrong, Ehud had escaped from the palace and was nearly home. The minute he reached Ephraim, he took out a trumpet and gave the signal to go to battle. The Israelites swooped down on the Moabite soldiers and slaughtered 10,000 of them. Finally, they had won back the Lord's favour and their freedom.

❀ THE JUDGES OF ISRAEL ❀

OTHNIEL *(1374-1334BC)*
From Kiriath Sepher in Judah.
Saved the Israelites from the armies of western Mesopotamia.

EHUD *(1316-1236BC)*
From Benjamin.
Saved the Israelites from the Moabites, the Ammonites and the Amalekites.

SHAMGAR
Was a judge during the early rule of Deborah. Killed six hundred Philistines.

ABIMELECH
Ruled for three years. From Manasseh.

TOLA *(1126-1103BC)*
A minor judge.
From Issachar.

JAIR *(1103-1081BC)*
A wealthy man and a minor judge.
From Gilead, in east Manasseh.

IBZAN *(1100-1093BC)*
A minor judge.
From Bethlehem, in Judah.

ELON *(1093-1083BC)*
A minor judge.
From Zebulun.

ABDON *(1083-1077BC)*
From Ephraim. A minor judge.

SAMSON *(1103-1083BC)*
From Dan.
Attacked the Philistines.
Was betrayed by Delilah.

ELI *(ruled for 40 years)*
Was the priest at the tabernacle at Shiloh. Became Samuel's guardian.

SAMUEL *(1059-1043BC)*
The last judge and a prophet. Brought the nation of Israel together. Under him, the Philistine invasions ended.

Deborah the Judge

THE Israelite people knew that from the very earliest times in their history, each time they had turned away from God and broken His commands, they had brought a severe punishment upon themselves. Surely the years that the Lord had allowed the ruthless Moabites to rule over them – the worst sentence yet – should have taught them a lesson they wouldn't forget? Unfortunately, this wasn't so. When Ehud died, the people quickly fell back into their old habits. Yet again the furious Lord turned his back on His people, leaving them to their own fate, and yet again they were conquered by an enemy: this time King Jabin of the Philistines. Now Jabin's army was feared far and wide – not only because it was under the command of the famous General Sisera, but also for its squadron of 900 indestructible iron chariots. The threat of his crack troops hovered over the Israelites, and King Jabin ruled the nation harshly for 20 years.

At that time, there was a prophetess called Deborah, who lived in the hill country of Ephraim. Deborah had been appointed one of Israel's judges and she was well respected by the people for her wise counsel and just decisions. Totally unexpectedly, a man called Barak received a message that Deborah wanted to see him and, although he was very puzzled, he went at once to meet her. "The Lord commands you to gather 10,000 men and go to Mount Tabor," Deborah told him. "There, God will bring General Sisera and King Jabin's army out to fight you, and you will win!" Barak was more than a little startled; he was totally amazed! However, he agreed to do as he was told – just as long as Deborah went too. "Of course I will go with you," she assured him. "But, even though you will be victorious in the battle, the greatest glory will not be yours. Sisera himself will be defeated by a woman." Undeterred, Barak steeled himself to his task and set about finding soldiers.

The news reached General Sisera that the Israelites were gathering on the slopes of Mount Tabor, intent on rebelling, and he at once prepared his forces for war. How frightened the Israelites must have been, facing rank upon

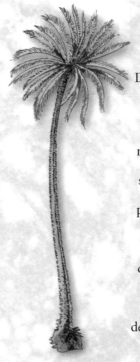

❧ ABOUT THE STORY ❧

Once again, the Israelites have forgotten God and are worshipping the gods of the Canaanites. So, once again, God removes His protection, and the Israelites come under the rule of King Jabin. After 20 years of hardship, Deborah comes to the rescue of her people, instructing Barak to gather an army. Deborah joins him, and together they defeat Jabin's army. Jael deceives General Sisera and kills him.

Deborah the Judge
Deborah is one of the few women in the Bible to hold a position of power. She was a prophet who was also one of the Judges. Like most of the Judges, she was a military leader, but she was also a judge in the modern, legal, sense of the word. According to the Bible, she sat under "the palm tree of Deborah", and the Israelites came to consult her there when they wanted to have their disputes settled. She was well known throughout all the tribes of Israel, and highly respected. In the Bible, she is described as "a mother in Israel".

rank of chariots and row on row of accomplished, professionally trained soldiers! But Deborah urged them on and inspired them with faith. "Up and fight, Israel!" she cried, before they went into attack. "Today, the Lord will deliver this great army into your hands."

Deborah's words proved true and, quite against all the odds, Sisera's army was utterly routed. But when the fighting was finished and there was not a single Canaanite warrior left alive, the most important corpse of all was not to be found on the battlefield. Sisera had escaped.

Stumbling through the hills in a panic, the general was completely shocked by the defeat and physically drained. Yet somehow he managed to dodge all the Israelite troops combing the area, trying to hunt him down. In a clever move, he made for the tent of a woman called Jael – an unlikely hiding place since Jael was originally Israelite. However, her husband – a direct descendant from Moses's father-in-law – had changed his loyalties, having split from his tribe and made peace with King Jabin. As Sisera had hoped, Jael readily smuggled him inside her tent – which was just as well since he was utterly exhausted and could go no further. Kindly, Jael covered the slumped army chief with a rug, assuring him that he could sleep safely while she kept watch. Little did the general know that he was never to wake up. While Sisera dreamt, Jael hammered a tent peg right through his skull.

Even though Jabin's army was gone and his warlord dead, Barak and the Israelites didn't rest. The warriors carried on fighting until they had slain the Canaanite king himself and destroyed his palace at Hazor. Now surely this time the Israelites would make sure they did everything as the Lord wanted. Alas, no. Within the space of 40 years the obstinate people had again turned to wicked ways, and an enraged God left them to be conquered by the Midianites.

> *The Lord will sell Sisera into the hands of a woman.*

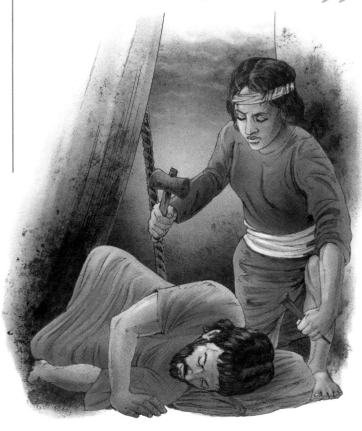

∼ THE SONG OF DEBORAH ∼

MOST BLESSED OF WOMEN BE JAEL,

THE WIFE OF HEBER THE KENITE,

OF TENT-DWELLING WOMEN MOST BLESSED.

HE ASKED WATER AND SHE GAVE HIM MILK,

SHE BROUGHT HIM CURDS IN A LORDLY BOWL.

SHE PUT HER HAND TO THE TENT PEG

AND HER RIGHT HAND TO THE

WORKMAN'S MALLET;

SHE STRUCK SISERA A BLOW,

AT HER FEET HE SANK, HE FELL;

WHERE HE SANK, THERE HE FELL DEAD.

∼

The Song of Deborah
The Song of Deborah is one of the earliest passages in the Old Testament. It is a victory song – a celebration of the Israelites' victory over General Sisera. The song explains the details of the battle and Sisera's defeat.

Flooding of the river
Part of *The Song of Deborah* tells exactly how the Israelites won the battle. God sent a storm, which caused the River Kishon to flood. Sisera's chariots, which were in this area, were swept away. The Israelite soldiers were unharmed, as they were positioned on higher ground, on Mount Tabor.

Gideon and the Angel

THE Midianite tribes hated the Israelites with a passion and treated them more cruelly than any enemy before. They made life as miserable for the Israelites as possible: they attacked their homes whenever they had the chance; and they burnt their crops and killed their flocks, leaving the land wasted and the Israelites starving.

In these difficult times, the Israelites were forced to go to great lengths to try to outwit the Midianites, such as threshing any small amounts of wheat they could save in the wine press to keep it out of sight. A young farmer called Gideon was doing just this one day when a man appeared beside him out of nowhere. "You have a brave heart," the man told Gideon. "God is with you."

Gideon thought the man's words were even more odd than the weird way he had suddenly arrived. "If the Lord is indeed with us, how come we live under such terror?" he answered, bitterly. "Why doesn't God perform some amazing miracle to save us, like He did for our fathers? I tell you, the Lord has given up on us and left us to be punished by our enemies."

The stranger looked at Gideon without blinking. "You will take on the Midianites and set Israel free," he said.

"How on earth can I do that?" he scoffed. "My clan is the weakest, and I'm the youngest in my family!"

"The Lord will be with you," replied the stranger.

Still full of doubts, Gideon went off to find some food and drink to offer the uninvited guest. But when he laid down the meat and bread in front of him, the man only touched it with the tip of his staff. Instantly, the food burst into flames and the stranger disappeared. Gideon realized that he had been face to face with an angel.

Later that evening, a voice spoke to Gideon out of the darkness: it was the Lord Himself, instructing him to destroy his own father's altar to Baal and erect one to God instead. Gideon was afraid – he knew he'd be in very serious trouble. But that night, he did as he had been told. The people were furious when they saw what had been done and immediately suspected Gideon. Joash, Gideon's father, refused to punish his son as he felt sure that there must be a good reason for his son's outburst.

From that day onwards, Gideon was somehow different. But it was only when the Midianites, the Amalekites and all the other Eastern tribes crossed the Jordan and gathered ready for a battle, that Gideon showed exactly how much the Spirit of the Lord had altered him. Sounding a trumpet to call the Israelites to arms, he roused the people to strike back. A massive force

Gideon and the angel
This picture shows Gideon talking to the angel. At first, Gideon is doubtful about the angel's message that he will save Israel. He does not think himself worthy. He asks for a sign from God, and when he sees the food burst into flames, he accepts God's will.

> *With the 300 men that lapped I will give the Midianites into your hand.*

of 32,000 men quickly formed – but the Lord told him the army was too big! "If this many Israelites defeat the Midianites, they'll think that they've done it," God told Gideon, "I want them to know that the victory is my work." Gideon gave permission for all those who were afraid to return home, and soon only 10,000 soldiers remained. "They are still too many," God sighed. "Take them down to the water and watch how they drink. If anyone laps the water like a dog, take him to one side. Tell those who scoop up the water with cupped hands that they're no longer needed." Before long, Gideon's army was down to a mere 300 men, and God was satisfied that with this number in their army, they would know who to thank for their victory. So Gideon prepared his battle plan.

That night, three squads of 100 men crept from all directions up to the Midianite camp, each with a trumpet and a pitcher with a blazing torch inside. On Gideon's signal, the men blasted away and smashed their pitchers so that their torches flashed from all around in the darkness. In the confusion, the troops thought they were being attacked by a mighty army, and they ended up fighting among themselves. As panic spread, the troops began to flee, but they could not escape. Gideon sent messengers to Ephraim, where fighting men joined the chase.

The Israelites gave pursuit until the enemy were utterly defeated. The rejoicing nation begged Gideon to become their sole leader, but the young man refused. "I will not rule over you, and my son will not rule over you; the Lord will rule over you," he told the people. And Israel lived in peace for the rest of Gideon's life.

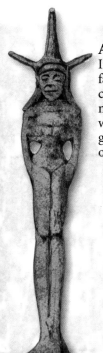

Asherah
In the Bible, God tells Gideon to destroy his father's altar to Baal, the Canaanite god, and to cut down the "asherah" beside it. Asherah is the name of a Canaanite fertility goddess associated with Baal, and an asherah pole is an image of that goddess, which would generally have been carved out of one big tree-trunk.

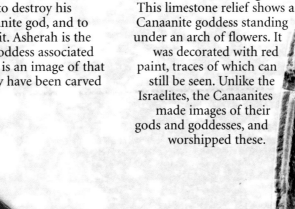

Pottery jars
The picture to the left shows the type of pottery pitcher, or jar, that Gideon and his men would have taken with them on the night that they attacked and defeated the Midianites.

Canaanite goddess
This limestone relief shows a Canaanite goddess standing under an arch of flowers. It was decorated with red paint, traces of which can still be seen. Unlike the Israelites, the Canaanites made images of their gods and goddesses, and worshipped these.

111

Jephthah

IMMEDIATELY after Gideon died, Israel's troubles began once more. One of Gideon's sons, Abimelech, couldn't get over how his father had passed up the chance to be ruler over all Israel. He was tormented by thoughts of the missed opportunity, so he tricked his kinsmen out of a lot of money and paid thugs to kill all 70 of his brothers, before setting himself up as the King of Shechem and Bethmillo. But his supporters began to argue and fight among themselves, and after things in his country got worse, Abimelech was eventually killed when a woman dropped a millstone on his head.

> " *Jephthah crossed over to the Ammonites and he smote 20 cities.* "

Within 50 years the Israelites faced yet more chaos. The Ammonite people declared war on the Israelites. As the Israelites had done in the past, they cried out to the Lord for help. At first the Lord hardened His heart, but just in time He decided to give them another great war leader.

The man the Lord chose as His new hero might have been considered unsuitable in many ways. Jephthah was the son of a man called Gilead, but, as he had been born illegitimate, he was despised by all the members of Gilead's lawful family. As soon as his brothers had grown old enough to gang up against him, they had driven him away from home. Left to fend for himself in the land of Tob, Jephthah had made a name for himself as a fearsome bandit. Under his leadership, a band of villains had plundered the countryside, terrorizing the local people.

Jephthah's daughter
Human sacrifice was not something God would be pleased by, so this element of the story is surprising. It has been suggested that, instead of sacrificing his daughter, Jephthah sent her away to live a life of celibacy, in service to God. Other sources argue, however, that this is incompatible with the fact that the Bible clearly states that Jephthah kept his vow.

Timbrels and cymbals
Percussion instruments, such as cymbals and timbrels, or tambourines, were used to accompany singing and dancing. During the Exodus from Egypt, Moses's sister, Miriam, played a tambourine while she and the other women sang and danced. Israelite women would often celebrate the return of victorious armies by coming out of the town, singing and dancing with their timbrels.

Spoils of battle
This picture shows a gold amulet, or charm, in the shape of a flying falcon. It is now in the Israel Museum, Jerusalem. This is the type of valuable ornament that Jephthah and his men would have plundered from the towns they conquered.

Now the Israelites faced the full force of the Ammonite army, and a ruthless warrior such as Jephthah was just the sort of commander they needed to organize their counter-attack. The elders of the tribes hurried to the land of Tob to beg the man who had been disowned by his Israelite brothers to come back and lead their troops into battle. "I will only return with you on one condition," Jephthah demanded. "That if the Lord grants us victory, you will make me your leader." The panic-stricken Israelite elders quickly agreed to his demand.

Messengers soon arrived from the King of the Ammonites, demanding the return of land the Israelites had taken when they had originally invaded Canaan. Jephthah wasted no time in sending a clear message straight back that they would not do so. "The Lord will judge this day between the people of Israel and the Ammonites!" he cried, rousing the soldiers to fight. Then Jephthah prayed to God and made a solemn vow, "Lord, if you deliver these enemies into our hands, I will sacrifice to you whatever I see first when I reach home." And so Jephthah and his army went to war and slaughtered the Ammonite forces.

News of the warlord's great victory travelled before him, and as Jephthah drew near to his house his daughter came out to celebrate his return, playing a tambourine. Jephthah couldn't believe his eyes. Instead of rushing to throw his arms round his daughter, he howled with grief, throwing himself down into the dirt and tearing at his clothes in despair. "I have vowed to the Lord that I would sacrifice the first thing I saw on my return," he wept, unable to meet her eyes. "And I cannot take back my promise," he

moaned. Jephthah's daughter bore the dreadful news with courage and faith. "It is right that you keep your bargain with God," she said quietly. "Only grant me some time to prepare myself."

After two months had passed, Jephthah paid the price for the wicked things he had done in the past, slaying his daughter by his own hand. But each year afterwards, on the anniversary of her death, the Israelite women gathered together to remember her.

The journeys of Jephthah

When Jephthah was rejected by his family, he fled north from his home to the land of Tob. Here he made a name for himself as a great leader and a fearsome bandit. When Israel was being threatened by the Ammonites, the elders of the threatened tribes thought that Jephthah was the person to help them out. So they went to see him to ask if he would rescue them. Jephthah led his armies throughout the area to the east of the Jordan, destroying and burning the Ammonite towns, such as Abel-keramim, and defeating the Ammonites at every stage. With God on his side, the Ammonites could not win. But his foolish attempt to make a deal with God proves his undoing, when on his return to Mizpah his daughter is the first person that comes out of his door to meet him, so he has to sacrifice her as he vowed.

~ **ABOUT THE STORY** ~

After more years of trouble, God chooses a new leader, Jephthah. When the Israelites ask him to lead their troops into battle against the Ammonites, he makes a bargain with them, that he remain their leader if he is successful. However, his bargain with God is not so clever. Unfortunately for Jephthah, the first thing he sees on returning from battle is his daughter. He cannot break his vow to God, so he has to kill her.

Samson and the Philistines

FOR decades the Israelites had struggled with the war-like Philistines for control of the Promised Land. No matter how many defeats each nation suffered, they both refused to give up; and even though Barak and Deborah had previously crushed the entire Philistine army, the Philistines had slowly regained their strength. Now Israel once again fell into Philistine hands.

Yet God didn't entirely abandon the Israelites. He blessed a childless couple with a very special baby, Samson, sending an angel to tell them that one day he would stand up against the Philistines. The angel also warned the parents never to cut his hair.

Samson grew into a tall and exceptionally strong young man. But when he fell in love with a Philistine girl, his mother and father were utterly dismayed. They didn't know

that it was all part of God's plan, and begged Samson to reconsider. But the wedding plans continued.

A grand wedding feast took place with 30 Philistine guests of the bride invited. Everyone threw themselves into the celebrations and Samson decided to add to the fun by asking a riddle. He thought back to the time when he had been travelling to visit his bride-to-be and a lion had jumped out at him. The mighty Samson had killed the

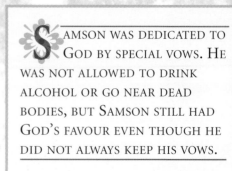

Jaffa
This picture shows a view of Jaffa, on the Mediterranean coast of Israel. Today, it is part of the city of Tel Aviv but in Old Testament times, it was part of Philistia (the land of the Philistines). In the Bible, it is called Joppa.

SAMSON WAS DEDICATED TO GOD BY SPECIAL VOWS. HE WAS NOT ALLOWED TO DRINK ALCOHOL OR GO NEAR DEAD BODIES, BUT SAMSON STILL HAD GOD'S FAVOUR EVEN THOUGH HE DID NOT ALWAYS KEEP HIS VOWS.

The Philistines
On the left is a Philistine warrior's coffin. The Philistines were the Israelites' greatest enemies. According to the Bible, they came from the Greek island of Crete and settled on the southern coastal plain of Canaan in the 12th century BC. The Philistines had five main cities, each with its own ruler. The country of Palestine takes its name from the Philistines.

surprised lion with his bare hands. Later, on his return, Samson had seen that a swarm of bees had made a hive in the lion's carcass, and without fear he had reached in and taken a piece of the delicious honeycomb. These events made a nicely perplexing riddle:

"Out of the eater came something to eat,
Out of the strong came something sweet."

"Solve it by the end of the week," Samson challenged the Philistines, "and I will give each of you a set of fine clothes. If you fail, you must buy me rich clothes instead."

For days the guests racked their brains, until they were almost driven mad. As the baffled Philistines ran out of ideas, they decided to cheat. They went to the bride and told her that her life depended on telling them the secret.

Samson's young bride was so scared that she plagued her husband desperately for the answer to the riddle. On the seventh day, when she broke down and wept, Samson gave in. And before the sun went down, the Philistines had their answer.

> *The Spirit of the Lord came mightily upon him and the ropes became as flax.*

When Samson realized that he had been tricked by his guests he was furious. He stormed over to the nearest Philistine town and killed 30 citizens. He took the clothes that they were wearing, and he gave them to the Philistine wedding guests to keep his side of the bargain. Then, broken-hearted, he returned all alone to his father's house.

The Philistines turned on his sweetheart and her father and burnt them inside their house. Samson was grief-stricken. "I swear I shall not stop until I have taken my vengeance on the whole nation," he vowed solemnly. But first he had to deal with the lynch mob who had arrived looking for him. Cunningly, he allowed the Israelites to tie his hands and lead him to his captors. There he broke free and seized a large jawbone that was lying at his feet. He attacked the Philistines in a frenzy, and by the time he stopped, he had killed 1,000 of his greatest enemies single-handed.

The Philistines didn't give up trying to catch Samson. When they found him sleeping one night, he escaped by simply lifting the city gates and walking away with them! It seemed as if it would never be possible to conquer the man with the strength of the Lord Himself.

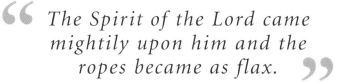

Chosen by God
Samson was singled out by God from birth as special, so could ask God to perform a miracle and supply water to quench his thirst in the desert at Lehi.

Samson the Nazirite
Samson was a Nazirite – one who is dedicated to the service of God by special vows. Nazirites were not allowed to drink alcohol, nor to eat raisins or vinegar. They were forbidden from cutting their hair, and they had to avoid going near dead bodies. As the episode with the lion shows, Samson did not take his Nazirite vows very seriously.

❦ ABOUT THE STORY ❦

The Israelites have fallen under the rule of the Philistines. God sends a saviour in the form of a baby boy. As a young man, Samson disappoints his parents by marrying a Philistine girl, but this is part of God's plan for him, and the alliance is short-lived. Samson is furious that he has been tricked into revealing the riddle about the lion, and he takes revenge. This is the first of Samson's personal battles against the Philistines.

Samson and Delilah

NEWS of Samson's feats of strength against the hated Philistines spread like wildfire through Israel and the people's hero found himself made a Judge. This only inflamed the Philistines' hatred further, and they put Samson even higher on their 'wanted' list.

While the Philistine leaders plotted and schemed, Samson fell in love with a girl called Delilah. But Samson hadn't learnt his lesson. Like his former wife, Delilah was a Philistine. And unknown to him she was soon bribed by Philistine chieftains to use her charms to get Samson to reveal the secret of his strength. She was completely snared by the promise of enough silver to make her very rich, and she did all she could to captivate the great

Israelite Judge. Often when they were alone together Delilah would cuddle up to Samson and ask, "Why won't you tell me how someone could take away your power?" Her innocent eyes and frustrated, enquiring tone gave her a childish air, and Samson never dreamt that Delilah was a cunning woman intent on deceiving him. She nudged and nagged, coaxed and cajoled, until Samson was forced to tell her something just to keep the peace! But he decided to have a little fun, and tease her for a while.

Little did Samson know that he was playing very dangerous games indeed. "If I am tied with seven new bowstrings, I will lose all my strength," he whispered to Delilah, with no idea that Philistine soldiers were hiding in the very next room. "Let me try, just for fun," begged Delilah, and bound him as tightly as she could. Then she stood back and put Samson to the test, crying out, "The Philistines are coming!" and daring him to break free. Imagine the disappointment on Delilah's face when the laughing Samson snapped out of his bowstrings as if they were threads of cotton. "You fibbed!" she cried, stamping her foot. "Please tell me the real secret of your strength!"

"All right, all right," Samson shrugged. "If I'm bound with new, unused ropes, all my strength will leave me." Delilah clapped her hands with glee and rushed to tie him just as he had instructed. Yet once more Samson burst free, and the Philistine ambush stayed where they were.

"You're just mocking me," Delilah pouted. "Stop fooling around, now, and tell me the truth."

Samson pretended to be serious. "Take the seven braids of my hair and weave them into your loom, then you'll find my strength will fade." Very carefully, Delilah did as

Samson and Hercules
This picture shows a statue of the head of Hercules. In Greek and Roman mythology, Hercules was a hero of incredible strength and courage who performed 12 difficult tasks, or labours. After his death, he was made a god. In general, the word "Hercules" is used to mean a man of exceptional strength.

Parallels have been drawn between Samson, the strong man of the Bible, and Hercules, the strong man of Roman myth, comparing Samson's many feats of strength with Hercules' labours. However, while Hercules is a mythological character, there is strong historical evidence for Samson's existence. His birth and death are carefully documented, and the story of Samson as told in the Bible is closely connected with known historical events.

Dagon
Dagon was one of the main Philistine gods. He is often depicted as a fish god, but this is believed to be because of a confusion with the Hebrew word *dag* which means "fish". Another Hebrew word, *dagan* means "grain" and it is possible that Dagon was a vegetation or grain god. He was first worshipped in Mesopotamia from at least 2500BC onwards.

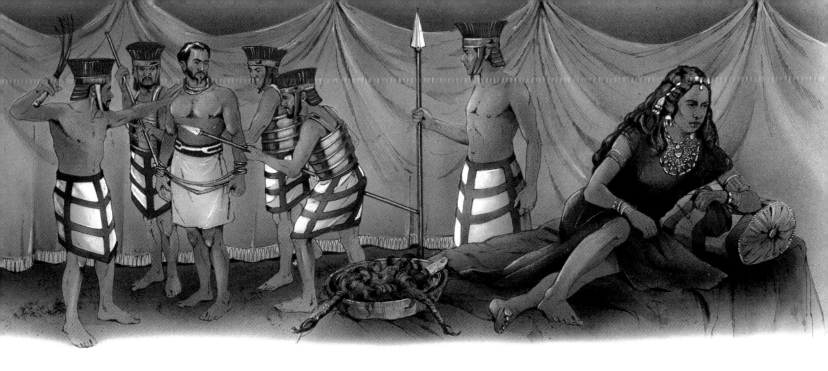

> ## 'If I be shaved then my strength will leave me and I shall become weak.'

she was told. But when she was finished and had made the weaving secure, Samson simply broke the loom with a flick of his head, enjoying the joke more than ever.

"How can you say you love me when you tell me nothing but lies!" Delilah sobbed. She sulked for weeks, making life so awful for Samson that in the end he could bear it no longer.

"If my hair is cut, I shall be like any other man," he confided. And Delilah knew he was telling the truth.

This time Delilah planned everything down to the last detail, so nothing could go wrong. She was so confident of success that she sent messages to the chieftains to come and collect Samson – bringing her money, of course – before she'd even taken him prisoner. First, she soothed Samson to sleep in her lap. Then, when he was snoring soundly, she gave the signal for a servant to creep in and cut off his precious long braids. Finally, with a small self-satisfied smile, she breathed in his ear to wake him. "Samson! Samson!" she whispered. "The Philistines are really coming!" Without realizing that his hair was gone, Samson sprang up to face the soldiers. But the strength of the Spirit of the Lord had indeed left him, and he was soon overpowered. As Samson stood before the Philistines in chains – knowing helplessness for the first time in his life – the cruel, merciless warriors blinded him by gouging out his eyes. Then, rejoicing at the great Israelite leader's misery, they flung him into the jail at Gaza.

Betrayed by Delilah
The name Delilah means "flirt", and the word has come to mean "a temptress". Delilah's greed for money leads her to collaborate with the Philistines and to betray Samson.

> ### ⮞ ABOUT THE STORY ⮜
> Samson is persuaded by Delilah's charms to reveal the secret of his strength. When Samson's hair is cut, one of his Nazirite vows is broken. Until now, this was a vow he had kept. The vow is a sign of his dedication to God. Though Samson is physically strong, he is morally weak. His weakness symbolizes the weakness of all the Israelites, who have repeatedly broken God's laws and turned to other gods.

Destruction of the Temple

IN the double darkness of the prison dungeons and his blindness, Samson was put to work grinding corn, which hurt him at every move because of the shackles round his wrists and ankles. He had no family with him, no friends, and no possessions – only God and time. And as time passed, Samson's hair began to grow again without him even realizing.

The day came when the Philistines held an important festival in praise of their god, Dagon. Every man, woman and child was out in the streets to watch the sacrifices and join in the rejoicing, and this particular year the celebrations were better than ever. The Philistines had something really special to thank Dagon for, and they were determined to throw a party to remember. For Dagon had delivered into their hands the powerful Israelite leader who had single-handedly been the cause of thousands of Philistine deaths.

The merry-making went on and on, and the worshippers grew wilder and wilder. Voices began to call for the famous prisoner to be brought up out of the jail and paraded for all the Philistines to see, so they could enjoy mocking and jeering at him to their hearts' content. Then the word went round that Samson was to be displayed in the temple itself, and the size of the crowds swelled immediately. How the Philistines longed to look down on their once dreaded enemy and sneer at him and show him in person just how much they hated him!

As soon as the first people caught sight of the wretched, blind Samson shuffling into the temple, they began to yell insults and ridicule him, and soon the noise and excitement was at fever pitch. The Philistine chieftains ordered Samson to be positioned right in the middle of the temple floor, between the two main supporting pillars, in order to give as many of their subjects as possible a good view. And the Israelite champion stood there as he

> **Strengthen me, I pray, this once that I may be avenged upon the Philistines.**

was told, quite broken and slumped, trying to block out the insults and obscenities that came hurtling through the darkness to his ears.

But as if from nowhere, a small spark of an idea suddenly began to glimmer in the blackness that now floated permanently before Samson. Slowly he bent down to the boy who was there to lead him about, and said, "Will you help me feel where the pillars are, so I can lean on them." Samson felt the lad take his hands and guide them out on to the cool rock on either side of him. Then silently Samson called out to the Lord with all the passion that was inside him. "O Lord, God, remember me, I pray," he beseeched, as he stood all on his own in the midst of his enemies. "I pray to you, O God, please give me my strength back just one more time – so I can be avenged

Samson's story
This picture of Samson dates from the 13th century. This means that it is not a realistic painting, but can tell the story of Samson to people at the time who could not read.

Grinding grain
Grinding grain would have been humiliating for Samson, as it was a job normally done by slaves. Samson, though, was probably put to work at a large mill, usually worked by oxen.

upon these people for the loss of my eyes." And Samson drew himself up and braced himself against the pillars, suddenly feeling the Spirit of the Lord flooding as strongly through his body as ever.

"Let me die with the Philistines!" he cried out, and heaved with all his might.

Not one of the Philistines had been able to hear above their own commotion what Samson had said. Yet they had seen him open his mouth and cry to Heaven, and had watched with mounting horror as the crushed, dejected prisoner had straightened

up into a broad-shouldered warrior. Now their scornful cries of derision at once changed to howls and screams of terror as the pillars began to tremble and dust came crumbling down upon them from the ceiling. Before anyone could flee, Samson broke the pillars with an almighty crack and the roof and walls of the huge temple came crashing inwards, burying the thousands of people inside under tonnes of rubble.

That day, the mighty Samson died along with the Philistines. But he killed more enemies by dying than he had killed during all his life.

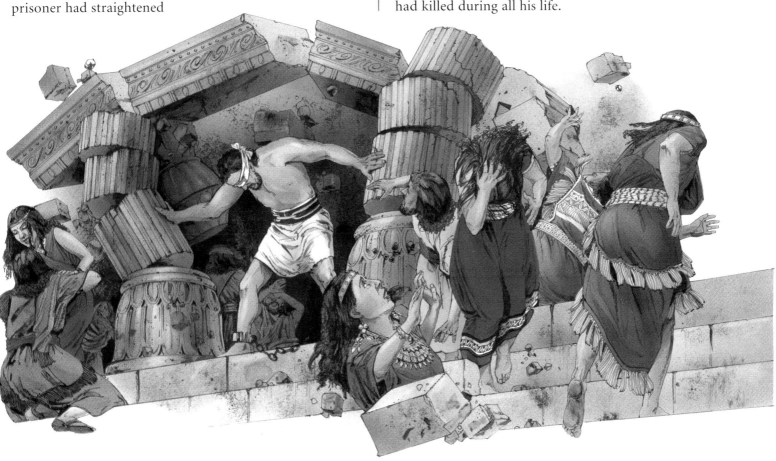

❖ ABOUT THE STORY ❖

Samson appears to be a broken man, but his faith is still strong, and God answers his prayer. Through Samson, God finally releases the Israelites from Philistine rule. Samson's destruction of the temple is symbolic of the Israelites' defeat of the Philistines.

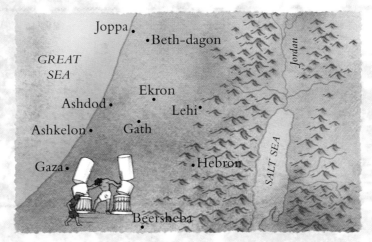

Samson
This map shows the area of Samson's war with the Philistines. It shows Lehi, where he killed the Philistines with the jawbone. You can also see Gaza from where he took the city gates, and Hebron where he left them. Finally, there is the Temple of Dagon at Gaza that he destroyed as he died.

The Book of Ruth

DURING the days when the Judges ruled Israel, there was once a great famine that struck the land. Many people were forced either to leave their homes and settle elsewhere, or stay and starve. One man who chose to take his family away to safety was Elimelech. With his wife, Naomi, and his two sons, he went to live in Moab, where the crops were much more plentiful. There they were very happy at first, both boys taking Moabite wives: one called Orpah and the other Ruth. But in the space of.ten years, all three men died, leaving their widows sad and lonely. Naomi longed to return to Israel, and made up her mind to go back. The brave widow talked to Orpah and Ruth about her difficult decision. "I consider you both my own daughters, but I shall go back to Israel on my own," she told the two young women. "There's no need for you to come too. You both belong here with your own people." Orpah and Ruth were devastated, but Naomi was insistent. Finally, sobbing with grief, Orpah agreed to remain in

> "*Where you go, I will go, your people shall be my people and your God, my God.*"

Moab. Ruth, however, flatly refused. "Wherever you go, I will go," she told Naomi, determinedly. "Your people will be my people, and your God my God. Only death itself will keep me from your side." So the two women set out on the long journey to Naomi's home town of Bethlehem.

They arrived at Bethlehem in the middle of the harvest, so Ruth managed to find work straightaway. As was the custom, she went with the other women of the city into the fields to gather the barley that the reapers had left behind. Ruth worked hard from morning until sunset. Her efforts were noticed by a landowner called Boaz, who asked his professional reapers who the young woman was. When Boaz heard that Ruth was Moabite and discovered how faithful she had been to her mother-in-law, he summoned Ruth to see him. "Stay in my fields, under my protection," he told her. "Whenever you get thirsty, help yourself to the water drawn for my reapers."

Ruth was quite overcome with his generosity. "Thank you," she blushed, quite embarrassed by the special treatment. "But why are you being so kind to me?"

Boaz smiled and told her gently that he had heard all about her kindness to Naomi. "May God reward you well for all that you have done," he praised her.

Later on, when the harvesters stopped to eat, Boaz not only called Ruth to come and join them but also gave her more than enough food. The young woman could hardly believe her good luck and hurried back to her work.

"Where on earth have you been working?" marvelled Naomi when she saw the huge sack of grain and the large bundle of food her daughter-in-law had brought home.

✤ ABOUT THE STORY ✤

Although the Israelites have been turning away from God, this story illustrates how, for many individuals, faith in Him remains strong. It also shows that God is just as concerned with the lives of ordinary people as He is with the affairs of great leaders. Ruth discovers her new faith through her love for her mother-in-law. She goes on to produce a son who will become the grandfather of David, the first King of Israel.

Everyday life
The picture shows Ruth working in the fields. While this story relates to the same period as the stories of the Judges before it, its tone and content are very different. It deals with ordinary life, which would have been relevant to many people of the time. Most people during the period of the Judges still had to make a living from the land.

Meeting place
Business deals often took place at the town gates, like the gates of Damascus shown here, as there were plenty of people around to act as witnesses. Boaz was not Ruth's nearest male relative, so he had to meet the man who was, called a "kinsman-redeemer", and buy the right to acquire Naomi's land and marry Ruth. The kinsman-redeemer gave his sandal to Boaz as a sign of the agreement.

"The landowner's name is Boaz," she began, but could get no further before Naomi interrupted her.

"Boaz?" the widow cried, her face lighting up with excitement. "Boaz is one of my dead husband's closest relations! This has to be the Lord's work! Thanks to God!" And the two women's hearts were filled with gladness.

When the harvest was over Ruth found herself out of work.

"We'll have to tell Boaz that we're family and maybe he will take pity on us," Naomi told her. Ruth put on her finest clothes and went off to find Boaz.

Boaz was sleeping by his grain to protect it when Ruth arrived. She silently went to the end of his sleeping mat and covered herself with the corner of Boaz's robe. When Boaz woke, he was deeply moved by Ruth's plea. "I will do everything in my power to look after you," he said.

The next day, Boaz formally took Ruth and her mother-in-law under his protection. He met Ruth's "kinsman-redeemer", Naomi's nearest living male relative, and bought the right to marry her, sealing the deal, as was customary, by receiving his sandal.

Boaz cared for Ruth and Naomi from that day onwards. He married Ruth, and in due course she gave birth to their son, Obed, who was to become the grandfather of David, the greatest of all the Israelite kings.

Ruth and Naomi
Ruth decided to make the long journey with Naomi to Bethlehem. Although she thought that she was giving up the chance to remarry and settle down, her first loyalty was to Naomi. She was still rewarded, though, by her marriage to Boaz, and the birth of their child.

Threshing and winnowing
After the barley had been harvested, it was beaten with a threshing board, then winnowed – tossed into the air with a fork so that the grain separated from the stalks. The light stalks blew away while the heavy grain fell straight to the floor.

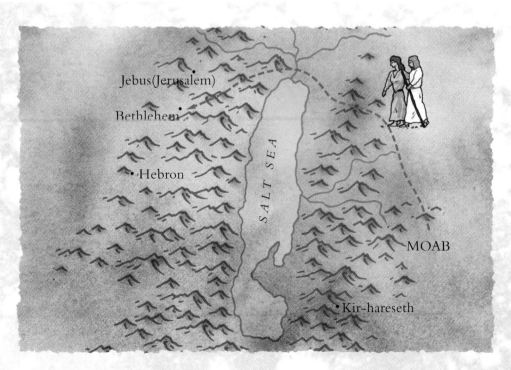

Moses

MOSES is one of the great leaders in the Bible. His life was eventful from the very start. Desperate to save her baby son from the Pharaoh's decree that all Hebrew male babies should be killed, Moses's mother put him into a reed basket and hid him among the bulrushes that grew beside the Nile. Found by one of Pharaoh's daughters, he was brought up by her at the royal court.

As a young man, Moses felt sympathy for his fellow-Israelites, who were often ill-treated by their Egyptian masters. When he witnessed an Egyptian overseer beating an Israelite slave, he was so angry, he killed the man. The news reached Pharaoh's ears and Moses fled to safety outside Egypt's borders. During this time, he received a sign from God, in the form of a burning bush, telling him that he was to become the saviour of the Israelite people.

After battling against a great deal of opposition from Pharaoh, Moses finally succeeded in leading his people out of Egypt, to search for the land God had promised them. On Mount Sinai, Moses spoke directly with God and received the Ten Commandments and other laws.

During the 40 years of exile in the wilderness, Moses remained loyal to his people and to his God. Despite the Israelites' regular lapses of faith in God and their rebellions against Moses's own leadership, he stood by them, frequently pleading to God for mercy on their behalf. When Moses's own sister, Miriam, complained about him, claiming that God had spoken to her as well as to Moses, God rebuked her, explaining that although he appeared to other people in visions or dreams, the way in which he appeared to Moses was different. He said, "With him will I speak mouth to mouth, even clearly, and not in dark speeches" (Numbers 12:8).

Although he devoted his whole life to God, Moses was not above sin himself. On one occasion, in the wilderness, he used his rod to bring forth water from a rock, instead of just speaking to the rock, as God had ordered. For this disobedience, he was forbidden entry into the Promised Land, though he did climb Mount Nebo to view it from a distance, shortly before his death.

A man of God

Throughout his life, Moses's faith in God never wavered. He was a trusting and obedient servant until the day he died. Despite all his achievements, and his status as God's chosen one, he remained meek, humble and patient, always putting his people's needs before his own. He was both a great man and a great leader.

The death of Moses

The book of Deuteronomy describes the death of Moses, finishing with the following words about one of the greatest of Old Testament prophets. "And there has not arisen in Israel a prophet since like Moses, whom the Lord knew face to face, none like him for all the signs and wonders which the Lord sent him to do in the land of Egypt, to Pharaoh and to all his servants and to all his land, and for all the mighty power and all the great and terrible deeds which Moses wrought in the sight of all Israel."

Deuteronomy 34:10-12.

The Battle of Beliefs

ON their arrival in the land of Canaan, the Israelites fought many battles with the local people, in an attempt to take over their land. Alongside the war over land, another war was also being fought – a war of religion.

God had instructed the Israelites to drive the Canaanites away from their lands. He knew that the local people worshipped different gods, and that their religion might influence the Israelites. At first, the Israelites obeyed God, but as the years went by, they grew tired of constantly fighting the Canaanites and began to live alongside them as neighbours. As God had predicted, they also began to worship their gods.

Gideon and the angel
In this picture, the angel of the Lord commands Gideon to destroy his father's altar to Baal, together with its statue. Gideon was appointed by God as one of the Judges who would save the Israelites from their enemies.

One aspect of Canaanite religion that the Israelites would have liked was the idea of worshipping an image, such as a statue, of a god or goddess. It would have been far more satisfying to worship something they could actually see, as the Israelites were forbidden to worship idols by Moses's second commandment.

The other reason the Israelites turned to the local gods was their apparent control over the fertility of the land. Once the Israelites settled down to become farmers, their crops were very important to them. Many of the Canaanite gods were linked to nature and fertility, and, because of this, they seemed to the Israelites to have more direct influence over their daily life than their own God did. The Canaanites were very successful farmers; some took this as evidence of the superiority of Baal.

Statue worship
Many Israelites were attracted to the Canaanite gods because they could worship statues, which was forbidden by their own God.

Destroying the altar
Gideon destroyed his father's altar to Baal and built a new altar to God. He went on to defeat the hordes of invading Midianites with an army of only 300 men.

Canaanite gods
These are three of the main Canaanite gods. Dagon is believed to be a god of grain or vegetation. Baal, which means lord, is a weather god associated with thunderstorms and rain. He is often shown holding a bolt of lightning. Asherah is a fertility goddess associated with Baal.

DAGON   BAAL   ASHERAH

Battling on
While the physical battles of clashing swords and shields raged noisily around Canaan, the quieter battle of beliefs was also going on.

The Judges

THE officials called Judges were originally appointed by Moses during the wilderness years. His father-in-law, Jethro, suggested that they could take some of the burden of responsibility from Moses's shoulders. These were Judges in the legal sense, in the way that people use the word today. After the death of Joshua, no single leader took over, and the Judges took on the role of rulers in peacetime and military leaders in wartime. So the word "judge" came to mean "leader" or "governor".

Ehud and Eglon
Ehud was one of the early Judges. He saved the Israelites from the Moabites by killing their king, Eglon.

Deborah's wisdom
Deborah used to sit under a palm tree and hand out advice to Israelites who came to her for help with settling their disputes.

The Book of Judges in the Old Testament tells of the lives of these Judges. Their main role was to save the Israelite people from their enemies and to try and keep them faithful to God's laws. During the time of the Judges, a pattern of events kept repeating itself. The Israelites turned away from God and started to worship the Canaanite gods so God punished them by letting them fall into the hands of a foreign ruler. The people repented and begged for mercy, promising to change their ways so God appointed a Judge to save them. For a period of time, the people mended their ways, but after the death of the Judge, they slipped back into their sinful habits.

There were 14 Judges, the first being Othniel and the last Samuel. Some ruled for a very short time and achieved nothing of great importance. Others were more significant, including Deborah, a woman Judge who, together with Barak, saved the Israelites from the Canaanite General Sisera. Gideon took on the mighty army of the Midianites with a force of only 300 men, and there was Jephthah, a brigand who defeated the Ammonites. The most famous Judge is Samson, who made many attacks on the Philistines. Under Samuel, the last Judge, and the first Kings, the nation of Israel was eventually brought together and the Philistines were finally defeated.

TIMELINE 1400BC TO 1000BC

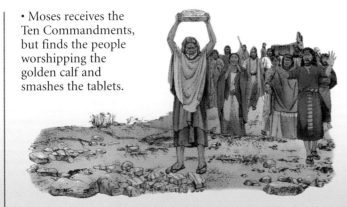

• Moses receives the Ten Commandments, but finds the people worshipping the golden calf and smashes the tablets.

1400BC   MOSES SMASHES THE STONE TABLETS

THE ISRAELITES CROSS THE RIVER JORDAN

• Moses, Israel's greatest leader, dies.

• Joshua is appointed leader of the Israelites.

• Joshua takes the Israelites across the River Jordan into Canaan, and leads them in victory against Jericho.

1300BC

1200B

Samson and the Nazirite Laws

THE Judges were chosen by God to lead and judge his people. It is confusing, therefore, to see that some of these appointed leaders, who are held up as examples to their people, lived their own lives in a way that was far from what people might expect, and seemed to disregard many of God's laws.

The most obvious example is Samson. He was a Nazirite which meant that he was dedicated from birth to the service of God by special vows. Nazirites were not allowed to cut their hair nor to come into contact with dead bodies. Samson broke most of his Nazirite vows, by allowing Delilah to cut off his hair, and by eating honey from the carcass of a lion he had killed.

Although it is hard to accept the behaviour of Judges like Samson in positions of authority, we must remember that all the Judges are instruments of God and their actions are part of God's plan. For example, it is because Samson allows Delilah to cut his hair that he is captured by the Philistines. In their temple God gives him back his strength so he can kill several thousand of them at once. God's purpose for Samson is to defeat the Philistines, so He allows some of His laws to be broken in order to achieve something more important.

Forbidden food
Samson broke his Nazirite vows by eating honey from a nest bees had made in a lion's carcass.

Tricked by a woman
Delilah tricked Samson into revealing the secret of his strength and then betrayed him to the Philistines.

The strongest man
When Samson was found in Gaza, he escaped by uprooting the city gates and walking away with them.

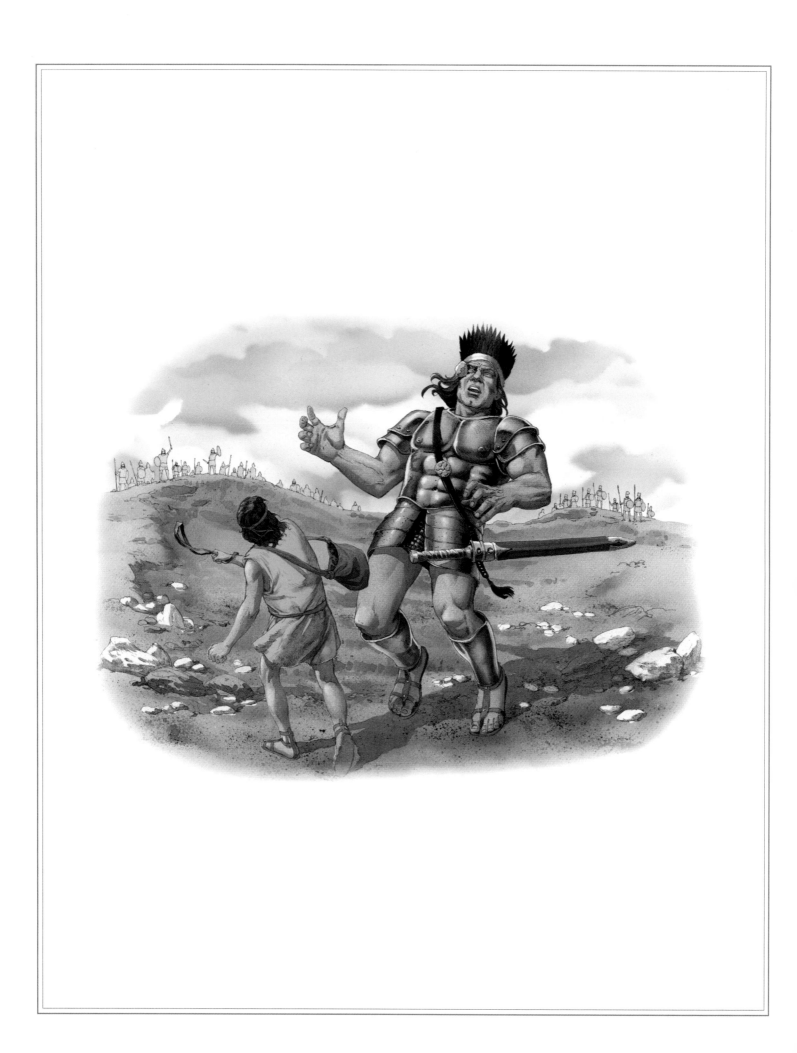

THE GREAT KINGS

*The reigns of Saul, David and Solomon,
the great kings of Israel*

The Great Kings

HERE you can read about the Israelites' battles amongst themselves and with their neighbours, and charts the rises and falls of their faith in God. It covers the period of time from Samuel through the reigns of the first kings of Israel, to the division of the kingdom into two nations, Israel and Judah.

The story starts with the story of Samuel, who, brought up by Eli the High Priest, was called by God as a prophet at an early age. He went on to rule Israel as a Judge, a ruler of Israel called by God. Under Samuel's leadership the Israelites' faith in God was restored. When he got older the people asked him for a king, so God instructed Samuel to anoint Saul the first king of Israel.

Saul was very popular with his people and successful in war, but things soon started to go wrong. Saul disobeyed God several times. He was eventually punished when God rejected him as king, and Samuel anointed a shepherd boy called David as Israel's next king. David became very popular after killing the Philistine giant Goliath. Saul became so jealous that he tried to kill David who escaped to safety in the wilderness where he lived for many years. He only returned to Israel after Saul and his four sons died during a battle with the Philistines.

After Saul's death, David eventually became king over all Israel. He captured the city of Jerusalem and made it his capital, setting up the tabernacle there, and bringing back the ark. It was David who wanted to build a temple, a permanent home for the Ark of the Covenant containing their sacred laws, but God decreed this would be done by the next king, David's son, Solomon.

Jerusalem
David decided when he became king that he wanted Jerusalem as his capital. It is now known as the "City of David"

When Solomon took the throne on David's death, his main aim was to maintain the peace that his father had achieved. Solomon concentrated on developing trading links with his neighbours, and he channelled his energies into huge building projects, the most important of which was the temple in Jerusalem. As part of his plan to forge links with his neighbours, he married many foreign women, but his wives reintroduced pagan gods into Israel and Solomon joined them in their worship. God's punishment to Solomon was to split the kingdom in two, and only two of the 12 tribes were given to his son. The other ten crowned a government official called Jeroboam as their ruler.

Until the era of the kings, the Israelites had been led by Judges or priests. The first king, Saul, was requested by the people. Samuel tried to persuade them to be content to worship God as their king, but they wanted to be like their neighbours. God gave His consent, but warned that a king would make demands on his people, and a king would not be as forgiving as God had been.

The king's role developed as it passed from Saul, to David, to Solomon. Saul was a fine warrior king but never quite established his position as religious leader – it was Samuel who performed this role during his lifetime. David was very successful, he was in many ways the ideal king. He established Israel as a nation state and founded a dynasty that lasted for over 400 years. Because he had been involved in warfare he was not allowed to build a temple – that role fell to Solomon who was wise, peaceful, but was not, and could never be perfect.

David is very significant in Jewish history. The Star of David is the symbol of Judaism and features on the Israeli flag today. After David's death, the Jews hoped for a Messiah (an "anointed one"), a righteous leader descended from David, who would reunite the tribes of Israel and restore Israel's position in the world. The message of the New Testament is that this hope was fulfilled in Jesus Christ, and the lineage from David to Jesus is traced at the beginning of Matthew's gospel.

❧ THE GREAT KINGS ❧

This section covers the life of Samuel, the last of the Judges and first of the prophets, and the lives of the Israelite kings he anointed.

THE EARLY LIFE OF SAMUEL
First Book of Samuel, Ch. 1 to 7.
KING SAUL
First Book of Samuel, Ch. 8 to 15.
SAUL AND DAVID
First Book of Samuel, Ch. 16 to 31.
BATTLE FOR THE CROWN
Second Book of Samuel, Ch. 2 to 4.
KING DAVID
Second Book of Samuel, Ch. 4 to 20.
KING SOLOMON
First Book of Kings, Ch. 1 to 11.
THE KINGDOM IS DIVIDED
First Book of Kings, Ch. 12.

David and Jonathan
The fugitive David was the closest of friends with Jonathan, even though Jonathan was the son of King Saul, who wanted to kill him.

Judea and the Dead Sea
The Salt Sea, now called the Dead Sea, and the River Jordan are at the centre of the Promised Land, and have been important since the miraculous crossing of the river by Joshua. The shores of the Salt Sea are actually 400m below sea level.

Israel in the Time of Samuel

THERE were great changes to the state of Israel during the life of Samuel. When he was first called by God, the Israelites had long since fallen into sinful habits. They were worshipping other gods, the same gods that the Lord told them never to worship when they first arrived in Canaan under the leadership of Joshua.

When Samuel became the last Judge of Israel, the Israelites were fighting a losing battle with the Philistines, one of the tribes already living in Canaan. The Philistines were one of the first people to use iron in their weapons. They had a better organized army and were winning land from the Israelites. This stopped when Samuel took command. His first battle with the Philistines, with help from God and the Israelites with their renewed faith, was a huge success. For the rest of Samuel's life the Philistines were forced further and further east towards the sea.

All the lands around Israel at this time were kingdoms, and most were successful in battle, much of the time against the Israelites. Many of the people thought that this was because the Israelites did not have a single, strong leader to stand at the head of their army. They asked Samuel for a king, and he anointed Saul.

Saul won his first victory against the Ammonites who were laying siege to the city of Jabesh-gilead. This was the first of many victories for Saul, who won many cities for Israel. He won a great victory in the battle at Michmash, when his son Jonathan led the outnumbered Israelites against the powerful Philistine army. Saul also met with success in the south of the kingdom, winning battles with other tribes like the Edomites and the Moabites.

Despite his military successes for the Israelites, Saul was never as successful in leading the Israelites in their worship of God. Samuel was always the religious head of the country. This led to problems for Saul, who offended God and Samuel time after time. God eventually abandoned Saul as king, and blessed David instead. After Saul's death at Gilboa, and a brief civil war for the crown between David and Saul's surviving son, Rehoboam, David ruled the whole of Israel as the sole king.

David first made sure that the land Saul had gained from the surrounding tribes was safe, and went on to win more land, from the Philistines, the Edomites, the Ammonites, the Moabites, and the Arameans in the north. When he captured Jerusalem and made it his capital, the Israelites' conquest of Canaan was finally complete.

David did not stop there. He had extended the kingdom, but he also expanded the 'vassal territories' of Israel. These were states or kingdoms that paid sums of money to David so that he would not attack them, and David would also provide them with protection from other invading states. David extended the empire from Ezion-geber in the south, to Damascus in the north. At his death, he handed on to his son Solomon an empire larger than any that the Israelites would ever see again.

Solomon was not the man of war that his father had been. He secured the lands that his father had gained, and made peace treaties with the surrounding powers to ensure that his kingdom was safe. Solomon divided his kingdom into twelve districts, each with its own governors to collect taxes and organize the forced-labour schemes, where people had to leave their land and work for Solomon for one month in three. By getting the country organized like this, he could claim taxes from the people, which funded his building work. But the heavy taxes and forced labour made him unpopular.

When his son, Rehoboam came to the throne and told the people he would be even worse than his father, ten of the tribes rebelled and crowned Jeroboam, one of Solomon's governors, their king. This split Israel into two countries. The northern country kept the name of Israel, and built their capital city at Samaria. The southern country was made up of the two tribes of Benjamin and Judah. They took the name of Judah, with their capital at Jerusalem.

The Promised Land
The picture on the left is an old map of the Promised Land. It shows the Salt Sea, the River Jordan and the Sea of Chinnereth on the right-hand side. You can also see Egypt and the River Nile on the left.

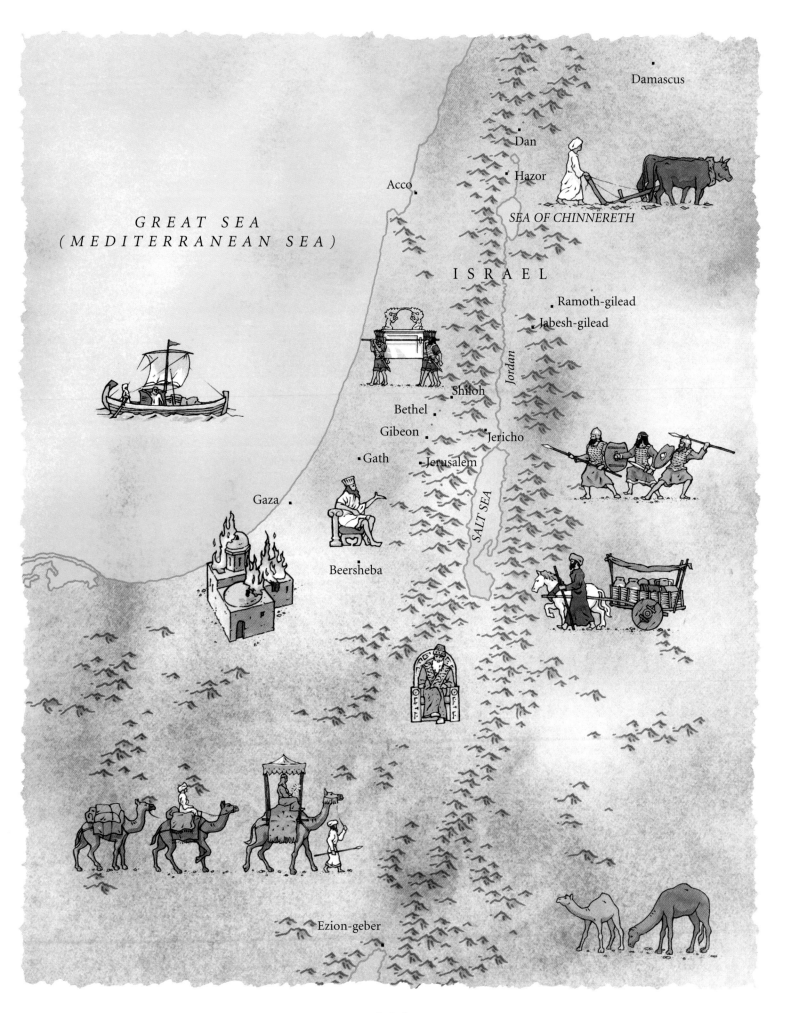

GREAT SEA
(MEDITERRANEAN SEA)

Damascus

Dan

Hazor

Acco

SEA OF CHINNERETH

ISRAEL

Ramoth-gilead

Jabesh-gilead

Shiloh

Jordan

Bethel

Gibeon

Jericho

Gath

Jerusalem

SALT SEA

Gaza

Beersheba

Ezion-geber

The Birth of Samuel

AFTER the Israelites had settled into the Promised Land, they began to forget God. People ignored the warnings of the Judges. They sank into sinful habits, worshipping false idols. Eventually, few God-fearing families were left. Even old Eli – the high priest in the tabernacle at Shiloh – had two wicked sons. Hophni and Phinehas were priests themselves, but they had no respect for God. They were dishonest and violent, and even took the sacrifices worshippers brought for the Lord, beating up anyone who resisted.

Only a few people still kept the Lord's commands. Among them were Elkanah and his two wives, Peninnah, who had many children, and Hannah, who had none. Each year, the family would travel from their home in the hills to worship God in the tabernacle at Shiloh. And each year, Hannah would pray with all her heart that the Lord would grant her children. One year, after Peninnah had teased her about being childless, Hannah was more distressed than usual. She stood in the house of the Lord begging God to answer her. "Lord," she vowed, "if you'll grant me a son, I promise I'll give him into your service."

When Eli noticed her muttering under her breath, he was furious. He was always having to throw thugs out of the shrine, and now a drunk had wandered in. "Get out of God's house and don't come back till you've sobered up!" he yelled furiously at Hannah.

"Please forgive me, my lord, I'm not drunk," sobbed Hannah, and poured out her heart to the old priest.

"Go in peace," he said kindly, "and may you have your wish. I'll add my prayers to yours."

Imagine Hannah's joy soon after when she realized she was pregnant! She called the boy Samuel, and a couple of years later, she kept her promise to God. Hannah went back to Shiloh and gave the boy into Eli's hands. God rewarded Hannah's loyalty by sending her five other children, and each year she returned to Shiloh to see her firstborn son.

Samuel grew up pure-hearted and strong. He loved the old priest as if he were his real father, and Eli was as proud of Samuel as he was ashamed of his own sons. "Why do you commit these terrible crimes?"Eli raged at Hophni and Phinehas. But they just ignored the old man and carried on regardless.

One day a man arrived in Shiloh, asking for Eli. The days of great prophets such as Moses and Joshua were long gone. However, Eli knew the stranger was a prophet. The prophet's, message made Eli's blood run cold.

"Centuries ago, God appointed your family as priests to serve Him for ever. Now your sons are sinning against

Priests and worshippers
As priests, Eli's sons were entitled to some of the sacrificial offerings brought to the tabernacle. They abused their position by taking more than their proper share, and because of their sinful acts, God put a curse on Eli's family.

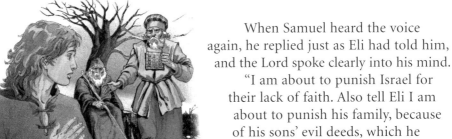

Him. Know then that sickness, poverty and misery will soon arrive at your door. Both your sons will die on the same day, and the Lord will raise up a new, faithful priest who will serve Him truly."

From then on, Eli had a heavy heart. And as his spirit sank, he started to lose his sight, but Samuel was always close at hand to help the old man.

One night when Samuel was lying in bed he heard someone calling his name. Samuel ran to the high priest straight away. But the old man was puzzled.

"I didn't call you," Eli said. "Go and lie down again."

Samuel had just settled down when the voice came again. "Samuel! Samuel!" Once more, Samuel leapt up and raced round to Eli's room.

> ❝ *'I will fulfil against Eli all that I have spoken concerning his house.'* ❞

"Here I am, father," he told the old man.

"I didn't call, my son," replied Eli. "Go back to sleep now." But when it happened a third time, a shiver ran down Eli's spine. He suddenly realized what was going on.

"Go and lie down," he told Samuel gently. "If someone calls you again, say, 'Speak, Lord, for your servant is listening.'"

When Samuel heard the voice again, he replied just as Eli had told him, and the Lord spoke clearly into his mind.

"I am about to punish Israel for their lack of faith. Also tell Eli I am about to punish his family, because of his sons' evil deeds, which he knew about but failed to stop."

Samuel was worried. How could he possibly give the old man such dreadful news? "You must tell me everything that the Lord said," Eli insisted. Sadly, he listened to everything that was going to happen. He sighed wearily. "It's the Lord's will," murmured Eli. "He must do whatever He sees fit."

Sacrificial fork
This sacrificial fork would have been used by the priests to scoop up the parts of the sacrifice to which they were entitled.

Hannah's song
When Hannah took Samuel to Shiloh and gave him into God's service, she sang a song of praise and thanksgiving to the Lord. The words of the song suggest that she was a prophetess. Hannah's song has been compared to the song of thanksgiving that Mary sang when an angel told her she would become the mother of Jesus.

∼ THE SONG OF HANNAH ∼

THE LORD MAKES POOR
AND MAKES RICH;
HE BRINGS LOW, HE ALSO EXALTS.
HE RAISES UP THE POOR
FROM THE DUST;
HE LIFTS THE NEEDY
FROM THE ASH HEAP,
TO MAKE THEM SIT WITH PRINCES
AND INHERIT
A SEAT OF HONOUR.
FOR THE PILLARS OF THE EARTH
ARE THE LORD'S,
AND ON THEM HE HAS SET
THE WORLD. ∾

Home of the tabernacle
This is Shiloh, where the tabernacle was kept, and where Hannah went to pray. Its modern name is Seilun. The tabernacle was set up here by Joshua when the Israelites conquered Canaan and did not move until the time of King David.

Philistines Capture the Ark

As Samuel grew up, he became known far and wide as a true prophet. Eli the high priest was getting frail and blind. His one hope was that Samuel would prove to be God's chosen new leader. Everything else looked gloomy.

The Philistines wanted to win back their land and were about to attack once again. The Israelite army was going to meet them, confident that God would be with them and give them victory. However, despite Samuel's rousing preaching, many people still worshipped idols. In the past, whenever the Israelites had turned away from God, God had turned His back on them too. Now, He left them to face their worst enemy alone.

At the end of the first battle 4,000 Israelite soldiers lay dead at the feet of the cheering Philistines. The elders were shocked. "Why did God allow us to be crushed like this?"

they groaned. "We'll have to bring the Ark of the Covenant here. We must have God with us on the battlefield if we are to be saved from our enemies."

The two wicked sons of Eli brought the holy ark from Shiloh. As the ark entered the camp, the soldiers cheered so loudly that the Philistines heard it in their own base. When they found out the cause of the commotion, they shook in their shoes. "The Israelite God who struck down the mighty Egyptians has come to help them!" they howled. "We're doomed!" However, instead of waiting in despair, they looked death straight in the eye. "Fight, Philistines!" came the command from their generals. "Don't be taken like slaves, but die with honour!" The soldiers launched a sudden, courageous attack.

Later that day, Eli was sitting worrying about the ark. "I should never have let them take it," he murmured. Then, he heard wailing, and footsteps hurrying towards him. "I come from the battlefield," the messenger panted.

Eli gripped his seat and tried to steady himself. "What's happened?" he asked.

"There's been a terrible slaughter!" the messenger wept. "30,000 foot soldiers have been slain and your sons are among them!"

Eli's heart was pounding. "What news of the ark?" he yelled, in a frenzy.

The messenger looked up at the high priest. "It has been

❧ ABOUT THE STORY ❧

The Ark of the Covenant contained the Ten Commandments that God had given to Moses. It symbolized God's presence, so when it was captured it seemed as if God Himself had left the Israelites. But He did not intend people to think that the ark had any magical properties. This event was like a visual aid to show that God was more powerful than Dagon, the false god of the Philistines.

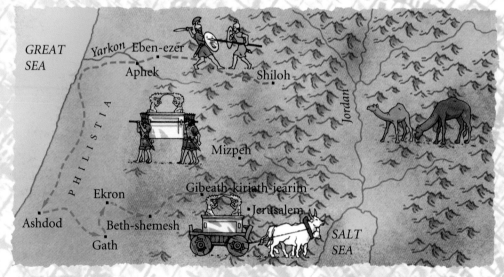

Travels of the ark
The ark was moved from Shiloh when the Israelites wrongly tried to use it as a good luck charm in battle. The Philistines captured the ark at Eben-ezer, but plagues infested each city it was kept in, so it was sent back to the Israelites at Beth-shemesh.

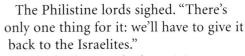

captured!" he whispered. Eli gasped and toppled backwards as if he'd been punched. There was a snap as the old man's neck cracked and Eli died, God's judgement on his family fulfilled.

The Philistines carried the ark to Ashdod, where their lords displayed it in the temple of their god, Dagon. However, next morning, the people found the statue of Dagon fallen face down on the floor before the ark. The Philistines set their god back in its place and dusted him off. The following day Dagon was again found lying in front of the ark, with his head and hands broken off. Soon ordinary people discovered lumps growing inside them and their skin breaking out in boils. Then thousands of rats scuttled into the city. "It's the ark!" the people wailed. "Get rid of it!"

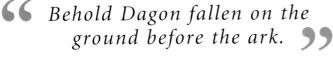

> ## *Behold Dagon fallen on the ground before the ark.*

"They may be right," the lords agreed. "We'll send the ark to Gath instead."

The people of Gath fared no better. No sooner was the ark within their walls than the tumours and boils began to plague them too. "Take it away!" the inhabitants screamed.

The people of Ekron heard of plans to transfer the ark to them, and immediately they sent a committee to stop them. "Don't you dare send us that cursed thing!" they raged.

The Philistine lords sighed. "There's only one thing for it: we'll have to give it back to the Israelites."

The lords consulted magicians on how to return the ark. They built a cart to carry it, with an offering of ten golden statues. They hitched up two cows that they'd separated from their calves. "Set the cart off without a driver," the magicians instructed. "If the cows go to the border, it will prove the Israelite God really is in charge. If they return to their calves, we'll know it's all a load of rubbish."

The Philistines were stunned to see the cows plod straight down the road to the Israelite city of Beth-shemesh, just as if the cart had an invisible driver. The Israelites in the fields couldn't believe their eyes. Weeping with joy, they ran to receive their nation's treasure. And the ark stayed in a safe-house at nearby Gibeath-kiriath-jearim for 20 years, for the people dared not move it.

Plagues
The offering of golden statues mentioned in the story included five gold rats, each one representing one of the five Philistine rulers. The Philistines hoped that by sending out statues of the rats that were carrying the plague, they would succeed in getting rid of the plague itself. The gold offerings were placed in the cart, in a box beside the ark.

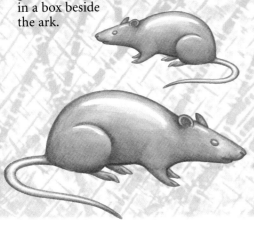

SOME PEOPLE REFUSE TO HONOUR OR SERVE GOD. THE BIBLE TELLS US THAT EVENTUALLY EVERYONE WILL HAVE TO ADMIT THAT HE EXISTS AND IS WORTHY OF WORSHIP. ALL WILL BOW BEFORE HIM – AS THE STATUE OF DAGON DID.

Ark in battle
The ark was the Israelites' most precious possession. By using the sacred ark as a talisman to protect them from the Philistines, the Israelites showed disrespect to God. Their punishment was to lose both the battle and the ark.

Samuel in Command

SAMUEL grew up a strong man, full of faith in the Lord. He became the Judge, or leader of Israel, just as Eli had hoped. The great prophets of the past – Abraham, Moses and Joshua – had all spoken to the nation and inspired the people, and Samuel was no exception. One of the very first things he did was to call a huge meeting at Mizpah. "There is only one God," he told the hundreds of thousands of people gathered there. "You have seen what dreadful things you bring upon yourselves when you abandon the Lord. Now, if you really want to turn back to God, you must get rid of all the pagan idols you've been worshipping. You must beg the Lord's forgiveness and feel truly sorry in your hearts. Make up your minds that you're going to serve the one true God. Do your very best to obey every single one of His commandments and laws. Then the Lord will save you all from the threat of the Philistines and raise the whole nation of Israel above all its enemies."

As the people listened, they looked up with awe at the young man who stood in front of them. Samuel's eyes shone as he spoke of God, his whole body was alive with passion. "It's true!" they shouted. "We've sinned against the Lord! Help us to find forgiveness!"

Filled with hope, Samuel gave great thanks to God. Then he instructed the nation that everyone was to begin a long fast right there and then as part of their penance, and Samuel led the crowd in prayer.

Meanwhile, news of the massive gathering was reaching the ears of the Philistine lords. "You'll never get another chance like this," the spies reported. "Nearly all of the Israelites have gathered together in one place, and they're mostly unarmed! To top it all, Samuel is there too!" Without a moment's delay, the Philistine lords mobilized their troops and marched on Mizpah.

Samuel was right in the middle of making a sacrifice when a terrified Israelite scout came dashing up to him with word that the full might of the Philistine army was drawing near. Panic rippled through the crowd like wildfire. The people began to jump up in terror, turning this way and that, not knowing which way to run. Samuel, however, calmly continued making his offering to God. He didn't flinch even when the Philistine soldiers suddenly appeared on the crests of the hills all around, endless dark figures against the sky.

> *The hand of the Lord was against the Philistines all the days of Samuel.*

As the Israelites screamed, the Philistines began to charge down the slopes towards them, spears aloft, swords glinting in the sun. At the very last minute, when the Philistines were close enough for the Israelites to see their faces, Samuel finished his sacrifice and looked up to heaven, praying for help. The wave of roaring troops suddenly disintegrated into a confused mob of bent figures, who stumbled about with their hands to their ears. The Israelite screams died away into a stunned silence. While they heard nothing but the beating of their own

hearts, the Philistines rolled on the earth in agony at the mind-splitting thunder that came from the skies.

Once the Israelites had recovered from the shock, they rushed on the soldiers with renewed confidence that the Lord was with them. And victory was theirs. It was a sign that God was willing to forgive the sinning nation.

For the rest of Samuel's life, the Israelites defeated the Philistines in every battle they fought. All the cities the

Philistines had won back were recaptured by Israel, too. The nation's other enemies sensibly stayed well away.

The Israelites looked up to Samuel as one of their greatest ever leaders; they respected him as someone very close to God. But Samuel didn't keep his distance from the people. Each year he toured round the country, going from place to place among them. And the prophet won back the Israelites' hearts for the Lord.

Samuel

Not only was Samuel a Judge and a prophet, but his name is also given to the two books of *Samuel* in the *Old Testament*. When he was a baby, his mother dedicated him to God and he was brought up by the high priest, Eli, at the temple at Shiloh. He was first called upon by God while still a child. His leadership was later challenged by those who wanted a king as leader instead of a Judge. After some resistance, Samuel anointed Saul as the first king of Israel. He later anointed David as the next king. Samuel died in a place called Ramah, north of Jerusalem, and was buried there.

❖ ABOUT THE STORY ❖

Samuel gives us here the perfect example of the supreme faith in God that the Israelites have been lacking. Even as the Philistines bear down on the unarmed Israelites, Samuel knows that the Lord will protect them, so he puts the Lord first, completes his sacrifice and God saves them.

Saul is Made King

IN his old age, Samuel made his two sons, Joel and Abijah, Judges over Israel. But like the sons of Eli, they were corrupt. They took bribes from the people, and ignored the way the rules should have been applied. Bad actions were frequently said to be right and good deeds to be wrong.

Eventually the elders of Israel visited Samuel at Ramah. "Samuel, you are a great man. But we know that you are too old to lead us now," they told him. "However, your sons are dishonest. We don't want Judges anymore, we want a king to govern us, like all the other nations."

When the elders had gone, Samuel wearily closed his eyes. "A king, Lord," he sighed. "You'd think that to have you for a king would be enough."

"The Israelites are rejecting me, just as they have before," God replied. "If the people want a king, they shall have one. But make sure they know what they're getting."

Samuel called a great assembly of the people. "Listen to the Lord's warning," he told the Israelites. "A king will force you to work as his servants. He will tax you and take a tenth of all your grain and wine, flocks, and workers. You will weep and wail at how your king rules over you, but the Lord will not answer your cries. For in having a king, you are pushing God aside."

"All the other nations have a king," the people protested. "Why shouldn't we?"

Samuel realized they weren't going to listen. Inside his head he heard the Lord's voice. "Give these Israelites what they want," God said.

Samuel shook his head. "Go home, all of you," he said quietly.

Months later, up in the hill country, a landowner called Kish told one of his sons, called Saul to track down some escaped donkeys. Saul searched for days without any luck until his servant told him that Samuel happened to be nearby. "He might help us," he said.

As the two men approached the city gates, they were surprised to see a stranger coming out to meet them. They were even more shocked when the old man said, "I am Samuel, who you are looking for. God told me yesterday that you would be coming. Your donkeys have been found, so stop worrying about them. In any case, a few donkeys are nothing compared to the whole of Israel." Saul was puzzled. Whatever did Samuel mean? He was even more puzzled when Samuel took Saul and his servant to be guests of honour at a great feast, and insisted they stay the night with him.

Next morning, the prophet anointed Saul with oil. "The Lord has declared that you are to be king of Israel," Samuel announced. "You will rule over all the people and

save them from their enemies. As a sign that this message comes from God, on your way out of the city two men will give you news about your donkeys. At the large oak tree at Tabor, three men will offer you bread. Finally, near the Philistine garrison at Gibeah, you'll meet a group of prophets singing hymns. Then I'll meet you at Mizpah."

Everything happened just as Samuel had predicted, but Saul was no longer amazed at these strange events. He had changed and had a new faith in the Lord.

Nevertheless, at the meeting the prophet called at Mizpah Saul was terrified. He'd never seen so many people in one place before. "Hear me, Israelites!" Samuel shouted to the crowd. "It is time to select your king." He told the people to draw lots, so everybody would know that nothing unfair had gone on. Although it seemed like chance, Samuel knew that God was in control. First, the Israelites drew lots for the tribe the king should come from – Benjamin was chosen. Next, the tribe drew lots – and the Matrite families were picked. Out of all the Matrite families, Kish's was chosen. And finally, from Kish's family, Saul's name was pulled out of the hat.

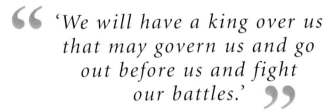

> '*We will have a king over us that may govern us and go out before us and fight our battles.*'

Saul was nowhere to be found! The excited Israelites searched the area for their new king. Finally someone spotted him hiding among a heap of bags, and he was pushed forward. "Here is the king God has chosen for you!" bellowed the prophet.

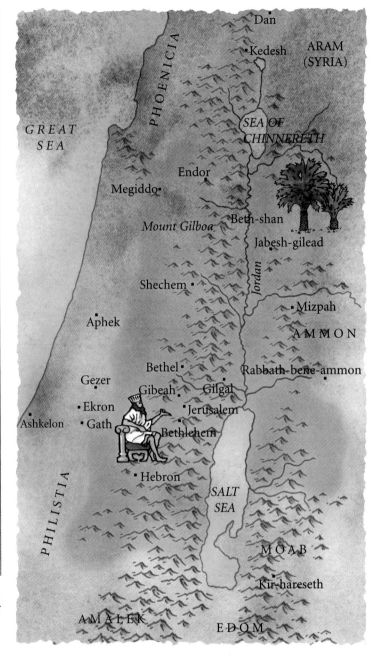

The kingdom of Saul
This map shows in orange the extent of Israel during the reign of King Saul. The Israelites had held on to a lot of Canaan, but they had never defeated the Philistines or the tribe of Moab.

Horn of oil
Samuel anointed Saul by rubbing a special holy oil onto him. This ceremony was a sign that Saul had been chosen by God. Samuel would have used olive oil mixed with spices, such as cinnamon and nutmeg. The oil would have been contained in a horn made of ivory and gold.

SOMETIMES PEOPLE DO THINGS WHICH THEY SHOULDN'T. THIS STORY REMINDS US THAT GOD ALLOWS US TO USE OUR FREE WILL TO MAKE MISTAKES. HE ALWAYS STAYS WITH US TO HELP WHEN THINGS GO WRONG AND WHEN WE ARE IN NEED.

❖ **ABOUT THE STORY** ❖
God had intended the Israelites to be a model nation, showing others what it was like to trust God completely. But the Israelites found it hard to trust God when they couldn't see Him. They thought a king would be better, but forgot that kings are often selfish.

Saul's First Victory

NOT long after Saul became king, part of his new kingdom found itself in trouble. When the Israelites had first arrived in the Promised Land, they had conquered many territories belonging to the Ammonites. Ever since, the Ammonites had been intent on taking back their land, and sometimes they attacked Israel's borders. Now, under the command of Nahash, Ammonite warriors had

besieged the Israelite city of Jabesh-gilead. The outnumbered citizens tried to save themselves by making a treaty with the Ammonites. "If you allow us to surrender peacefully," the Israelite messengers pleaded with Nahash, "we promise to serve you as slaves."

But Nahash was ruthless. "We will allow you to live," he announced coldly, "on one condition: that we put out the right eye of every Israelite in the city."

The inhabitants of Jabesh-gilead were devastated, and the elders begged for seven days to think about it. What a terrible choice they had to make: either face starvation and eventual slaughter by the Ammonites; or suffer torture, endure life in bondage, and bring utter shame on the whole nation. Messengers raced out of the city towards Gibeah and King Saul, knowing that the lives of their families and friends depended on their getting through.

When the panic-stricken riders burst into King Saul's palace, he wasn't at home. Even though Saul was king, he still worked as a farmer and he was busy in the fields. That evening, as Saul returned from his ploughing, he heard weeping and wailing in his courtroom.

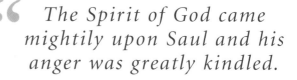

> **The Spirit of God came mightily upon Saul and his anger was greatly kindled.**

Hearing the news from Jabesh-gilead, Saul's anger rose with the outrage of God Himself at the brutal Ammonite threat. With his own hands, he slaughtered two oxen and hacked them into pieces. Then he sent them to every tribe

Saul's victory
Saul's palace was at Gibeah, but the first time his people needed him to lead them in battle was against the cruel Ammonites at the city of Jabesh-gilead. Saul mustered troops and made his way north through Shiloh, Tirzah and Bezek, gathering men. By the time the army reached Jabesh-gilead, Saul had a huge army and easily defeated the enemy forces.

Working the land
At this time, farmers like Saul would have used wooden ploughs. Poorer farmers had no metal, but wealthier ones had ploughs with iron blades. As a pair of animals (usually oxen) pulled the plough along, the blades turned the soil over and cut furrows in it so that seeds could be planted there. A light plough was an advantage as the fields were often stony. It was useful to be able to lift the plough over boulders. Large stones were used instead of fencing to mark the boundaries of a field.

Meanwhile, Saul split his forces into three battalions. Early next morning they attacked the Ammonite camp and took the tribespeople completely unawares. Just as the king had promised, by midday the fighting was finished. The ground was littered with the lifeless bodies of the Ammonites, and the people of Jabesh-gilead wept with relief at their narrow escape.

How the Israelites rejoiced! They had hoped for a king who would put their enemies to rout. Saul was the answer to their prayers. "Where are those unfaithful few who refused to pay our king tribute?" the people began to shout. "They should die for their lack of loyalty!"

"Calm down!" cried Saul. "You're not going to lay hands on anyone. This day is a day of celebration, for the Lord has saved Israel once again." The soldiers marched triumphantly back to Gibeah, with their glorious king at their head. They sacrificed peace offerings to the Lord and carried on the celebrations.

in Israel with the message: "Anyone who doesn't follow me into battle will find the same thing happens to his herds."

Israelites across the country felt the Lord was calling them to defend the land. Every fit man came out to fight. When Saul mustered his army at Bezek, he had 300,000 Israelite troops to face the 30,000 Ammonite soldiers.

Within the city, the terror among the people was growing quickly. "Don't be afraid," came the reassuring message from their new king. "By midday tomorrow, I promise you that it will all be over."

The people of Jabesh sent an envoy to tell Nahash that they would surrender the next day at noon. At best, the message would trick the Ammonites into a false sense of security. At worst, they would have to give themselves up and face the appalling consequences.

Defending a town
Towns in ancient times had to be carefully defended because of constant battles over land. Most towns were surrounded by walls which were 3 m wide and 6–9 m high. The walls prevented enemies from entering and formed a platform from which to attack. The picture shows a battering ram being used against the walls of a besieged city.

❧ ABOUT THE STORY ❧
This victory helped the Israelites to see that they could rely on God to rescue them from their enemies. It also reminded them that He did not want them to become slaves again, as they had been in Egypt. Unfortunately, although this victory was entirely due to God's help, Saul began to think he had special powers too – and this pride led to his later downfall.

Saul and Jonathan

SAUL'S son Jonathan inherited his father's fighting spirit, and his battalion of 1,000 soldiers took the Philistine garrison at Geba. The nation's hopes soared. They could recapture more of the land taken by the Philistines! All Israel followed Jonathan's example and rallied to their king. But the Philistines sent for reinforcements, and soon 30,000 chariots and 6,000 cavalry had amassed at Michmash, vastly outnumbering Saul's army. Many of the Israelite volunteers lost their nerve and hid in the hills.

Saul didn't move until the prophet Samuel arrived to offer sacrifice to the Lord. After waiting a whole week, Saul decided to delay no longer. Even though only priests were allowed to offer sacrifices, he'd have to do it himself.

Just as he finished, Samuel arrived. "You have done a very foolish thing," the angry prophet told Saul. "Because you have gone against the Lord's commandments, He will take the kingdom away from you and your sons. Instead, a new king will be crowned." Then Samuel left the camp.

Things were bad. Only 600 Israelite soldiers remained, and only Saul and Jonathan had proper weapons – everyone else had axes and scythes from their farms. The Philistines were in no hurry to attack; they knew they could crush the Israelites at any time.

Jonathan could not bear the waiting any longer. "Let's go over to the Philistine garrison and see what happens," he urged his armour-bearer one day. Trusting the Lord, Jonathan decided that if the Philistines challenged them to come up to the camp, it would be a sign that God was with him, and they would defeat the Philistines.

The Philistine look-outs laughed when they saw the two Israelites approaching. They were sure they had nothing to fear. "Come here!" they mocked, drawing their swords. "We've got something to show you!"

Jonathan felt a surge of confidence. "God is with us!" he whispered. The two men attacked and soon 20 Philistine soldiers lay dead. They turned and began to make for the main Philistine camp.

At the sudden sight of the two Israelites, the Philistines were thrown into utter confusion. It seemed as if the enemy had appeared out of nowhere. The Philistines ran to and fro in panic, and in the chaos they ended up fighting each other.

❖ ABOUT THE STORY ❖

When Saul became king, Samuel explained that God was still in charge; Saul was simply His servant. Therefore, the human king had to obey God's laws. To show that he did, the king was not allowed to offer sacrifices – that was the job of priests. Saul, however, decided that he could do what he liked. He tried to take God's place, and as a result lost the right to be king.

SCYTHE   ADZE   CHOPPER   SICKLE

Israelite weapons
These are some of the tools the Israelites might have used as weapons. A scythe was normally used for cutting the crops at harvest time. An adze was a tool with a wooden shaft and a metal blade used for planing large pieces of wood to a smooth finish. An axe was used mainly for cutting down trees and chopping wood roughly into shape. The sickle here was also used to cut crops. It is made of wood with flint teeth.

Next day, King Saul went with a priest to ask God for guidance. Saul's prayers were met by silence. "Someone has sinned and so the Lord has closed His ears to us," the king announced. "Whoever it is will die." Imagine Saul's horror when he found out that it was Jonathan who had disobeyed him. The army yelled, "We don't want Jonathan to die for his mistake! Our victory over the Philistines is all due to him." The whole army fell on their knees, praying to God and offering all they had as a ransom for Jonathan. The king's son was spared, and the soldiers carried him home in triumph.

> ❝ *'Cursed be the man who eats food until it is evening and I am avenged on my enemies.'* ❞

Back in the Israelite camp Saul noticed the commotion. and sent his troops on the attack. When the Philistines saw Saul's soldiers coming, they ran for their lives. "No one is to stop for food until every Philistine is dead!" cried Saul. On and on went the battle until nightfall when, faint with hunger, Saul was forced to make camp. But Jonathan hadn't heard his father's command not to eat. When he found some honeycomb as they marched he ate it.

Saul's disobedience
Saul's arrogance in taking over the role of the prophet and offering a sacrifice cost Saul dearly – his sons would not inherit their father's throne. The picture above shows priests offering a sacrifice.

Saul's command not to stop for food was foolish. It caused people to suffer and nearly cost Jonathan's life. The Bible tells us not to say things we might later regret. It is important that we are honest with ourselves and others, but we must be aware of other people's feelings and respect them.

Jonathan
This story illustrates the courage of Jonathan as a warrior, but he is mainly remembered for his loyalty to his friend David, who succeeded Saul as king of Israel. Jonathan was the eldest son of King Saul, and his loyalty to David conflicted with his duty to his father, who wanted David dead. Although Jonathan made several attempts at peacemaking, he was forced to disobey Saul to protect David. Jonathan died with his father during a battle against the Philistines at Mount Gilboa.

Saul the Warrior King

KING Saul went on to win victory after victory. But he and Samuel hadn't spoken since the day the king had offered his own sacrifices at Michmash. So Saul was surprised when the prophet Samuel arrived at the palace. Samuel had a message from God. "When Israel moved from Egypt to Canaan, the Amalekite people attacked us.

God now commands you to go and destroy them. Have no mercy. Don't even spare their cattle or possessions."

Saul marched 210,000 fighting men to a valley near Amalek. He attacked the city and killed the people. However, the Amalekite king, Agag, begged Saul to spare him. Saul also had second thoughts about slaughtering the Amalekite sheep and cattle. He added them to his own flocks.

Even before the king returned, the Lord had told Samuel that

SAMUEL'S STATEMENT "TO OBEY GOD IS BETTER THAN TO SACRIFICE" IS OFTEN REPEATED IN THE BIBLE. IT MEANS THAT RELIGIOUS ACTS ALONE DON'T PLEASE GOD: WE MUST OBEY HIM IN OUR DAILY LIFE. ❧

Destruction of Amalek
This picture shows the destruction of Amalek. The Amalekites had been enemies of the Israelites since their years in the wilderness. God ordered Saul to destroy them as a punishment for their repeated attacks on His people. He also wanted to ensure that the Amalekites would no longer be a threat to Israel.

Sparing the Kenites
The Kenites were a tribe who had once shown kindness to the Israelites by guiding them in the desert. Because of this, they were spared by Saul. The name "Kenite" means "smith". The region the Kenites inhabited was known to contain copper, shown above, so they are thought to have been coppersmiths.

Saul had defied God. At once Samuel set off to find Saul.

"I've done it!" Saul lied. "I did what the Lord wanted."

"Why then can I hear the noises of cattle?" said Samuel.

Saul piled lie upon lie. "We took the animals so we can sacrifice them to God." he said.

"Stop!" Samuel bellowed. "You've disobeyed the Lord's commands! Why did you take some things for yourself, when you knew it was wrong?"

Saul still wouldn't own up. "I *have* obeyed God," he insisted. "My mission was to crush the Amalekites. King Agag is in my control, and I've wiped out his city. We've left the best of the livestock to sacrifice to the Lord."

Samuel was furious. "You should know that to listen to God and obey Him is much more important than offering Him sacrifices! Rebellion and stubbornness are terrible sins. You have rejected the word of God, and He has rejected you as king."

At that Saul panicked. "I'm sorry. I have sinned," he confessed, falling on his knees before the wise old prophet. "I know I should have listened to the Lord, and not worried what the people thought. I beg you, please ask God to forgive me."

The prophet was stony-faced. "The Lord no longer sees you as the king of His people." Samuel turned to go and Saul tried to stop him. He caught the edge of the old man's robe and it ripped. "Just as you have ripped my robe," Samuel declared, "so today the Lord has torn the kingdom from you. He is going to give it to a better man."

Even though Saul was king, Samuel was still the Judge of all Israel. He called for a sword and killed Agag, king of the Amalekites, on the spot.

Samuel returned to his home and Saul went back to Gibeah. The prophet grieved for Saul, but he would have nothing further to do with him. God was sorry that He'd ever chosen Saul to be king of Israel.

> *And Samuel hewed Agag in pieces before the Lord in Gilgal.*

God's rejection of Saul
Samuel ordered Saul to destroy all the Amalekites, including all their livestock– their cattle and sheep. Instead of killing the Amalekite king, Agag, Saul took him prisoner. He also kept the best of the animals for himself instead of destroying them. Because of this disobedience, Saul was rejected by God as king and Samuel never saw King Saul again. Samuel had predicted that if Israel had a king, troubles such as this would arise. However, instead of being pleased at his accurate forecast, he grieved for Saul. The picture shows God telling Samuel that He is rejecting Saul as king, while Saul looks on.

✦ ABOUT THE STORY ✦

Saul had grown greedy. He wanted to add to his wealth, and it seemed wasteful to destroy everything. He had not understood that God had ordered the complete destruction of the Amalekites to show that He is a God who punishes sin – the Amalekites had opposed God in the past. Before the battle, Saul had spared the Kenites who lived among the Amalekites, because they had once helped God's people.

The Choosing of David

THE time came when the Lord told Samuel to stop feeling sorry for Saul. "He is no longer king of Israel," God told the elderly prophet. "I want you to take some holy oil to Bethlehem. Visit Jesse, for I have chosen one of his sons to be Israel's new king."

Samuel was worried. "If Saul hears about this, he'll kill me," he told the Lord.

"Pretend that you are in Bethlehem to make an important sacrifice," the Lord suggested. "Invite Jesse to the ceremony and then I will show you what to do."

When the elders of Bethlehem heard that the great prophet was coming, they hurried to meet him, wondering why he had come. "Welcome," they greeted Samuel. "We hope there's nothing wrong." Everyone feared the awe-inspiring man of God.

"Of course there's nothing wrong," Samuel assured them. "I'm here to hold a special prayer service and offering, and you're all invited."

The leaders of Bethlehem must have been surprised to see that the prophet invited Jesse's household, a mere family of farmers to the important service. However, they must have been even more jealous when, after the prayers and the singing and the sacrifice were all done, Samuel drew Jesse and his family to one side for a quiet word. "I'd like to meet your family," the prophet said. The embarrassed farmer felt very honoured, and introduced his sons one at a time.

First was Eliab. As soon as Samuel laid his eyes on Jesse's broad-shouldered, good-looking eldest son, he thought to himself, "Surely this is the new king of Israel." But God immediately spoke clearly into his mind.

"Don't be deceived by how handsome or tall these young men are. Remember Saul – he looks like a hero, but he's not a true king. I see people differently from the way you see each other. I value someone not on their outward appearance, but on their inner worth. I look at human hearts and judge people on what they're like inside."

Next, Abinadab came forward. The prophet studied his face. "No, not this one," he thought.

Then Jesse called Shammah. Again Samuel thought, "No, not him either."

Four more of Jesse's sons passed under the all-seeing eyes of God's faithful servant, but Samuel knew that none of them was the right man. "There must be someone else," thought Samuel to himself, and said out loud to Jesse: "Are those all your sons?"

"There's one more," the puzzled farmer stuttered. "My youngest, David. But he's out looking after the sheep."

"Go and fetch him," Samuel urged gently.

When David arrived, the prophet at once heard the voice of the Lord saying, "Get up and bless him, for this is the one." So, to the complete shock of Jesse and his family, Samuel drew out his precious ceremonial horn filled with holy oil and anointed Jesse's youngest son David as the future king of Israel.

> " *The Spirit of the Lord departed from Saul, and an evil spirit tormented him.* "

After the prophet had gone, Jesse's family remained puzzled by what had happened. However, no one could deny that David seemed different, wiser, and sure of himself, with a strange fearlessness.

At the same time that David was filled with God's grace, the Spirit of the Lord left King Saul. Instead, an evil demon came to drive him mad with worries, doubts and fears, and thrust him into deep, black depressions.

Saul's servants suggested a companion to lift his spirits. "David, the son of Jesse of Bethlehem, can play the harp quite brilliantly. He's also a brave young man – a good fighter. And above all, people say that he's close to God."

Saul sent for Jesse's youngest son to come to the palace, never dreaming that the boy would one day replace him on the throne. David seemed to be the only person who could relieve the king of any of his depression, and Saul grew to love him dearly. He made David his honoured armour-bearer and kept him close by his side. Whenever Saul felt gloomy, David would play the harp and bring some moments of peace to the troubled king.

Anointing

This picture shows Samuel anointing David as king by rubbing holy oil on to him. In the Old Testament, a person was anointed to show that they were in some way holy or special to God. Objects such as pillars, shields and the tabernacle, could be anointed too. It was a sin to use anointing oil for any other purpose. Anointing was an act of God and, because of this, was a solemn and important event. In the New Testament, Jesus anointed sick people as a way of healing them.

❧ ABOUT THE STORY ❧

The Bible implies that David did not know exactly why he was anointed. If it had been known, Saul would have tried to kill David, and others could have tried to capture the throne for David. The young shepherd still had much to learn before he was ready to be king.

David and Goliath

It wasn't long before the Philistines waged war on Israel again. King Saul gathered the army together, and young men from all over the country hurried to the king's camp.

David returned to his former job of looking after Jesse's sheep while three of his older brothers enlisted with Saul. Jesse worried about them continually; his eyes always looked dull and tired. One day, David noticed his father packing some grain, bread and cheeses. "Take these things to your brothers, David," Jesse urged his youngest son. "Then hurry home and tell me how they're doing."

When David reached Saul's camp, he found the soldiers retreating in a panic, running from the battle line as fast as they could. David couldn't believe his eyes. He was nearly trampled underfoot as the last soldiers swarmed past him. Then he saw the enemy, and he understood. On the far side of the battlefield, standing alone, was the biggest man David had ever seen. He was nearly as tall as two men with colossal legs like tree trunks. He carried a spear the size of a battering ram, and his mighty body was clad in enormous bronze armour. "Who is that?" David gasped, rooted to the spot. The soldiers nearby explained.

"It's Goliath of Gath," they told David. "Each time we're ready to attack, he strides out and challenges us to settle things by a duel. He says that if any puny Israelite can beat him, then the Philistines will be our slaves. If he beats our champion, then the Philistines will take all of us into slavery. The king has offered a huge reward to anyone who'll fight him, including his daughter's hand in marriage. But who could beat such a giant?"

"I'd give anything for the chance!" shouted David defiantly, and he went to find the king.

At first, Saul was reluctant to let the young shepherd face the huge warrior. But there was something about the way David spoke that convinced the king he might not be sending the boy to his death after all. "God has given me the strength to fight lions and bears when I am looking after my father's sheep," David said, "and now I know He'll give me the strength to beat this giant!" So Saul gave David permission to go and try.

The king dressed the shepherd for the battle, but David wasn't very big and Saul's armour totally swamped him. David could hardly move. And the weight of Saul's hefty sword and shield made his arms ache. So David took off all the equipment again, until he stood there in his simple shepherd's robe, holding only his sling, his crook and a bag of five smooth, round stones.

When he saw the tiny figure coming out to meet him, Goliath threw back his head and laughed. "Am I a dog, that you come with a stick to beat me?" he roared. "Come on then," he taunted. "I'll mince you into little pieces and feed you to the wild beasts." David was completely unruffled by the huge soldier.

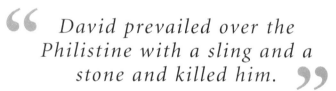

David prevailed over the Philistine with a sling and a stone and killed him.

"You may have mighty weapons, but I'm armed with the most mighty weapon of them all, the name of the

David's anger was because Goliath was mocking God, not just frightening the people. The Israelites had forgotten that God was more powerful than any enemy. David had known God's protection and help in the past and was convinced that God would not let him down. David's faith in the power of God meant that, armed only with a sling and stones, he could single-handedly do what the whole Israelite army could not.

Single combat
The practice of single combat was sometimes used to decide who should win a war or battle. In single combat, each side chose an individual to represent them. The above picture shows two knights fighting this sort of duel, with the armies facing each other.

Lord God of Israel! It's you who will be fed to the birds and wild beasts, not me!"

At these cheeky words, Goliath gave a mighty roar and strode forwards. David reached into his bag for a stone, took aim and slung it. The little pebble hit right in the centre of the giant's forehead, and it sank into him. Without even realizing what had hit him, Goliath keeled over like a felled tree and crumpled into the dust. David took Goliath's own huge sword, ran up to the massive body and hacked off Goliath's head.

On the far side of the battlefield, a stunned silence descended over the Philistine army. Then the jubilant Israelites charged, and the Philistines ran for their lives, all the way back to their cities.

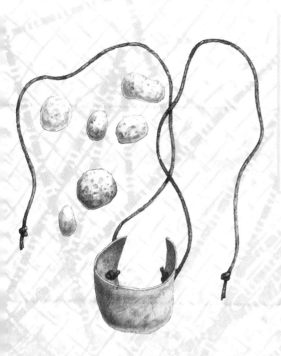

DAVID ACTED IN FAITH, TRUSTING GOD TO HELP HIM. THE BIBLE ENCOURAGES CHRISTIANS FACING TASKS WHICH THEY BELIEVE ARE IN LINE WITH GOD'S WILL TO TRUST HIM TO OVERCOME DIFFICULTIES.

Slings and stones
The sling was a weapon used by many armies. It consisted of a wide pad with a string attached to each side. The soldier put a stone on the pad, held the ends of the strings in one hand and whirled the sling around very quickly. When he let go of one string, the stone flew through the air towards the enemy.

Bears
In the Bible, David tells Saul that he killed a bear and a lion that came to attack his sheep. For most of the year, wild bears eat plants. They only attack livestock during winter when they cannot find enough food on the ground.

David in Danger

KILLING Goliath of Gath turned David into the Israelites' new hero. As the army marched home, the people of each city lined the roads, singing and dancing for joy. Everyone wanted to see the young shepherd who had killed a giant. The noise was almost deafening. "Da-vid! Da-vid! Da-vid!" the crowds chanted.

Saul had come to love David as though he were his own son, and Saul's son, Jonathan, was as fond of David as if he were his own brother. While the procession went on, Saul's old doubts began to niggle the king. The cries of

"We love you David!" were drowning the shouts of "God bless King Saul!" Saul became jealous. "If the people prefer David to me, it won't be long before they want him as king," he thought.

Next day, Saul sat slumped in a chair, snarling at anyone who approached him and muttering angrily under his breath. As usual David and his harp were sent for. David was gently plucking the harp strings when he felt a rush of air. A spear came flying at his head, and he ducked just in time. David tried to ignore the king's display of violence and continued to play as if nothing had happened. Then a second spear came hurtling at him. David again managed to dodge it, but he was deeply shocked.

The atmosphere in the palace grew worse. Since God had abandoned Saul, the king increasingly felt that his life was empty and meaningless. It was even more frustrating for him to see how David seemed to be always at peace, full of a quiet faith and courage. Eventually Saul could no longer bear to have the young man around him, and began to dream of killing David. Saul didn't want to stain his hands with the sin of murder, so Saul made David commander-in-chief of his troops, secretly hoping that he would be slain in a skirmish with the Philistines. However, David never came to any harm. Wherever he went, he led his men to victory and his troops idolized him. All over the

✦ ABOUT THE STORY ✦

The sad story of Saul's madness is told in the Bible to show two things. One is that when someone deliberately closes their heart to God, they open it to all sorts of evil forces. The other is that God looked after David in many ways. These narrow escapes show that God was protecting him so that one day he would be able to do the special job for which Samuel had anointed him.

WHEN GOD CALLS SOMEONE TO SERVE HIM, HE ALLOWS NOTHING TO STOP THEM DOING THAT WORK. DIFFICULTIES DO NOT MEAN GOD HAS ABANDONED US. THEY MEAN THAT GOD CAN SHOW US HIS WORK.

A broken promise

Saul had promised that whoever killed Goliath could marry his daughter. When David asked for his daughter's hand, Saul broke his promise and demanded an extra gift of 100 dead Philistines. He was sure David would be killed, but he returned unharmed and presented Saul with twice as many Philistine bodies.

country, Saul's subjects loved David more than ever before. The king just became more and more jealous.

One day, the scheming king was presented with the perfect plan to remove David for good. Saul discovered that David and his daughter, Michal, were in love. To David's utter astonishment the king said he'd like them to get married. After all, he was only a farmer's son. There was no way he could afford the traditional expensive present, especially for a king's daughter.

Saul grinned. "All I ask in payment for the bride is that you single-handedly slay 100 Philistines." The wicked king was sure that this time David would not survive. Once

> **Saul thought to make David fall by the hand of the Philistines.**

again, David did the impossible. He killed not 100, but 200 Philistines. And Saul was forced to watch David marry his beloved daughter.

For Saul, this was the last straw. Now, above everything else, the king wanted David dead. He no longer cared how it was done or by whom. He was even ready to do it himself, never mind that it was a sin. Saul began to draw up a murderous plot with his courtiers.

Jonathan heard the palace rumours and raced to tell his best friend that his father wanted to kill him. He hid David away and then begged his father not to go ahead with his terrible plan. Although the king's icy heart

melted at first, it wasn't long before he was being driven mad with hatred again. Saul sent officers to arrest David and then, without a trial, to kill him.

Saul's daughter Michal was suspicious. She noticed strangers hanging around outside the house one night and immediately warned her husband. "My father's spies are everywhere. You must go," she wept. After a tearful farewell, David quietly climbed down a rope from the window and escaped into the night.

Next morning, when soldiers battered down the door, all they found in David's bed was a life-size statue wearing a goat-hair wig. David was far away, in the safe hands of God's faithful old servant, Samuel.

Evil spirits

After Saul disobeyed God, the Spirit of God left him and evil spirits began to torment him by whispering in his ear. These evil spirits were sent by God to punish Saul. Saul lost control of his mind and became depressed and violent. His jealousy towards David drove him to attempt to kill him. David was no longer able to soothe the king's troubled mind with his harp-playing.

David's harp

There were several different types of harp. The picture shows a Jewish harp, also called a nebel. It is made out of animal skin stretched over a round soundbox. The word "nebel" means "skin bottle". Another type of harp is the kinnor, a small stringed instrument with a wooden frame. David's harp could have been either of these.

A Faithful Friend

SAMUEL sent David to a safe house at Naioth in Ramah. But Saul found out and sent soldiers after him. When they didn't return, the baffled king sent another group ... and then another ... Finally, wild with frustration, he set out after his son-in-law himself. But when Saul reached Naioth, he met the same strange fate as his soldiers. God's Spirit overcame him and he fell into a trance and took off his clothes. This allowed David to escape.

Apart from his wife, Michal, and the prophet, Samuel, there was only one other person David could trust to help him: the king's own son, Jonathan. He arranged a secret meeting with his best friend.

When the two men met safely, they hugged each other. "What have I done to make your father hate me so much?" David asked Jonathan.

Jonathan shook his head in dismay. "I still can't believe that my father wants you dead. If there's anything I can do to help, just say the word." David had an idea.

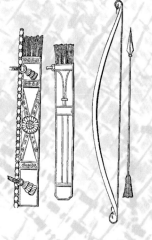

❧ ABOUT THE STORY ❧

Many of the Bible's teachings are revealed in practical situations rather than given as a series of ideas. One of its chief teachings is that God is faithful to His people and that He expects us to be faithful to Him and to each other. In this story, Jonathan shows that faithfulness in a dramatic way. The story encourages us to trust God and to care for each other as Jonathan cared for David.

Bows and arrows
Jonathan's bow would have been made of wood, together with animal horn and sinews. His arrows were probably made of reed, with metal tips. Arrows were carried in a leather holder called a quiver, which held about thirty arrows.

Saul's trance
When Saul arrived in Naioth, the Spirit of the Lord came over him and he went into a type of trance. God made him strip off his clothes because they were symbolic of his royal status, whereas in God's presence he was powerless. The Bible describes Saul's behaviour as "prophesying", which means revealing or interpreting God's will.

"It's simple!" he cried. "The new moon festival begins tomorrow and Saul will expect me at court. I'll stay here in the country. If your father asks where I am, say that I asked your permission to go and make a sacrifice with my family. If this doesn't bother him, I'll be reassured that I'm no longer in danger. However, if he's angry, then I'll know that I've spoiled some evil plan to get his hands on me."

"Yes!" cried Jonathan, eagerly. "I'll wait and see how he reacts, then I'll go out for my archery practice. Hide near the range. Once I've shot my arrows and my servant is collecting them, listen carefully to what I shout to him. If I yell, 'The arrows are near you,' it's a sign you have nothing to fear. But if I say, 'The arrows are further on,' then you're in danger and must get away fast." The two friends made a vow in the name of God that they would always remain loyal to each other, no matter what might happen.

Next day, at the feast, David's place at the king's table was empty. Saul didn't let it spoil his fun, but on the third day, when the king saw David's vacant chair, he exploded. "Where is David?" he demanded. Jonathan told his father the excuse David has asked him to give Saul.

David and Jonathan's plan didn't fool him. "You traitor!" he raged. "I know you're best friends! As long as he's alive, you'll never ascend to the throne that's rightfully yours!" Saul brandished a spear. "Bring David to me!"

Jonathan was seething. Stubbornly he replied, "Why should I? What has he done?"

The king roared and hurled his spear at his own son.

Next morning, full of sadness, Jonathan went out to the archery range. He shot his arrows past his servant, and as the lad searched for them, Jonathan called out, "The

66 *'The Lord shall be between me and you for ever.'* 99

arrows are further on. Hurry up, don't hang about."

Jonathan sent the servant away, and David came out. Instead of greeting his friend with the usual embrace, David bowed low. It was the only way he could show Jonathan his gratitude for the great loyalty he had shown. The two friends knew it might be the last time they ever saw each other. "Go in peace," Jonathan said, "and may the Lord keep our friendship firm for ever." Then the two men turned away from each other and went their separate ways, Jonathan went back to his tyrant father at the palace, and David, the outcast, to life on the run.

❋ RELIGIOUS FEASTS ❋

During religious feasts people gave thanks to God, repenting of their sins and offering sacrifices. These are the main feasts mentioned in the Old Testament:

The Feast of Weeks *was later known as Pentecost. It was celebrated on the fiftieth day after the Sabbath that began the Passover. It was marked by the offering of sacrifices.*

The Feast of Tabernacles, *which was also called the Feast of Booths, lasted for seven days. It commemorates 40 years in the desert at the time of Moses. Fruit was gathered and people lived in booths, or tents, made of branches.*

The Day of Blowing of Trumpets, *begins the new year. Sacrifices were offered and work stopped.*

The Day of Atonement *is when the high priest makes sacrifices to God to make up for peoples' sins. It took place on the tenth day of the seventh month.*

The Feast of Purim *commemorates the events of the book of Esther, when Queen Esther saved the Jews from a plot by the prime minister to kill all the Jews.*

David the Outlaw

WHEN David left Saul for good, he disguised himself as an ordinary Israelite and fled to Nob. The head priest Ahimelech recognized him instantly and was suspicious. David pretended he had come without all the pomp of the royal household on the king's business. Ahimelech believed him.

Unfortunately, David saw in Nob, another of Saul's officers called Doeg. David knew Doeg recognised him, and David was unarmed. "The king sent me off in such a hurry that there wasn't time to gather my equipment," David pretended to Ahimelech. The only weapon the priest possessed was Goliath's sword. It was the sharpest and most deadly David had ever seen. David was pleased as he himself had won the sword from Goliath in battle.

It wasn't safe to stay in Nob, so David decided to hide among Saul's enemies. He fled to King Achish, the Philistine king of Gath, but his fame had gone before him. "Isn't this Israel's champion?" Achish's servants murmured, hauling David before the throne. He was among his enemies, and in grave danger, so he pretended he was mad. Luckily Achish believed David was mad, and threw him out of the court.

David was so famous that no matter how he disguised himself, he risked being recognized. He tried to avoid people altogether by going to the wilderness around Adullam. But first his brothers hurried to him, and then runaways sought him out. Eventually, David found himself leading about 400 men, many on the run, just like David.

Saul was furious that David was still free. One day he commanded everyone to assemble before him.

The king strode up and down the ranks, his face as black as thunder. "You are all so loyal to David that not one of you will tell me where he is?" he accused his men, in a cold rage. Doeg seized his chance to gain favour.

"I saw David at Nob," he told Saul. "Ahimelech gave him some food, and Goliath's sword." Saul's face lit up.

"You will be well rewarded," the king promised the smug Doeg. "Go and kill Ahimelech and his priests, then slaughter everyone else in the treacherous city," he commanded, "or die yourself."

Only one citizen in Nob managed to escape Doeg and his murdering troops, that was Abiathar, Ahimelech's own son. He brought the outlaws news of the terrible massacre. David wanted revenge at once, but the Israelite city of Keilah was besieged by the Philistines and God asked

Cave shelter
The cave where David and his men hid, and where he cut off part of Saul's robe, was at a place called En-gedi, a fresh water spring west of the Salt Sea. The Hebrew word "en-gedi" means "spring of the kid" A "kid" here means a young goat. The place was home to wild goats, but the rugged ground and availability of water made it equally good as a hiding place for people. During excavations that took place in 1949 and 1961-5, several fortresses and a synagogue were discovered on the site.

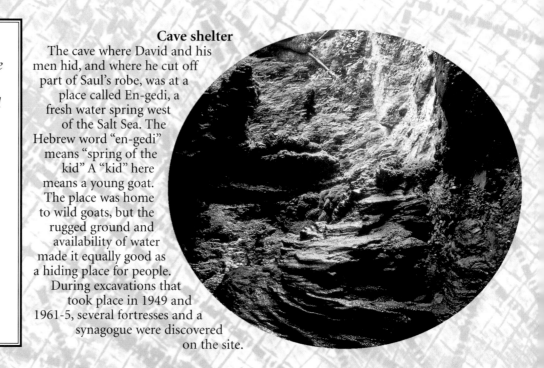

The king broke down and wept. "You have repaid evil with kindness," he sobbed, "and you will truly be a great king one day. I ask you only to vow that you won't destroy my family for the evil that I have done to you." David gladly gave Saul the promise he wished for and the two men parted in peace, at least for the time being.

> ❝ *'The Lord gave you today into my hand in the cave, but I spared you.'* ❞

David to rescue it. David's fighters saved hundreds of Israelites, even though they were risking their lives by leaving their hiding place in the hills.

Saul was overjoyed. "How stupid David is to walk into a walled and gated city," he laughed. Saul sent soldiers to Keilah, to capture David, but David and his band raced away. God had warned them of the king's approach.

Saul kept looking for David. As he was walking out of a dark cave he heard a familiar voice shout his name. Shocked, he spun round to see David at the cave-mouth, waving a piece of cloth. The outlaws had been hiding in the gloom, and David had crept up to the king and cut off a piece of Saul's robe without him knowing. David bowed down, as always. "Why do you listen to those who say I would hurt you?" he called out to Saul. "See, today I could have cut your throat, but I cut only your robe instead."

IT IS OFTEN TEMPTING TO GRAB IN A WRONG WAY SOMETHING WE BELIEVE SHOULD BE OURS. THE BIBLE TEACHES THAT WE CANNOT ACHIEVE GOOD ENDS BY USING BAD MEANS.

David runs from Saul
David escaped from Saul at Gibeah and was taken by Samuel to Ramah. He met his friend Jonathan at Horesh, before he fled to Nob. After seeking refuge with the Philistine king at Gath, David hid in the wilderness around Adullam, before he rescued the town of Keilah. He finally found Saul in the cave at En-gedi.

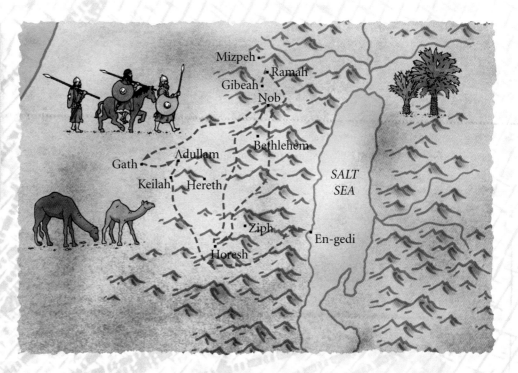

David and Abigail

THE time came when the elderly prophet Samuel knew that death was near. Samuel was revered through the all Israel. Grief-stricken people gathered at Samuel's house in Ramah one last time to hear what he had to say.

"I have listened to all your complaints and answered your request for a king," the old man wearily told the crowds. "Now your king walks before you, leading you on, and I must stop here. Always remember that God was deeply offended by your demand for a king on earth. You must still strive to serve God as best you can, or He will sweep you aside as he would a pestering fly, both you and your ruler. As a sign that what I say is truly the word of God, the Lord will today send thunder and rain to destroy your wheat harvest."

Later that day, colossal black clouds blotted out the skies and towered over the land. Spears of lightning stabbed through the gloom, thunder rumbled like chariot wheels across the heavens and raindrops like arrows flattened the crops in the fields.

The people of Israel trembled. King Saul shuddered. Samuel, the prophet and last Judge of Israel, passed away.

When David heard the news of his old friend's death, he was deeply saddened. He was also now in even more danger. With the great prophet gone, there was no one with any power to stop King Saul doing exactly what he wanted. Even though Saul had called off the hunt for his rival, David knew that the

demons which tormented the king wouldn't leave him alone for long. It was only a matter of time before they drove him mad with jealousy and fear once again, and then Saul would surely set out once more to find his rival and kill him.

David told his band of men to move camp. They set off, never staying too long in one place and living off their wits. Sometimes they would risk approaching a nearby village to ask for food and drink. At other times, they would simply plunder flocks of sheep and herds of cattle that were grazing out in the open, taking animals they thought their owners could spare.

When the outlaws reached the pasturelands around Carmel, they encountered many shepherds, each with a massive flock, who all said that they worked for an important farmer called Nabal. David could have simply allowed his hungry outlaws to help themselves to a few of Nabal's sheep. After all, the farmer seemed to own thousands! He thought it would be better to strike a bargain with such a wealthy man, rather than make enemies by stealing from him. David sent ten men to the sheep-shearing at Carmel to find the landowner and politely put forward their requests.

Now Nabal was a thuggish type of man, puffed up with his own importance and used to throwing his weight around. When David's messengers were shown in by his servants, he hardly gave them a glance. "Who is this David? I don't know any 'son of Jesse,'" he scoffed, pretending not to have heard of the great hero. "He's probably just another runaway servant. Do you really expect me to welcome a complete stranger and his band of criminals into my home and invite them to share my food? Now go away and don't come back!"

Nabal's servants were shocked. How could their master humiliate the great hero like this? David was putting out his hand in friendship, and Nabal was slapping it away. The servants knew that Saul's former army commander

place. She was even more angry to find that Nabal was completely unconcerned; in fact, he had thrown a great feast. There he was, right in the middle of all the merry-making, and roaring drunk. Fuming with rage, Abigail pursed her lips and stormed off. Next morning, when Nabal was sobering up with a head-splitting hangover, she told her husband what she had done. Nabal was instantly filled with a cold fury. His face turned white, his eyes glazed over, his hands gripped the arms of his chair like icy claws, and his spluttering mouth froze into silence. He was paralysed like stone, and he died ten days later.

> ❝ *Nabal's wife told him these things, and his heart died within him.* ❞

When David heard that Nabal had died, he simply nodded. "The Lord has repaid Nabal for his own evil-doings," he said. "Things have come to a just end." But he couldn't get thoughts of Nabal's wife out of his head. David had lost his wife, Michal, because when he had first gone on the run, the outraged King Saul had forced his daughter to marry another man. Now David was reminded of Michal by Abigail's loyalty and beauty. It wasn't long before the outlaw began to woo Nabal's widow, and soon Abigail became his wife.

wouldn't put up with their master's insults. Though they begged Nabal to change his mind the stubborn man wouldn't listen. The servants imagined how David and his men would be putting on their weapons and galloping towards them at that very moment. In desperation, one of Nabal's servants went to confide in their master's wife, Abigail.

Abigail was as good-natured and beautiful as her husband was arrogant and ugly. She knew that Nabal's rudeness would be the cause of all of their deaths, unless she went quickly to beg for mercy. Hurriedly, she loaded several donkeys with 200 loaves, five sheep, sacks of raisins, grain and fig cakes, and two wineskins. And without telling her husband, she set off down the mountain towards David's camp.

Abigail had not got very far when she saw a cloud of dust approaching. As David and his men drew into sight, she leapt down from her saddle and knelt before them, begging forgiveness for what her husband had done.

David was touched by the beautiful young woman's pleas. "Go in peace," he told her kindly. "I am glad that the Lord sent you to me this day."

Abigail raced home, full of relief that she'd saved her whole household from death, but cross that her husband had put them in such a desperate position in the first

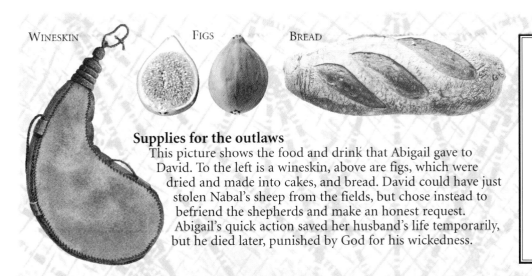

WINESKIN   FIGS   BREAD

Supplies for the outlaws
This picture shows the food and drink that Abigail gave to David. To the left is a wineskin, above are figs, which were dried and made into cakes, and bread. David could have just stolen Nabal's sheep from the fields, but chose instead to befriend the shepherds and make an honest request. Abigail's quick action saved her husband's life temporarily, but he died later, punished by God for his wickedness.

> ❖ **ABOUT THE STORY** ❖
> *David had been forced by Saul to live on the edge of the law. He never wanted to steal from anyone unless there was no alternative. He offered many landowners protection from the Philistines in return for food and drink for him and his men.*

The Witch of Endor

King Saul once more lapsed into an angry, black depression and once again he ordered his troops to find and kill his rival.

The king fared no better than before. Under cover of darkness, David and two of his men crept boldly into Saul's base, right up to Saul's very bedside. Neither Saul nor his soldiers stirred. His army commander Abner and royal bodyguard slept all around him. Once again, David chose not to slay Saul. Instead, he stole the spear and water jar from his bedside.

Next morning, David called across the valley. "Abner! Why weren't you watching over the king properly last night?" Both Saul and his general trembled at David's mercy and goodness in sparing Saul's life.

Back at their hideout, David told his followers, "Saul will hunt me down wherever I go within Israel. The only way for us to have any sort of freedom is if we go and live among our enemies, the Philistines." So David returned to King Achish of Gath, this time as the leader of a 600-strong band of soldiers. Achish had no reason to think that David was trying to trick him as they were both enemies of King Saul. The cunning king gave the outlaws land on the border of Gath and Israel. He hoped that David would stir up trouble by raiding Israelite settlements for supplies. David was also crafty. He attacked Philistine towns instead, and made sure that there were no

survivors left alive to report the events. When Achish asked him who he had been attacking, he lied. The king trusted David completely. He thought David had begun to attack his own country and his people would never forgive him.

One day the Philistine leaders joined forces to attack Israel, and Achish asked David to ride with his army. David pretended that he was pleased. Achish rewarded him by appointing him his personal bodyguard.

Meanwhile, in the Israelite camp, Saul watched the arrival of the enemy forces with growing dread. His own army was hopelessly outnumbered, and his prayers were unanswered. He felt that God had abandoned him, and he could no longer ask Samuel for advice. He was desperate. According to God's law, Saul had banished everyone who practised magic, but now he sent his servants to seek out someone with magic powers. They found a clairvoyant at Endor who claimed she could talk with the dead. Saul disguised himself and hurried with two men to the medium's house. "I'll pay you well for a message from the spirit world," Saul told her. But the woman was wary.

"If the king hears that I have been practising witchcraft, I'll be put to death," she protested. Saul swore in God's name that no harm would come to her. Nervously the woman asked who he wanted to contact.

Swallowing hard, Saul whispered, "Bring up Samuel." The woman shivered at the name. All her instincts told her not to try, but Saul insisted. So the woman closed her eyes.

Suddenly she leapt up away from Saul in alarm. "You've tricked me!" she gasped. "You're the king himself!"

"Have no fear. Please tell me what you see," Saul begged.

Trembling all over, the woman shut her eyes once more. "I see an old man wrapped in a robe," she replied. "He wants to know why you've disturbed his rest." The king bowed down. Though he couldn't see Samuel, he knew it was the holy man.

> " *Samuel said, 'Why then do you ask me, since the Lord has become your enemy?'* "

"I face my biggest battle with the Philistines yet," Saul said to Samuel. "God no longer speaks to me through either prophets or dreams. So I've come for your advice."

Samuel's reply was grim. "Since the Lord has turned away from you, why do you come to me for help? The Lord has already told you He has taken the kingdom away from you and given it to David. Moreover, the Lord is about to give Israel into the hands of the Philistines. Tomorrow, you and your sons shall find yourselves here with me!"

Saul was shocked to the core. If Samuel was right, then nothing in heaven or earth could save him or his nation. Samuel had never been wrong before.

Magic

In the Bible, magic is defined as attempting to influence people and events by supernatural means. Black magic, such as witchcraft, tries to achieve evil results. White magic tries to undo curses and spells, and to use supernatural forces for the good of oneself and others. According to the Bible, all kinds of magic are wrong and must be overcome by the power of God. Magic is not compatible with a relationship with God and living a life that pleases him. This picture shows a breastplate that was worn by Egyptian magicians.

> ❖ **ABOUT THE STORY** ❖
>
> *The Israelites had been forbidden by God to consult people who claimed to be able to influence the course of events through magic. They were to rely on God alone. Asking spirits questions was dangerous, as it could bring the Israelites into contact with evil forces.*

The Death of Saul

THE Philistine and Israelite armies hurried to prepare for battle. Tension rose in both camps. The Philistine commanders boiled with rage when they saw David and his men riding with King Achish of Gath. "What are these Israelites doing here?" they demanded.

"I can vouch for him completely," Achish explained. "David is Saul's greatest enemy and has lived in my lands for years now." The Philistine chiefs weren't convinced.

"We don't trust him," they said determinedly. "For all you know, he might make it up with Saul and turn on us in the fighting. Send him away at once, where he can be no risk to us!"

The king of Gath couldn't change their minds so he told David that he was to have no part in the fighting. David was secretly relieved. He hadn't wanted to fight Saul.

Everything happened as Samuel had warned Saul through the witch of Endor. A Philistine victory was never in doubt. Their mighty army slew the Israelites in their hundreds. Among the dead and dying were three of Saul's four sons, including Jonathan, David's best friend. Saul himself had fallen under the showers of Philistine arrows, and was terribly injured. Saul's armour-bearer struggled to lift him up and help him limp away, but Saul was bleeding badly and in too much pain. "I'd rather die than be taken alive by the enemy," he groaned to his servant. "If you love me, help me to kill myself and escape being tortured by these ungodly savages." His armour-bearer broke down, unable to carry out the dreadful task. So Saul summoned the last dregs of his energy. Moaning with agony, he hauled himself to his feet and heaved up his sword. Then with one final effort, he fell forward on to the sword, gasping his last breath. Once Saul's armour-bearer was sure the king was dead, he killed himself too.

> **"** *Saul said to his armour-bearer, 'Draw your sword and thrust me through with it.'* **"**

As the news spread that their leader was dead, the exhausted Israelites turned and fled. The Philistines hacked off Saul's head and stripped his corpse of his armour, sending the trophies in triumph to the temple of their god, where they were put on display. Then they hung the dead king and his sons high on the town walls of Beth-shan.

Next morning, the royal bodies were gone. The brave people of Jabesh-gilead had made their way through enemy territory in the night to rescue the corpses, remembering how Saul had saved them many years ago from having their right eyes put out. The body of the first king of Israel was returned to his country and buried honourably among his grieving people.

David was devastated when he heard the news, yet he could see how God's hand was behind everything. The Lord had prevented David from having any part in the death of the king. Now he mourned Saul, who had both loved him and hated him at the same time, who had grown arrogant with power and turned away from God, and who had been driven mad in the knowledge that God

DAVID'S LAMENT FOR SAUL MAY SEEM ODD. BUT DAVID TRUSTED GOD AND DID NOT ALLOW HIMSELF TO BECOME BITTER. IT IS AN EXAMPLE OF HOW GOD WANTS PEOPLE TO TREAT EACH OTHER.❧

The last days of Saul
Saul, worried about what would happen in the battle with the Philistines, found a witch at Endor to talk to the dead prophet Samuel. Samuel said he could not win as God was against him. Saul went with his army to meet the Philistines in the Valley of Jezreel, where he died.

had abandoned him. And David grieved for Jonathan, the friend he loved even more than his own brothers, who had defied his father to stay loyal to David.

David remembered how the king had loved to hear him play the harp, the one thing that was able to bring him peace. He thought of the perfect tribute for Saul and his son. He would compose a beautiful song in their honour, telling all about the mountain battle.

The song began:
"Thy glory, O Israel, is slain upon thy high places!
How are the mighty fallen!"
When David sang his song, gently plucking at the strings of his harp as he had done so many years ago in the palace for the king, he wept with sorrow that Saul would never again hear him play. He wept for the loss of his closest friend, Jonathan, a loss to David himself and to all Israel.

⮜ DAVID'S LAMENT ⮞

SAUL AND JONATHAN, BELOVED
AND LOVELY!
IN LIFE AND IN DEATH THEY WERE
NOT DIVIDED;
THEY WERE SWIFTER THAN EAGLES,
THEY WERE STRONGER THAN LIONS.
JONATHAN LIES SLAIN UPON THY
HIGH PLACES.
I AM DISTRESSED FOR YOU, MY
BROTHER JONATHAN;
VERY PLEASANT HAVE YOU
BEEN TO ME;
YOUR LOVE TO
ME WAS WONDERFUL.

Philistine figurine
This figurine was found in the Philistine city of Ashdod, and it represents one of the Philistine goddesses, probably a fertility goddess that they believed made all things grow, such as their crops.

David's lament
The song David wrote for his two friends, Saul and Jonathan, has been described as one of the most beautiful pieces of poetry in the Bible. It expresses great sadness at the loss of the men both as national figures and as personal friends of David.

⮜ ABOUT THE STORY ⮞

Once again, David had a lucky escape, reminding him that God was always protecting him. He could not get out of fighting with the Philistines without appearing disloyal and risking being killed by them as a traitor. God helped him and used the Philistines themselves to get David out of a tight spot. After this, few would question David's loyalty to Israel or his right to be king.

David Becomes King

WHEN Saul was dead, David prayed for guidance. He heard the Lord telling him to go back to Israel, to the south, and settle in Hebron. The people of Judah welcomed the hero with open arms, crowning David as their king.

The eleven other tribes in Israel did not accept David as their ruler. The general of Saul's army, Abner, with the backing of his troops, had set Saul's surviving son, Ishbosheth, on the throne to rule the rest of Israel.

King David ruled Judah and King Ishbosheth ruled the rest of Israel for several years. But everyone knew that Israel should be united with only one king.

One day the two armies fought, and David's soldiers won. Abner escaped, pursued by Asahel, brother of Joab, David's commander. Abner was forced to fight him and he stabbed Asahel with great regret.

After this there was full-scale civil war. Gradually support for David grew stronger. Ishbosheth was a weak ruler. He had never expected to be king as Saul had been grooming Jonathan for the throne. But power had gone to Ishbosheth's head. Eventually, Ishbosheth even confronted his most ardent supporter, Abner, because he had married one of Saul's concubines. Ishbosheth was trying to control everything. The general erupted. "After all I've done for you," he yelled, "you're rebuking me about a private affair!" Abner had only respected Ishbosheth because he was Saul's son; now he lost even that little regard. Abner did admire David as a servant of God and a great leader. "From now on, I'm going to support David," Abner bellowed.

"And God help me if I don't do everything I can to put him on the throne over all Israel." Ishbosheth stood trembling as Abner stalked off.

David threw a great feast to welcome Abner and Michal, his first wife, to the palace. Abner promised David that he would speak personally to the leaders of the 11 tribes and win their support for David. Abner set off immediately after the feast.

Soon afterwards David's commander, Joab arrived. He was appalled that the king had befriended the killer of his younger brother, Asahel. "David, Abner's deceiving you!" he cried. "He'll always remain true to the house of Saul." When David refused to listen, Joab sent a messenger to tell Abner to return. When the general arrived, Joab asked him

The murder of Abner
Abner was Saul's nephew, so he supported Saul's son, Ishbosheth, in preference to David. However, after quarrelling with his master, Abner transferred his loyalty to David. David's army commander, Joab, was angry when he heard that David had welcomed Abner, because Abner had killed his brother, Asahel. Without David's knowledge, Joab murdered Abner. The picture shows a medieval altar detail of the scene, dating from 1181.

Hebron
Hebron is situated 30km southwest of Jerusalem and is the highest town in Palestine. Many important figures in the Old Testament were buried there. So, apparently, were all the sons of Jacob, except for Joseph. Hebron was King David's capital for seven and a half years, until he moved to Jerusalem.

> **All the tribes of Israel came and said, 'You shall be prince over Israel.'**

for a private word. As Abner bent to Joab's ear, Joab stabbed him. "Now I am revenged for my brother's death!" Joab hissed.

David was furious. He cursed Joab and honoured Abner with fasting, and people tore their clothes in grief.

More tragedy followed. Two of Ishbosheth's captains had realised that without Abner Ishbosheth couldn't rule

for long. They wanted to gain favour with David, so they crept into Ishbosheth's house and stabbed him. Then they ran to David and proudly told him of their crime. To their shock, David was horrified. "Ishbosheth had done nothing wrong," he groaned. "You have killed an innocent man in his own house. You will die for your wickedness." The traitors were executed.

David was now the sole contender for the throne. The elders gathered together and anointed him. At last, the king God had chosen ruled all Israel.

Anointing oil
The oil used for anointing would have been oil from olives (below), mixed with myrrh and spices such as cinnamon (right) and cassia (bottom right). The recipe was made from instructions given to the prophet Moses. Ordinary olive oil was used in cooking, in lamps and as a medicine, but it was a sin to use the special anointing oil for any other purpose.

❧ ABOUT THE STORY ❧

Once again the writer wants to show how David lived according to God's laws. In ancient times, rulers often killed potential rivals, and took revenge on their enemies.

Joab was like that, but David wasn't. He didn't want to force his way to power. He knew that human life is precious. He had killed people in war, but when he had the chance to "live and let live" in peace time he did.

Bringing the Ark to Jerusalem

KING David wanted to mark the beginning of a new era for the unified country. He thought it would be wrong to remain at Hebron or move to Saul's palace at Gibeah. He decided to make Jerusalem his new capital city.

The Jebusites who lived there were afraid of being thrown out of their homes so they barred the gates against him. David sent some of his soldiers up a large water pipe into the heart of the city, and soon the gates were open. The king's men streamed in, and from that day onwards Jerusalem was known as the City of David.

Once David's new palace had been built, he wanted to make a proper home for the ark in Jerusalem. The holy chest containing the Ten Commandments had been kept in a village near the border of Israel ever since the Philistines had returned it.

David declared that the day the priests moved the ark should be a public holiday, and the people of Israel poured into the streets. The people sang and played tambourines, flutes and cymbals as the ark rolled along on its ceremonial chariot. King David himself led the way.

Then disaster struck! The oxen pulling the chariot stumbled on the rocky road, and the man guiding the cart, called Uzzah, reached out to steady the precious ark. Only the priests were allowed to touch it. As soon as Uzzah touched the ark, he fell lifeless to the ground. The shocked Israelites fell silent, reminded of God's holy power. The festivities were over for that day.

Uzzah's death made even King David nervous, and for three months he left the ark in the care of Obed-edom the Gittite. When he tried again to move it, he held a prayer service and offered sacrifices before the procession set off. The people came out to celebrate with even more energy than before. They sang and danced in the greatest carnival they'd ever held. Even King David took turns dancing with them. Quite carried away, he stripped off his clothes and leapt for joy before the ark of the Lord.

 David danced before the Lord with all his might.

Not everyone was enjoying themselves. Since Michal had returned to be the king's wife, she'd grown jealous of the other wives David had taken in her absence. She felt superior because she was King Saul's daughter, and she thought it beneath her to go and mingle with the common people in the streets. As the ark entered Jerusalem she stayed in her room in the palace, looking down on the revelry with disdain. Imagine her horror when she saw her husband, the king, half-naked and singing and dancing with everyone else! Things were never the same between Michal and David again. For the king loved his subjects and his subjects loved him, and he thought it right that he should be among them to pay homage to the God who ruled over all.

David and the priests brought the ark to where the tabernacle had been set up, the richly embroidered tent in which it had rested since the time of Moses. The king offered more sacrifices and prayers, and blessed the people. Then he distributed a gift of bread, meat and raisins to every person to commemorate the occasion.

❖ ABOUT THE STORY ❖

When Uzzah died, David was partly to blame. The ark should never have been put on a chariot. It was meant to be carried on poles, which the priests rested on their shoulders. That was how they carried it the second time. Uzzah's death showed the people that it was important to follow God's commands fully. David had thought he could improve on what God had said. He was wrong.

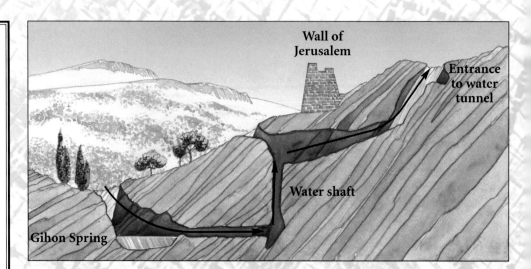

Surprise attack
Because of Jerusalem's position on a high plateau surrounded by deep ravines, the Israelites had never before succeeded in capturing the city. The Jebusites felt safe but David took them by surprise by entering the city via a water shaft. The picture above shows the possible route taken by David and his men.

When David was quietly resting in his palace, he thought, "Beautiful as the tabernacle is, we need a permanent temple. My own house is made of cedar wood and covered in gold and silver. The tabernacle is only a tent." He shared his idea with Nathan, a prophet. The next day, Nathan told David that God had spoken to him in a dream. "The Lord says that the tabernacle will do for now. You are a man of war, and you should not build the holy temple. But one of your sons will be a man of peace, and he will build a temple to the Lord so glorious that people far and wide will hear of it." At this prophecy from Nathan, David was content.

Death of Uzzah
Uzzah made the mistake of touching the holy ark, which not even the Levites were allowed to handle. God was so angry with Uzzah that He punished him with death. The second time David tried to bring the ark into Jerusalem, he made sure that the Levites carried it according to the instructions that had been laid down by Moses.

Jerusalem
This view of modern Jerusalem shows the city walls, the old quarter, which is the oldest part of the city and the mosque called The Dome of the Rock.

David and Bathsheba

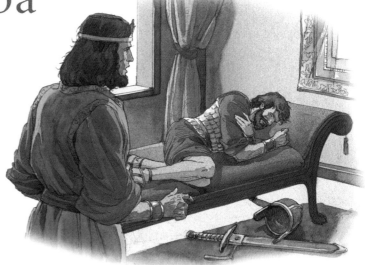

KING David ruled justly and fairly. He won victories over his enemies, but was capable of great acts of mercy, too. Saul's son Jonathan had himself left a son, called Mephibosheth, who was crippled in both feet. David commanded that Mephibosheth and Ziba, the servant who looked after him, be brought to the palace. "I'm giving back to you all the lands that belonged to your grandfather, Saul," David told the amazed boy, kindly. "Ziba will look after it for you while you live here at the palace with me. For I loved your father as my brother, and so I will love you as my son."

Although David was a good and great king, he was still just a man, capable of sinning like everyone else. The day

finally came when David offended God, during a time when the Israelites were fighting a tribe called the Ammonites. The king had put the army in the capable hands of his commander Joab, while he stayed in Jerusalem to take care of things at home. David liked to stroll on the flat roof of his palace in the evening, looking out over the houses and hills of his beautiful capital city. Late one afternoon, he was pondering matters of state and admiring the view as usual when his thoughts were interrupted. Bathing in a pool in one of the gardens below was the most beautiful woman he had ever seen. For the whole evening afterwards, he found it impossible to concentrate. He couldn't rest until he knew who she was.

David discovered that the woman's name was Bathsheba and that she was married to Uriah, a soldier in his army, safely away at the war. David gave in to temptation and began to woo Bathsheba. For several months the two

Amman – ancient Rabbah
Uriah and the rest of David's army were away fighting at Rabbah, the capital city of the Ammonites. Today, the city of Amman, the capital of Jordan, lies on the same site. The Ammonites had become a powerful people, but David and Joab succeeded in defeating the city and putting its inhabitants to forced labour. Later, after the death of Solomon, David's son, the Ammonites resurfaced as a threat to Israel. Today, many archaeological remains exist in and around Amman. Elsewhere in the city are ruins of cities from many different ages, including Roman and medieval. Among these ruins, sculptures and inscriptions from the 700s and 600s BC have been found. This picture shows a view across Amman from the citadel in the city. You can see the amphitheatre in the foreground.

Perfume pot
After bathing, Bathsheba would have rubbed perfumed oil into her skin. Perfume was a luxury and was kept in special containers like this pot dating from the 900s to 800s BC.

lovers enjoyed a secret, romantic affair, until Bathsheba told David that she was expecting his baby. The king panicked. If Uriah found out, he would know that the baby was not his because he had been away. Everyone would soon know that David had sinned by sleeping with another man's wife.

The anxious king tried to disguise his sins. He sent a message to his commander Joab to send Uriah home, pretending that he wanted an update on the war. Uriah gave the king his report, and David sent him home. But next morning, the king found that the gallant officer had not slept at home with his wife. He had vowed not to return home while his men were still fighting, so he'd slept at the door of the palace.

Next day the king held a banquet for the soldier and plied him with alcohol. Surely if Uriah was drunk, he'd forget his resolution and go back to his wife? That way, Uriah would not know that the child was not his. But Uriah curled up on one of the king's couches instead.

David could not own up to his terrible sin. However, his next plan involved committing an even worse one. When Uriah went to rejoin his troops, David gave him a letter for Joab, the army commander. It said: "I command you to put Uriah in the frontline. When he is in the thick of the fighting, withdraw your troops so he is left alone among the enemy." Joab did just what David had ordered.

A messenger was soon on his way to tell Bathsheba that her husband had fallen in battle. And as soon as her period of mourning was over, David married her.

The king must have thought that he had got away with his crime, but God sees everything. The prophet Nathan came to see him. "Listen to this story," he told David. "Once upon a time a rich man owned lots of sheep, and a poor man had one little lamb, which was like a pet. One day, when a visitor came, the rich man took the poor man's lamb and roasted it for dinner."

David was angry. "He deserves to die for this. Who is he?" he cried.

> **'Set Uriah in the forefront of the hardest fighting that he may be struck down, and die.'**

"You," the prophet said. "And the Lord will punish you. You have sinned in private, but all Israel will see you suffer. In the future, your own children will rebel against you. But first, the baby will die." Sure enough, Bathsheba's baby was born weak. Though David prayed and fasted, begging God to save its life, a week later the infant died.

ONE REASON DAVID SINNED MAY HAVE BEEN BECAUSE HE WAS TIRED – HE SHOULD HAVE BEEN OUT WITH HIS ARMY. TEMPTATION IS OFTEN GREATEST WHEN OUR RESISTANCE IS LOW AND WE BECOME WEAK.

Uriah's death
David's sin in sleeping with Bathsheba led to the second sin of murder. If Uriah had gone to his wife, the child could have been passed off as his and David would not have killed him. David hoped once Uriah was dead, no one need know what had happened. But Nathan exposed the truth, and David was punished.

❖ ABOUT THE STORY ❖
Until now, David has been shown as always loyal to God and anxious to do the right thing. In this case, though, it is Uriah who is right, and David who is very wrong. His lament over Saul could now be applied to himself: "How are the mighty fallen." The Bible never hides the failings of its greatest heroes. The stories are told to warn readers that everyone, even someone as great and as devoted to God as David, is vulnerable to sin.

Absalom the Rebel

NATHAN's prophecy that King David's children would rebel against him soon came true. David had many wives and children and was used to them all arguing among each other. But when his son Amnon attacked his daughter Tamar one day, it was serious. The family took sides and didn't forget the row. Two years later, another of David's sons, Absalom, took revenge for Tamar. He killed Amnon and fled to Egypt.

The king grieved for both his lost children. He couldn't bring back Amnon, but he could bring back Absalom. After five long years, David sent word to his son saying he was forgiven and that he could return safely to Israel, but on condition that he wasn't allowed to contact him at the palace.

For Absalom, this was worse than living in exile. He found it unbearable to think of all his brothers and sisters living as royal princes and princesses, while he lived in the same city as an outcast. Eventually, after three years had passed, David sent for Absalom. Absalom threw himself at the feet of the king, begging his father to receive him back into the family. David's heart melted, and he raised his son to his feet, hugging and kissing him. Absalom was disappointed not to feel the gladness he thought he'd feel. He remained full of a bitterness that wouldn't go away, and over time it grew and grew until it finally turned him against his father.

Secretly, Absalom decided to try to win the support of David's subjects for himself and overthrow his father. He was already a favourite with the people because he was a very handsome young man with long, thick hair. Each morning he presented himself at the city gate, standing on a horse-drawn chariot with fifty attendants around him. He would talk to the people and listen to their complaints, winning their hearts as a royal who did not mind shaking hands with ordinary people. "It's a shame the king doesn't come and chat to you all like this," Absalom would tell them. "He doesn't know about your problems like I do." And he'd heave a big sigh. "If only I were in charge, I'd fix things right away."

More and more people began to pledge their allegiance to the king's son, including those in the government such as David's trusted counsellor Ahithophel. Finally, even the bold Absalom thought that he was being a little too daring in organizing a rebellion right under the king's nose. He made an excuse to leave the city, telling his father that he wanted to go to the family city of Hebron to offer prayers and sacrifices for forgiveness. Then secretly he sent messengers to all the tribes telling his followers to come and gather there, for he was about to proclaim himself king.

However, many people still remained true to David, and word came to him of what his son was up to. He immediately fled out of danger by taking his court and leaving Jerusalem. Absalom moved in straightaway and set himself up on the throne. But what next? "Let me take some men and catch up with David," Ahithophel urged. "Your father will be unprepared and I can kill him without dragging anyone else into it. That way, you'll avoid civil war and your new subjects will be all the more pleased with you."

But a counsellor called Hushai gave quite the opposite advice. "No, you should bide your time," he told Absalom. "Your father is an experienced warrior and is probably hiding somewhere safe, away from his troops altogether. You have the throne now. Why not wait and gather a proper army around you? Then you can lead your men into battle and win all the glory for yourself."

Absalom liked the sound of that, and chose to follow Hushai. But unbeknown to him, the counsellor was one of David's men, working under cover to trick him with bad advice. And the king's son had fallen headfirst into the trap. Absalom's delay gave the king the breathing space he needed to rally his troops.

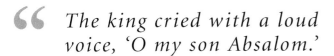

> ## *The king cried with a loud voice, 'O my son Absalom.'*

Even after all his treacherous son had done to him, David couldn't find it within himself to stop loving his son. And on the day that the two armies finally clashed,

the king instructed his captains to take Absalom alive and not to harm him.

The battle took place in the thickly wooded forest near Shiloh, a dangerous place full of quicksands, poisonous snakes and wild animals that claimed almost as many lives as the fighting itself. When countryman had finished slaying countryman, and the victory was David's, over 20,000 men lay dead among the trees.

Absalom was not one of them. He had leapt on to a mule and tried to escape. It proved impossible to dodge the branches that barred the galloping animal's way. As the terrified mule turned this way and that in the dense undergrowth, Absalom's hair got caught in the trees. And when his mount finally found a direction in which to bolt, the king's son was left dangling from a branch while the animal shot away from under him.

Back at David's palace everyone was rejoicing, except for the king himself who was waiting anxiously at the gate for a messenger to bring news of his son. When he heard that his own army commander Joab had found Absalom and killed him, despite his orders, he broke down and wept uncontrollably. "My son, my son!" he wailed. "I wish that I had died instead of you." David was paying a terrible price for sinning with Bathsheba.

In the years ahead there was more trouble to come, God sent a famine and then a plague to make the job of establishing peace within the nation extra hard. There was some happiness, too. Bathsheba gave birth to another baby boy called Solomon, who comforted his mother and father a little for the children they had lost. David loved Bathsheba as his favourite wife, and Solomon was to become his most beloved son.

Royal advisers
Kings were often dependent on their advisers to help them make decisions. Absalom takes the wrong advice when he listens to Hushai.

THE BIBLE ENCOURAGES ITS READERS TO WAIT PATIENTLY FOR GOD TO GIVE US NEW OPPORTUNITIES, AND TO BE CONTENT WITH WHAT WE HAVE. IF WE TRY TO FORCE OUR WAY, MANY PEOPLE CAN GET HURT.

❖ ABOUT THE STORY ❖

Absalom may have had his father's fighting spirit, but he had none of his patience and faith. Absalom became hungry for power and tried to force himself on to the throne. The writer wants us to notice that Absalom never asked what God wanted.

The Death of David

WHEN David was very old, he told everyone that he wanted Solomon to be king when he died. Another of David's sons had his own ideas. Adonijah wanted to be king and he talked several influential people into supporting him, including Joab, David's army commander, and Abiathar, the priest.

Adonijah thought that the old king no longer understood what was going on outside the palace walls, so he held a coronation ceremony for himself. Most of the royal officials of Judah attended the event. Nathan the prophet, who hadn't been invited, soon heard of it. He warned David's wife Bathsheba, and she went straight to David, who lay ill in bed. "You said our son

> " *All the people said, 'Long live King Solomon.'* "

Solomon would be your successor," she said, "yet Adonijah has made himself king. People are confused."

David took immediate action, which was quite the opposite to what Adonijah expected. Soon, Solomon was mounted on the king's own horse, wearing the king's crown, parading to Gihon with Nathan and Zadok the priest. There, they anointed Solomon as the new king, God's chosen successor to David. The appointment of the new ruler was proclaimed all over Israel.

People up and down the country celebrated. Adonijah heard the noise when he was in the middle of a party for his own coronation. As soon as his guests realised that the shouts of "Long live the king!" were for Solomon, they sneaked away. When David died and the rightful heir Solomon took the throne, no one dared argue with him.

∾ ABOUT THE STORY ∾

Although the Israelites' request for a king had not been according to God's purpose, this story reminds readers that God did not abandon His people. He continued to guide them in the choice of the next king. The Bible teaches that God keeps His "covenant" or agreement with His people even when they are unfaithful to Him. God had a very special purpose for the new King Solomon.

Crowns
Many different types of crown are described in the Bible. The crowns shown here are an Assyrian crown (left), above which are the red crown of Upper Egypt and the white crown of Lower Egypt. To the right is Ramses II's Egyptian double crown. Ramses had his own version of this crown made. In the top right corner is a simple Persian crown, and below this is a Syrian crown.

The Wisdom of Solomon

SOLOMON was only young when he became king. But he was ready to rule. He knew how the civil wars and the strife with Israel's neighbours had taken their toll on the nation, and he wanted to keep Israel at peace. First he had his rival Adonijah and his supporters executed. Then he married the daughter of one of his major enemies, Pharaoh, ruler of Egypt.

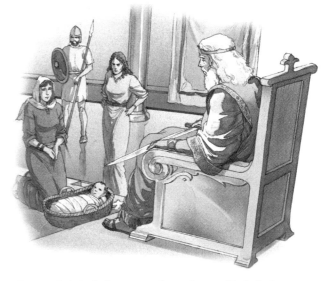

Solomon trusted God, just as his father had done. One night, during a religious festival at Gibeon, God spoke to the young king in a dream. "What gift would you like me to give you?" the Lord asked. Solomon thought hard.

"Lord," he replied, "I wish to rule well. Therefore give me wisdom, so I can judge between right and wrong, and govern my people with fairness." The Lord was delighted with Solomon's answer.

The wisdom of God was in him.

"Because you didn't ask for anything for yourself," God told him, "only for something that will benefit Israel, you will have your wish. I will also give you wealth, honour and long life."

One day, two women came to the king, begging him to settle an argument. They had both given birth, within three days of each other. But one night one of the babies had died. The first mother claimed that the other woman's child had died, and that she had swapped the dead baby for her live one while she slept.

"No I didn't!" the second mother yelled. "The living child is mine!"

"Enough!" bellowed Solomon. "Fetch me a sword." The two women waited. "The living baby will be cut into two and half given to each of you," he announced.

While the second woman nodded her agreement, the first woman fell on her knees before the king, weeping uncontrollably. "No, no, my lord! Do not kill the child," she wailed. "Please give it to her instead."

"Take your baby," Solomon smiled, laying the child in the first woman's arms. The king knew that the real mother would rather give up her child than allow it to be killed.

People were amazed by the king's good judgment, and he soon became known as "Solomon the Wise".

Royal wedding
Instead of marrying for love, Solomon used his marriage as a way of maintaining peace in Israel. He chose Pharaoh's daughter as his bride, as Pharaoh was unlikely to declare war on his son-in-law.

❧ ABOUT THE STORY ❧

In the Bible "wisdom" is the ability to understand, do and say the right thing, it isn't simply knowing things. Wisdom is always seen as a gift from God (in the New Testament the apostle James tells his readers to pray for it). In a holy sense, wisdom is knowing what God wants in any situation, and making decisions based on the way in which God wants people to live, not on what is easiest at the time.

Building the Temple

KING Solomon had new plans for almost everything, taxes, employment, the armed forces, trade, building. His greatest plan of all was for a great temple at Jerusalem, just as his father had wanted, a glorious home for the ark. It took four years just to lay the foundations of the temple. It was a similar design to the tabernacle, but twice as big. To complete the temple took another three years.

An enormous workforce was employed. King Solomon ordered many Israelites to leave their lands for one out of every three months to work for him. He also forced prisoners of war to become slaves. Soon thousands of men were cutting stone to size at the quarry. The great blocks were then heaved to the building site and hoisted into place so that not a single hammer or pickaxe was heard inside the holy building during its construction. For the really skilled work, Solomon hired expert joiners, carvers and metal workers from overseas.

Only the very best building materials were used. Rafts of the finest cedar and pine wood were floated down the coast from King Hiram of Tyre in Lebanon and taken inland by camel train. Merchants went to distant lands to trade Israel's foodstuffs and oil for gold and silver, rich fabrics and precious stones.

Eventually, all was finished. The temple was amazing. The walls and ceilings were made of elegant, sweet-smelling wood beams and planks. Rooms were lined with pure gold and carved with winged cherubim. Intricately carved doors of olive wood separated the sacred innermost chamber, the Holy of Holies from the outer room, the Holy Place, together with a shimmering veil that hung from delicate chains. The altar itself was made of gold.

Solomon dedicated the temple to the Lord with a grand ceremony. There were prayer services, and animals were sacrificed. The king prayed that God would make the temple a place that would inspire all who saw it to follow the Lord. He told the people that if ever they fell into the hands of enemies, they should look to the holy building, remembering what it stood for and who it served.

Finally there was a great procession as priests and elders of the tribes, with King Solomon at their head, brought the sacred ark of the covenant to its new resting place. As the priests laid it gently in the Holy of Holies, a cloud of God's glory filled the inner sanctuary. The Lord was present in the new house just as he had been in the tabernacle. The whole nation rejoiced.

> **" The glory of the Lord filled the house of the Lord. "**

When the celebrations were over, Solomon heard God say to him, "I have heard your prayers and requests and I have accepted this house you have built me. If you keep my commandments, I will establish your royal throne over Israel for ever, just as I promised your father, David. But if you turn aside from following me and worship other gods, then I will cause this temple to be destroyed and everyone will wonder how and why such a thing happened."

Tools of the trade
These pictures show an Egyptian stonemason's mallet (far right). Stonemasons cut and shaped blocks of stone. They used many of the same tools as carpenters, including saws, mallets, chisels and an adze, used like a modern plane (right).

The temple's rooms
The temple was divided into three areas: the entrance porch, the outer room (or Holy Place) and the inner room (or Holy of Holies). The outer room was a larger space, used by the priest for rituals and ceremonies. The inner room was smaller and was rarely used. Both rooms had wooden walls and doors, covered in decorative carving and overlaid with gold. Around the outside of the temple there were store rooms.

Worship is not only a matter of going to a religious service or ceremony. We worship God whenever we do something just because we love Him and want to honour Him.

Holy of Holies
The Holy of Holies was the sacred inner room of Solomon's temple. This was where the ark of the covenant was kept. When the ark was taken into the Holy of Holies, the whole room filled with cloud, which signified that God was present.

❖ ABOUT THE STORY ❖

Solomon's temple must have been a beautiful place. The king did not build it to show off his skill and wealth, but because he wanted to give the best he had to God. The temple became a symbol both of God's presence among the people, and also of God's blessings to them. It was an act of worship in itself, because Solomon and the people sacrificed time and money to build it.

Wealth and Splendour

ONCE the glorious temple was finished, Solomon's building plans were far from over. He built a new palace with a massive hall where he could sit in judgement. With splendid royal living apartments as well, the palace was even bigger than the temple. The mountain quarries swarmed with labourers. Sparks flew from the desert blast furnaces, the roads groaned at the weight of materials going in and out of Jerusalem. The magnificent palace was made entirely of cedar wood and the finest marbles, with three tiers of windows to let the sun stream in and high ceilings held aloft by rows of pillars.

Then Solomon started work on a mighty wall to circle Jerusalem, thick and high enough to stand firm against foreign armies. He sent his surveyors to oversee the reconstruction of cities such as Gezer that had been destroyed in Israel's many wars. New strongholds sprang up from these blackened heaps of rubble. They were even greater than before, with thriving markets and public buildings. Solomon built new store cities to hold all of Israel's supplies and treasures. The Israelites filled new warehouses with sacks of grain, nuts and figs, which Israel's farmers paid as taxes to the king. They stacked cellars with barrels of wine and vats of oil, and heaped treasures and gems into locked safe-houses. Housing and training grounds were built for King Solomon's 1,400 gleaming chariots and 12,000 horsemen. On the Red Sea coast, Solomon built an entire fleet of merchant ships that travelled far and away to seek treasures, and returned with cargoes of apes, peacocks and ivory, rare woods and metals, and gleaming jewels.

As Solomon's subjects heard each new demand from their king, it seemed he was asking them to perform the

❊ TREASURES FROM ABROAD ❊

The Israelites traded with many other countries and brought back all kinds of exotic treasures, such as gold, silver, jewels and ivory.

Bronze figure
This is a Babylonian bronze statuette of a figure carrying a basket full of building materials. Figures like this were put in the foundations of temples.

Stone lion's head
This stone lion's head came from Assyria. It might originally have been attached to the handle of a fan.

Silver goat
This silver goat is thought to have come from Persepolis in Persia. It dates from the 400s BC.

impossible. They grumbled and groaned at the high taxes and the enforced labour. The king certainly wasn't loved by his people as David had been. Even so, everyone was impressed and overawed. The sailors and traders carried news of the king's greatness abroad, so that even people who weren't sure where Israel was heard rumours of its wealth, splendour and its greatest marvel of all – Solomon's wisdom. The king seemed to know all there was to know about anything. He could recite over 1,000 poems and quote over 3,000 proverbs. Statesmen and philosophers travelled to Solomon's court from far away, to listen to the king and ask his advice.

> ❝ *God gave Solomon wisdom beyond measure.* ❞

One of the visitors was the Queen of Sheba from Arabia. She had heard all the rumours about the king and wanted to know if they were true. So she came to see for herself, travelling with a great retinue of servants and carrying gifts of gold and jewels.

Solomon showed the queen everything, from his golden palace, throne and dishes; to how he ran his court with fairness and administered justice to the people. He showed her how the Israelites worshipped in their glorious new temple. He said he could answer any question she asked. The Queen of Sheba was left speechless. "Israel is lucky indeed to have such a magnificent king," she told Solomon. When she returned home, Solomon gave her many souvenirs from Israel's treasure houses.

Solomon's kingdom

During the rule of Solomon, Israel was more wealthy than it had ever been before. On this map the orange colour shows the lands of Israel. The dark brown colour shows the lands that paid tribute to Solomon. By this time, Ammon, Moab and even Philistia had all been conquered.

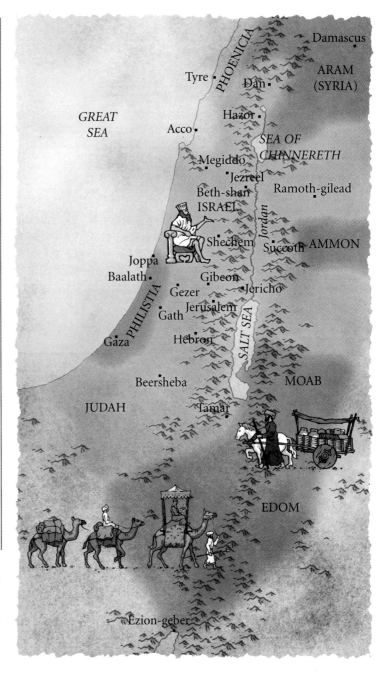

Trading ship

This picture shows a stone relief of a Phoenician trading ship. The Phoenicians were neighbours of the Israelites and, along with the Philistines, were leading powers at sea. The Israelites had little experience of the sea, so Solomon used Phoenician ships manned by Phoenician sailors to carry out his trading activities. The Israelites looked upon the ship as an object of wonder, and a safe journey was thought to be a demonstration of God's goodness and power.

✤ ABOUT THE STORY ✤

Solomon had prayed for wisdom rather than riches, but God promised him riches as well as a special sign of His blessing. At this time, people assumed those who became wealthy were favoured by God. Later, they realized this is not always the case.

Fall of Solomon

ONE of the ways that all kings in ancient times showed how great they were was by having many wives. Just as Solomon outdid everyone in the splendour and scale of everything around him, he also outdid everyone in the number of women he married. Including Pharaoh's daughter, Solomon had 700 wives altogether. He also had 300 mistresses. It was not just because he was greedy. The king knew that all his plans for making Israel great rested on peace. The only way to keep the peace was to make treaties with his enemies abroad. And over the years, Israel had made many enemies. So Solomon kept his ministers of foreign affairs busy negotiating deals at meeting after meeting, while he himself married princess after princess. After all, it was unlikely that one country would attack another if the rulers were father- and son-in-law ...

There was only one problem. King Solomon's wives were from peoples such as the Moabites, the Ammonites, the

Syrian storm-god
Solomon had wives from many foreign lands, such as Moab, Edom and Syria. These women continued to worship their own gods, instead of the Israelite God. This is a stone relief of the Syrian storm-god, Hadad, standing on a bull and holding his symbol of a forked bolt of lightning.

The Edomites
This is an impression of the king of Edom's seal, from 800 BC. The Edomites were one of the tribes that attacked Solomon during his reign.

SOLOMON MAY HAVE JUST BEEN BEING TOLERANT OF THE OTHER RELIGIONS SO THAT HE COULD KEEP ORDER. BUT THE BIBLE TELLS US WE CANNOT BE TOLERANT OF ANYTHING THAT GOES AGAINST GOD. KEEPING THE TRUTH IS MORE IMPORTANT THAN KEEPING THE PEACE. ~

Edomites, the Sidonians and the Hittites. These were all nations with whom the Lord had forbidden the Israelites to mix. God had commanded this from the first days of the Israelites' arrival in the Promised Land. The foreign tribes worshipped pagan gods, and the Lord knew that if the Israelites intermarried with them, they would be tempted to follow the pagan ways.

King Solomon was no more able to resist this temptation than anyone else. As he grew older, he allowed his beautiful, loving wives to sway his judgement. He allowed them to perform their own pagan rituals and worship their own idols (burning holy incense and offering sacrifices as only the priests were allowed to do), and he even built special places in which to do it! First, there was a temple to Chemosh, the god of the Moabites. Then there was a temple to Molech, the god of the Ammonites, which Solomon had built on the mountain east of Jerusalem, within sight of the mighty Israelite temple itself! Soon pagan temples were being built all over the country, and every one of them with the full knowledge, and even with the approval of the king. Even worse, the wives persuaded Solomon to go and worship with them too. He didn't stop going to the temple of the Lord, but he was also often seen praying at the temple to Ashtoreth, goddess of the Sidonians, and Milcom of the Ammonites.

God was furious with him. How could the man on whom He had bestowed the gifts of wisdom, wealth and honour, turn away from Him so easily! The Lord spoke to the king angrily. "Solomon!" He thundered, striking fear into the king's heart. "You have not kept my covenant and laws as I commanded you to! I promised to establish your royal throne over Israel for ever if you lived by my laws, but you have worshipped pagan idols. I am therefore going to tear your kingdom away from you. However, for the sake of your father David, I will not make you suffer this in your lifetime. I will do it to the son who succeeds you on the throne. He will be left with only a small part of your kingdom, while one of your servants will rule over the rest."

> *When Solomon was old, his wives turned away his heart after other gods.*

Even though Solomon was the most knowledgeable man in the world, he had no idea who the "servant" was that God was speaking of. It was a bitter pill to swallow. Instead of the kingdom he'd worked so hard to build going to his son, most of Solomon's efforts would be enjoyed by a stranger. Yet the king understood he had sinned. He had no choice but to accept the Lord's punishment and beg His forgiveness. The king realized that the period of peace, unity and prosperity he had brought to Israel was about to come to an end, all through his own fault. Despite all the efforts Solomon had made to live peacefully with his enemies, the last years of his reign were plagued with unrest. Two rulers in particular continually raided Israel, King Hadad of Edom and King Rezon of Damascus. The king knew that it was the way things would be for Israel in the future.

Shishak
The kings of Edom and Damascus were not the only ones to attack Israel during Solomon's reign – the Pharaoh Shishak also invaded. Shishak is the first Pharaoh to be mentioned by name in the Bible. This is a small silver pendant showing the Pharaoh, possibly worn on a necklace as jewellery.

Burning incense
This picture shows an incense burner from the 10th century BC. Incense was commonly used during religious ceremonies, as an offering to God. The word "incense" refers both to the substance used for burning (usually a spice or gum) and to the characteristic smell that is produced.

❧ **ABOUT THE STORY** ❧

Solomon failed God by allowing his wives to draw him away from God. Other nations worshipped many gods, and the temptation was great for the Israelites to do the same. Solomon, who loved God, foolishly allowed these other gods to be introduced into Israel.

The Kingdom is Divided

THERE was a high-ranking official in Solomon's government called Jeroboam, a very capable man who carried out his work quickly and efficiently. The king rewarded Jeroboam with promotion, making him minister over all the forced labour schemes in the territories that belonged to the tribe of Joseph.

Jeroboam was delighted. He immediately packed up his house and belongings, and set off out of Jerusalem to move to his new job. However, he hadn't long been on the road when he saw the prophet Ahijah coming towards him. To Jeroboam's astonishment, the prophet stripped off the new robe he was wearing and ripped it into twelve pieces. "I am here with a message for you from the Lord," Ahijah declared. "God is about to tear the kingdom away from Solomon and rip Israel apart, for the king has forsaken Him and turned to worshipping false idols. Solomon's son will rule over only two of the tribes, and the Lord will make you king over the other ten.'

Jeroboam was amazed. Though he was an ambitious man, he had never dreamed of being on the throne of Israel. How on earth was all of this going to happen, he wondered? He was an important man in the kingdom, but surely he wasn't important enough to be king.

Jeroboam knew that the dramatic prophecy was best kept to himself, but he couldn't resist confiding in his family and friends. They found it hard to keep the exciting

secret, and the news leaked out until people all over the country were whispering the rumour. Soon word reached the ears of the king himself. Solomon realized with dread that Jeroboam was the "servant" God had chosen to take over the kingdom. In desperation, the king sent men to kill Jeroboam, but he managed to escape and fled to the distant country of Egypt.

Finally, after reigning over Israel for forty years, King Solomon died and his son Rehoboam took the throne. Even though Solomon had made Israel a wealthy, famous country, life under him had been terribly hard. The exhausted people wanted to make sure that their new ruler would be less demanding than his father had been. They searched for a spokesperson to approach the new king, and there was no one more suitable than Jeroboam, who had returned from Egypt after Solomon died.

Rehoboam asked his counsellors what they thought he should do about the people's request. First he went to the advisers who used to be at his father's side. These old men knew how the people had suffered under Solomon's rule. They wisely advised the king to win the favour of his new subjects by showing them mercy and reducing the levels of taxation and forced labour.

Then Solomon's son went to his new advisers. They were inexperienced and counselled the king to show the people his authority by imposing laws that were even harsher than those of his father.

> " *'My father chastised you with whips, but I will chastise you with scorpions.'* "

The king thought for a while. Rehoboam was an arrogant young man who liked the idea of his subjects cowering in fear before him. He foolishly chose the advice of the younger men over that of his father's more experienced counsellors and advisers. "You have asked me to lighten your yoke," he announced to the anxiously waiting people. "Hear this. My father lashed you with whips, but I am going to lash you with scorpions!"

The tyrant had expected the Israelites to shut up and meekly shuffle away at this cruel threat. He was shocked to find that it had quite the opposite effect. Labourers all over the country downed tools and sat at home, refusing to work. On top of this general strike, there were demonstrations and organized protests. Several protests broke out into violent scuffles with the king's men, who had been sent to keep the rioting workers under control. In one demonstration the king's minister in charge of Israel's forced labour, Adoram, was stoned to death. "We will no longer serve the house of David," the people shouted. "We want a new king!" The ten tribes in the north of Israel crowned Jeroboam as their new ruler.

Only the tribe of Judah and the tiny tribe of Benjamin, in the south of the country, remained faithful to Solomon's son. From them he gathered 180,000 warriors to go and fight Jeroboam for the throne. A prophet called Shemaiah stopped him, bringing word from God. "The Lord says that no one shall fight against his countrymen. Everyone must return home, for this division in the kingdom has been brought about by the Lord himself."

So the kingdom that David had unified, and that Solomon had spent years building up, was once again split into two. The ten tribes of the north kept the name Israel, and the two small tribes of the south were called Judah.

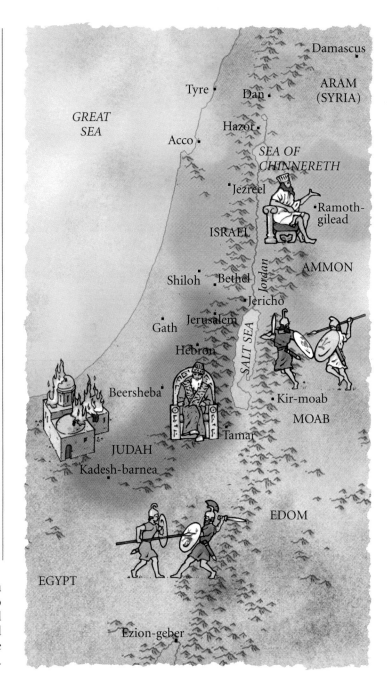

The divided kingdom

God punished Israel heavily for Solomon's disobedience. The two new kings ruled their separate tribes. Judah and Benjamin followed Solomon's son, Rehoboam, and all the other tribes crowned Jeroboam as their new king. Two kings were not as strong as one king would have been, and they lost land to the surrounding tribes.

Jeroboam's seal

In around 930BC Jeroboam became the first king of the separate Israel. The son of a wealthy landowner, he worked his way up in the royal court until he was in charge of many of Solomon's building projects. During one of these projects, Jeroboam led the workforce in a rebellion against the king's heavy-handed practices. Because of this, he was banished to Egypt, where he remained until Solomon's death. The picture shows Jeroboam's seal.

❧ ABOUT THE STORY ❧

This story marks the start of 200 years of feuding between Israel in the north and Judah in the south. The division occurred in 930BC, and the tribes were never re-united. Israel was destroyed in 722BC, and Judah in 587BC, but some Jews remained to pave the way for the New Testament.

The Book of Proverbs

FROM earliest times there were people in Israel and across the ancient world who studied what was called "wisdom". The writers of the *book of Proverbs* and other wisdom literature in the *Old Testament*, such as the books of Job and Ecclesiastes, discussed such difficult questions as: What is the purpose of life and why is there death, suffering and evil in the world? Some of these reflections on life are collected in the book of Proverbs.

Proverbs are short sayings that are easy to remember and which teach something about life and how people should live. They are general sayings, which means that they mean something to everyone and are relevant to all people in many situations. There are proverbs in many cultures all over the world.

Many of the wise sayings in *Proverbs* are basic common sense, but they are underpinned by the belief that wisdom comes from God:

"Trust in the Lord with all your heart and lean not upon your own understanding." (3:5–6)

The structure of the *book of Proverbs* varies. Sometimes several proverbs are linked by a single theme, such as the family or laziness.

Here are some examples of wise sayings from the *book of Proverbs*:

> ❝ *Let not loyalty and faithfulness forsake you.* ❞
> (3:3)

> ❝ *He who seeks good finds goodwill, but evil comes to him who searches for it.* ❞
> (11:27)

> ❝ *Even in laughter the heart is sad, and the end of joy is grief.* ❞
> (14:13)

> ❝ *A soft answer turneth away wrath, but a harsh word stirs up anger.* ❞
> (15:1)

> ❝ *Better a meal of vegetables where there is love than a fattened calf with hatred.* ❞
> (15:17)

> ❝ *Pride goes before destruction and a haughty spirit before a fall.* ❞
> (18:18)

> ❝ *Train up a child in the way he should go and when he is old he will not depart from it.* ❞
> (22:6)

Wisdom in Proverbs

The writers give a vivid picture of wisdom:

"Length of days is in her right hand, and in her left are riches and honour. Her ways are ways of pleasantness and all her paths are peace. She is a tree of life to them that lay hold upon her, and happy is everyone that retaineth her."

WISDOM

> **" A word fitly spoken is like apples of gold in a setting of silver. "**
>
> (25:11)

> **" Like cold water to a thirsty soul, so is good news from a far country. "**
>
> (25:25)

> **" Do not boast about tomorrow for you do not know what a day may bring forth. "**
>
> (27:1)

> **" As water reflects a face, so a man's heart reflects the man. "**
>
> (27:19)

SOLOMON AND THE BOOK OF *PROVERBS*

It is generally agreed that the book of *Proverbs* was compiled during the days of Israel's first kings, although editing continued for some centuries after this. It is not

> **" Let another praise you, and not your own mouth "**
>
> (27:2)

known exactly what Solomon's role was, but the book is introduced as 'The proverbs of Solomon, the son of David'. His name appears again at the beginning of chapters 10 and 25, and the collections of proverbs from 10:1 – 22:16 and 25:1 – 29:27 are usually attributed to him. Solomon was famous throughout the ancient world for his outstanding wisdom. Unlike the kings before and after him, he was wealthy, he had many international contacts and he was not engaged in warfare. He was able to collect and compose thousands of proverbs and songs. His court became an international centre for the exchange of learning.

❧ THEMES IN *PROVERBS* ❧

The themes dealt with in the book of *Proverbs* cover all aspects of life, including home, work, relationships, justice, attitudes and everything people do, say or even think. The sayings are based on practical observations of everyday life, and there is an underlying belief behind all the proverbs that wisdom comes from God.

The wise man and the fool
This is the main theme of the whole book and forms the subject of the first nine chapters. The proverbs highlight the contrast between the wisdom of obeying God and the folly of wilfully going one's own way.

The righteous and the wicked
The wise person will lead a good, or righteous, life, whereas the fool will always be

tempted by wrongdoing – in other words, he will become wicked. God loves and protects righteous people and is angry with those who are wicked. Although they may succeed for a while, it is only a matter of time before they arrive at death and destruction.

Laziness and hard work
Many of the proverbs describe the downfall of the lazy person. These people only realize their error too late, when they have achieved neither wealth nor status.

The family
This theme covers marriage, including unfaithfulness. It also covers the relationship between parents and children, including how they should be disciplined. Many of the sayings on this theme are still relevant today.

The Temple

ALTHOUGH it was King David's great ambition to build a temple, his son, Solomon, actually ordered the work to be done. Solomon built the temple in Jerusalem as a permanent home for the Ark of the Covenant – the wooden chest containing the Ten Commandments. The temple took seven years to complete. It was built as a house for God, rather than as a place to hold big gatherings of people. We have a good idea of what it looked like because there are detailed descriptions in the Bible. Solomon may have based his temple on the temples of the pagan tribes of the time. Ruins of these have been excavated that are similar in style to the Bible descriptions.

Solomon's temple was a rectangular building. It was about 30m long, 10m wide and 15m high. The temple probably stood on a platform above the level of the courtyard in which it was built, and was reached by a flight of steps. In the courtyard, in front of the temple, was a huge bronze altar for sacrifices and

an enormous bronze basin supported by twelve bronze bulls, which was used for ritual washings. There were store rooms along three sides of the building, which were probably used to keep sacred objects. The front entrance porch had a doorway with a giant bronze pillar on each side. These pillars were called Jachin and Boaz. It is not known what purpose they served as they were not part of the structure of the temple.

A pair of folding wooden doors led from the entrance porch to the outer chamber of the temple, which was known as the Holy Place. This was the larger chamber where the high priest performed ceremonial duties. The chamber was lit by five pairs of golden lampstands, and by a row of latticed windows high in the walls on each side.

A second pair of wooden doors led from the Holy Place to the inner chamber, which was known as Holy of Holies. This was a very sacred place. The doors

Solomon's temple
This picture shows the finished temple. In the Holy of Holies, the two guardian cherubim can be seen, their outstretched wings meeting above the Ark of the Covenant.

TIMELINE 1100BC TO 900BC

• Eli is Judge of Israel and High Priest in the tabernacle

• Samuel is born. He works in the tabernacle with Eli, before becoming a Judge himself

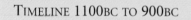

1100BC

MENORAH, A SACRED LAMPSTAND

SAMUEL RECEIVING THE CALL FROM GOD

• Saul is made king by Samuel

SAMUEL ANOINTING SAUL

• David flees from Saul

• Saul is killed at the Battle of Gilboa

1050BC

• David is made king of Judah

• David is made king of all Israel

THE DEATH OF SAUL AT GILBOA

1000B

to it were probably only opened once a year, for the high priest at the atonement ceremony. The Ark of the Covenant lay in the Holy of Holies, guarded by two wooden cherubim, each about 5m tall. When the ark was first put in place, the Holy of Holies was filled with a cloud, which signified the presence of God.

Both the Holy Place and the Holy of Holies had walls panelled with cedarwood and floors covered with cypress planks. The walls and doors were carved with flowers, palm trees and cherubim, and inset with gold. None of the underlying stonework was visible at all.

Solomon was assisted by neighbouring tribes in the building of the temple. He already had a friendship with King Hiram of Tyre, in Phoenicia. This alliance was strengthened by the agreement that Hiram would supply many of the materials for the temple, in particular the wood, and would take charge of the building work. In return for this, Solomon would provide him with foodstuffs, such as wheat, barley and oil.

Ancient cherubim
The figure shown on the right is actually what the cherubim in Solomon's temple would have looked like. Today we think of cherubim as looking like little children, but this figure has more in common with an Egyptian sphinx.

The tabernacle
The tabernacle was built during the Israelites' wilderness years, as a home for the Ark of the Covenant. It was a portable temple, which could be carried wherever they went. After the Israelites settled in Canaan, the tabernacle was kept at Shiloh, Nob and Gibeon, before Solomon built his temple, and the ark was transferred there.

The skill of many craftsmen, including stonemasons, carpenters and bronze-workers, was used to build the temple. Stonemasons sawed, hammered and chiselled stone blocks into shape, to make the basic structure. The blocks were worked on before being brought to the holy site so that no unnecessary noise was made. Even during the building stage, the place was regarded as holy. Ordinary woodwork was done by carpenters, but the woodcarving, such as the cherubim and the panelling on walls and doors, was carried out by specially skilled craftsmen. For the basic woodwork, local woods, such as cedar, cypress, oak, ash and acacia, were used, but for the carving work, hard woods, such as ebony, sandalwood and boxwood, were imported from abroad. King Hiram supervised much of the bronze casting himself, including the two decorative pillars for the entrance to the temple, and the huge basin, which was able to hold nearly 45,000 litres of water.

DAVID IS MADE KING

• Death of King David

• Solomon is made king of the united kingdom of Israel

• Solomon is blessed with wisdom by God

• The Queen of Sheba visits Solomon

DAVID AND NATHAN

• Death of King Solomon

• Solomon's son, Rehoboam becomes King of Judah

WEALTH OF SOLOMON

950BC

ASSYRIAN LION'S HEAD

• Jeroboam, Solomon's servant, becomes king of Israel

• The prophet Shemaiah tells Rehoboam he must not try to invade Israel

900BC

EXILE AND RETURN

The Israelites are driven from their land and are ruled by foreign kings, then return to Israel

Exile and Return

THIS section tells of the rise and fall of the kingdoms of Israel and Judah, of the people who lived there and the kings who reigned over them. It describes the enemy empires – Syrian, Assyrian, Babylonian and Persian – that posed a constant threat to the Israelite nation. It also follows the lives of the prophets, from Elijah to Ezekiel, who struggled through these difficult times to sustain the Israelites' faith in God.

The two main prophets who lived in the kingdom of Israel were Elijah and Elisha. Elijah received his calling from God during the reign of King Ahab. Ahab had been persuaded by his wife, Jezebel, to join her in worshipping the Phoenician god, Baal. As more and more people followed the king and turned to Baal and other pagan gods, Elijah had his work cut out trying to turn them back to God.

Even after Elijah proved God's supremacy in a contest, Ahab continued to sin against God. When a man called Naboth refused to sell him his vineyard, the king had him stoned to death, then took the land. Elijah reminded him that, in refusing to sell his birthright, Naboth had been obeying God, and predicted that Ahab and his family would die in dishonour. His prediction came true, when Ahab was killed in battle, and his blood licked up by stray dogs.

Elijah is one of only two people in the Bible not to die – the other is Enoch, a man who enjoyed a particularly close fellowship with God. When the time came for Elijah to go to heaven, he was carried upwards in a flaming chariot. This amazing spectacle was witnessed by Elijah's assistant, Elisha. As Elisha picked up the cloak dropped by his master, the mantle of power passed to him.

Nebuchadnezzar's Palace
These are the remains of the palace of Nebuchadnezzar in Babylon. The exile was when the Israelites were forced from their homes in Judah to live in Babylon, but it is also the time when the Jewish faith was properly established.

Beth-shan, Israel
There were two important pagan temples here that stood at the time of the good King Josiah.

Elisha continued the work of Elijah, but when he failed to eliminate Baal worship God was forced to punish the Israelites. The mighty Assyrians besieged Israel's capital, Samaria, for three years and eventually took control of the city. The kingdom of Israel had come to an end, and its people were scattered throughout the vast Assyrian Empire.

Meanwhile, the smaller kingdom of Judah was facing the same problems. Despite the efforts of the prophet Isaiah, the people continued to worship pagan gods, and most kings didn't stop them. There were some exceptions – God rewarded the loyalty of King Hezekiah by stopping the Assyrians taking over Judah and giving the king an extra 15 years to live.

Then the Babylonians besieged Judah's capital, the holy city of Jerusalem, for two years. They destroyed the temple, burned the city to the ground and took most of the inhabitants to Babylon as exiles, ending the kingdom of Judah.

The exiled people of Judah became known to the Babylonians as Jews. A prophet called Ezekiel gradually managed to get the Jews to pull together and follow the laws of Moses in an attempt to preserve their own identity. They were rewarded by God and their lives began to improve. Ezekiel predicted that they would return to the Promised Land to rebuild their temple. This came true when the Babylonian King Cyrus eventually decided to allow the exiled Jews to return to Jerusalem. They rebuilt the temple and the city, and threw out all the non-Jews living there. God's people were back in the Promised Land. They had their temple and holy city and they were once again one nation under God.

The book ends with the stories of Daniel, the prophet who interpreted the dreams of kings and survived being thrown into a den of lions; Esther, the beautiful young wife of King Xerxes, who saved the Jews from destruction by appealing bravely to her husband; and Jonah, the unwilling prophet, who was swallowed by a whale as a punishment for disobeying the call of God.

The main thread running through this section is the lives and teachings of the prophets. The role of these people was to remind the Israelites of the covenant they had made with God during the time of Moses, and to warn them of the consequences of disobedience. Prophets were known as "men of God", but God often referred to them as His servants. The person usually held up as the best example of a prophet is Moses. All the features which characterized prophets were found in Moses. He received a specific and personal call from God. He was warned in advance of events and of their significance by God. He was concerned about the welfare of his people. He played an active role in the affairs of the nation. His prophesying was made up of a combination of proclaiming about the present situation and predicting the future.

God usually spoke to His prophets by simply making them aware of His message, but He also used dreams and visions. A prophet was often associated with a group of disciples, some of whom may have been called by God, while others joined the prophet to learn from his wisdom. It is most likely to have been these disciples who recorded the words of their masters in the books of the Bible.

❧ EXILE AND RETURN ❧

This section covers the lives of two of the greatest prophets, Elijah and Elisha, and tells the stories of the later kings of Israel and Judah.

THE LIFE OF ELIJAH
First Book of Kings, Ch. 17 to 22.
Second Book of Kings, Ch. 1 & 2.
THE LIFE OF ELISHA
Second Book of Kings, Ch. 3 to 17.
KINGS OF ISRAEL AND JUDAH
Second Book of Kings, Ch. 11 to 25.
THE PROPHETS
Isaiah Ch. 1 to 9.
Jeremiah Ch. 1 to 36.
THE EXILE
Jeremiah Ch. 40.
Ezekiel Ch. 18 to 37.
Daniel, Ch. 1 to 6.
THE RETURN FROM EXILE
Ezra, Ch. 1 to 10.
Haggai, Ch. 1.
Nehemiah, Ch. 1 to 6.
ESTHER
Esther, Ch. 3 to 8.
JONAH
Jonah, Ch. 1 to 4.

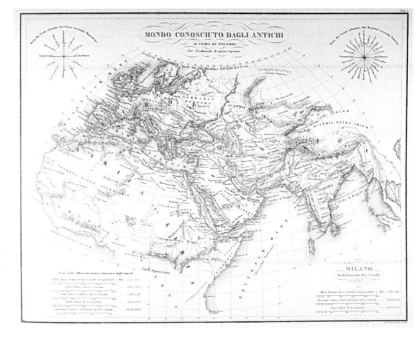

Jerusalem at the centre of the world

The picture on the right is an ancient map of what was known of the world at the time of Ptolemy, an Egyptian ruler who lived in AD100. Even at this time Jerusalem, capital of Judah, was a very important city. This world map places Jerusalem at its centre.

Divided Kingdoms and Exile

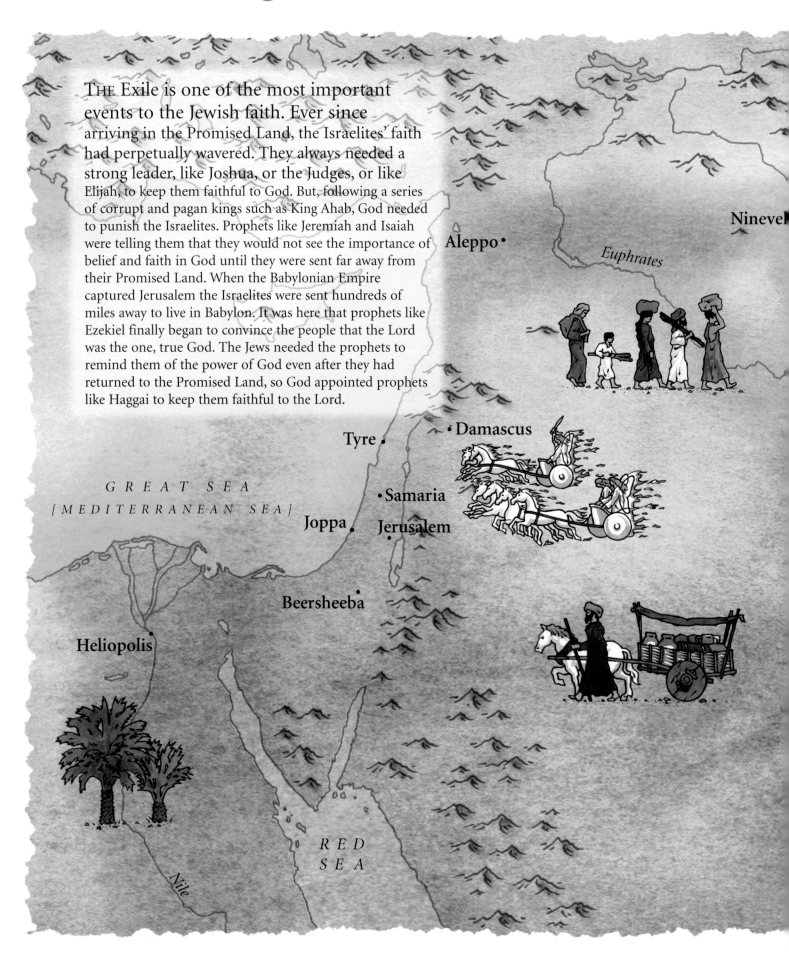

THE Exile is one of the most important events to the Jewish faith. Ever since arriving in the Promised Land, the Israelites' faith had perpetually wavered. They always needed a strong leader, like Joshua, or the Judges, or like Elijah, to keep them faithful to God. But, following a series of corrupt and pagan kings such as King Ahab, God needed to punish the Israelites. Prophets like Jeremiah and Isaiah were telling them that they would not see the importance of belief and faith in God until they were sent far away from their Promised Land. When the Babylonian Empire captured Jerusalem the Israelites were sent hundreds of miles away to live in Babylon. It was here that prophets like Ezekiel finally began to convince the people that the Lord was the one, true God. The Jews needed the prophets to remind them of the power of God even after they had returned to the Promised Land, so God appointed prophets like Haggai to keep them faithful to the Lord.

Nineve

Euphrates

Aleppo •

Tyre •

• Damascus

• Samaria

Joppa •

Jerusalem

G R E A T   S E A

[M E D I T E R R A N E A N   S E A]

Beersheeba

Heliopolis •

R E D
S E A

Nile

HYRCANIAN
SEA

Asshur

Tigris

• Babylon
• Nippur

LOWER
SEA

Persepolis

King Ahab the Bad

AFTER the reign of King Solomon, the Promised Land split into two kingdoms. The ten northern tribes kept the Promised Land's name – Israel. The smaller kingdom of Judah, formed by the two southern tribes, kept the capital, Jerusalem, and the temple built by King Solomon.

King Jeroboam of Israel was worried. He knew that his ten tribes would want to travel to the temple at certain times, as was the custom. And if his subjects felt that God's home was in Judah, wouldn't they eventually want to be ruled by the king of Judah instead? Jeroboam decided to set up two massive altars in his own country, at

Bethel and Dan, with a huge golden statue of a calf for each one. He appointed his own priests, with new prayer services and feast days. Then he appointed a new capital city for Israel, Samaria.

But in fact King Jeroboam need not have worried. The Hebrews in Judah were deserting the temple in droves and taking up pagan religions, which seemed to be much more fun. At pagan festivals the people ate and drank what they wanted, and danced with who they wanted – their gods didn't seem to mind at all. So statues of idols began to pop up all over Judah and their king did nothing to stop it.

For years, evil king followed evil king in both kingdoms. But Ahab, the sixth king of Israel, was one of the very worst. Ahab married Jezebel, the daughter of the king of Sidon, who worshipped the pagan god Baal. Jezebel persuaded Ahab to worship Baal too, and soon nearly all the Hebrews in Israel were worshipping Baal at a huge temple that Ahab built in Samaria.

> " *And Ahab did evil in the sight of the Lord more than all that were before him.* "

But not everyone abandoned God. The Lord called a faithful man named Elijah to take a message to King Ahab: "I am the God of Israel, whom you have forgotten. There will be no rain in the country until I say so."

The king just laughed. But before long, the weather got drier and drier. Ahab got angrier and angrier, and the Lord told Elijah to hide. Elijah headed east, as God instructed,

Jezebel
Jezebel was a Phoenician princess, married to King Ahab of Israel. When she arrived in Samaria, she continued to worship her native god, Baal. Jezebel encouraged her husband, his court and the whole of Israel to turn away from their God towards Baal. Ten years after Ahab died, Jezebel came to a violent end – she was thrown from the window of her palace by her servants, under the orders of King Jehu.

Elijah
The stories told in the Bible about the life of Elijah the prophet are mostly concerned with the clash between the worship of the God of Israel and that of Baal. Elijah has been compared with Moses and several elements of his life story support this comparison. For example, Elijah went to Mount Sinai, the holy place where Moses had spoken to God. He was also accompanied and succeeded by Elisha, just as Moses was by Joshua.

next day... and the next day... in fact, every day that Elijah was there. But despite the plentiful food, her son fell sick with a fever and, after several days, died.

"You say you're a man of God," she cried to Elijah. "Have I done anything wrong to deserve my son's death?" The prophet took the lifeless body to his own bed. He laid the boy down and knelt beside him. Three times Elijah cried out to God to give back the child's soul, and three times he listened for the child's heart to start beating again.

Soon, when Elijah carried the boy downstairs to his mother, he was alive.

until he reached the brook of Cherith. There, Elijah found a cave for shelter. The drought was so bad that there wasn't an animal or a blade of grass in sight. But the Lord didn't let Elijah go hungry. Morning and evening ravens arrived at the cave carrying meat and bread for him in their beaks. Then the brook dried up in the sweltering sun. "Go to Zarephath," came the Lord's voice. "There's a widow there who will look after you."

Sure enough, Elijah was taken in by a very poor widow who had only a handful of flour and a little oil left for herself and her son to eat. Nevertheless, she made Elijah a meal and resigned herself to starving to death. Yet the next day she was amazed to find that her flour jar and oil jug were full once again... and the

God the provider
This picture shows Elijah being fed by ravens. God demonstrates His superiority as He is able to provide for Elijah even in the heartland of Baal worship.

Samarian ivory
The building of Samaria was begun by King Omri and continued by his son, Ahab. This piece of ivory from the palace dates from the 9th century BC and shows the Egyptian god Horus.

> ❦ **ABOUT THE STORY** ❦
> *The reason why the people preferred Baal to the true God was that worshipping him was much easier and less demanding. However, the story of Elijah reminds readers that God always keeps a few people faithful to Himself and uses them to challenge others to return to Him. Believers may be few in number at times, but they are all very important to God's purposes.*

Elijah's Challenge

As God had commanded there had been no rain for three years. Elijah heard God telling him to go and find the furious King Ahab before Ahab found him. The king hated to obey Elijah, but he followed all his instructions: he needed the rain. He summoned the 450 priests of Baal and also the 400 priests of Asherah (Jezebel's other god) and ordered all his subjects to go to Mount Carmel.

The prophet was waiting for them. "The Lord God has brought this terrible drought upon Israel because you are sinning against Him and worshipping idols," Elijah told the king, sternly. "Let's settle this once and for all. I challenge your priests to a contest. Tell them to prepare a bull for sacrifice to their gods and I'll prepare another for sacrifice to the Lord. But no one must set either offering alight.

We'll all pray to our gods to miraculously light the fire themselves. And whoever has their prayer answered will obviously be worshipping the true god."

When everything was in place, Ahab and Jezebel's priests began to call upon Baal to light the offering. All morning they prayed, chanting themselves into a trance and dancing themselves mad. In their frenzy, they even slashed themselves with their sacrificial knives. But it was no use. Not a spark, not even a puff of smoke.

> **" *They raved on but there was no voice; no one answered, no one heeded.* "**

❧ ABOUT THE STORY ❧

Baal was said to be a god who controlled the weather and sent storms. So he already looked weak because there had been no rain. Then, when the fire (perhaps a lightning bolt) hit Elijah's sacrifice, it proved to everyone that Baal didn't really exist, but that the true God did. Elijah ordered the execution of the priests because they had led people away from God. This was a very serious offence in Israelite law.

Mount Carmel
This is a view down Mount Carmel, which is also the name given to a group of mountains in north-west Israel. It is believed to be the site of Elijah's contest with the prophets of Baal. In Bible times, it was covered in oak and olive groves.

Jezebel's seal
This picture shows a seal from the 9th-8th centuries BC. The name 'Jezebel' has been added in Phoenician letters. Jezebel was a Phoenician princess.

Elijah enjoyed watching the priests make fools of themselves. "Shout louder," he mocked. "Maybe your god is having a nap!" At midday the priests of Baal and Asherah gave up, exhausted. It was Elijah's turn. First Elijah took 12 large stones, one for each of the tribes of the Promised Land, and he rebuilt the altar to the Lord that had once stood at the top of Mount Carmel. He arranged the firewood and laid his bull on it, then he dug a deep trench all around. Elijah ordered the Israelites to fetch water and pour it over the altar. The astonished Israelites drenched the animal and the wood until the water filled the trench.

Then Elijah stood before the altar and prayed. The thousands of waiting men and women fell silent. "Lord, show these people that you are the one true God, and that I am your servant and have done everything at your command," the prophet called aloud. There was a mighty roar as the sodden heap burst into flame, and everything was burnt to ashes: not just the bull and the firewood, but the stones and the soil too! The terrified crowds were beaten back by the immense heat and fell to the ground to worship the one true God. Elijah pointed at the trembling priests of Baal and Asherah. "Kill them," he ordered. "Make sure not one of them escapes, for they have led you all into sin." At once the Israelites fell on the evil men.

King Ahab was enraged. But the prophet simply ordered him to calm down and have a meal.

Meanwhile, Elijah prayed while his servant watched the sky for rain. Suddenly Elijah's servant shouted out. "A little cloud as small as a man's hand is heading this way!"

"It is the rain," smiled Elijah. "Quick, Ahab! Get in your chariot and drive home before the storm overtakes you!" The king raced down the mountain as black thunder clouds chased him all the way to his royal city of Jezreel. As for Elijah, he was filled with the spirit of the Lord, and ran so fast that he beat the king back to the palace.

Fire from God
The illustration shows Elijah's sacrifice bursting into flames, while the prophet himself prays beside it. The sacrifice of the priests of Baal was not set alight.

Fleeing from the storm
In this picture, Ahab and Elijah are shown fleeing from the storm. Because the spirit of God came upon Elijah, he was able to run very fast and reached Jezreel before Ahab.

The Still Small Voice

WHEN King Ahab told Jezebel about Elijah's show of power on Mount Carmel, the queen turned purple. She shook with rage. She spat, she spluttered and finally exploded. "Find that trouble-making prophet!" she screamed at a messenger. "Tell him that by tomorrow he'll be in exactly the same place as my dead priests!"

In fear for his life, Elijah fled; first south into the kingdom of Judah and then into the desert. How depressed and worn out he was! All his efforts before the people at Mount Carmel had not been enough. He'd failed to turn the king and queen back to the Lord, and the Israelites would soon be back to worshipping their pagan idols once again. The prophet didn't have the will to go on any longer. He sank down under a broom tree. "Lord, I've had enough," he groaned. "Let me die right here." Exhausted, he fell into a deep, troubled sleep.

The touch of a gentle hand brought Elijah back to consciousness. Through his bleary eyes, he saw that the hand belonged to an angel, and at once the prophet was wide awake. "Get up now," the angel said, kindly. "You must be hungry." Elijah turned to look where the angel indicated and saw that a jug of fresh water stood next to some freshly baked loaves of bread. The smell was irresistible, and Elijah gratefully tucked in. With his stomach full and his mind much comforted, the prophet drifted off once more. But this time his dreams were easy. And when he awoke, the angel was there again. "Come and eat," came the soft voice, "or you won't be fit to make the journey." The journey that the angel wanted

Elijah to make was a long one – 40 days and 40 nights through the desert. But the special food and drink had revived Elijah more than he would ever have imagined, and he made it safely to Mount Horeb, the holy place where Moses himself had spoken to God. It was the perfect place to hide and wait for the Lord's instructions.

> ❝ *And behold, a voice said, 'What are you doing here, Elijah?'* ❞

Day after day Elijah sat inside a cave and wondered what would happen next. The prophet had totally lost track of time when he heard the Lord's voice calling him. It took him completely by surprise. "Elijah! Elijah!" God said. "What are you doing here?"

The prophet leapt to his feet and spoke aloud into the darkness. "Of all the people in Israel, only I remain faithful to you, Lord," Elijah called. "Because of this, they want to kill me."

"Go from this cave and stand outside on the mountain," God ordered.

Elijah had hardly stuck his nose out into the

open when the wind began to blow. First, a brisk breeze lifted the fallen leaves and swirled them around; then the wind howled into a gale that plucked trees out of the ground and ripped rocks from the mountainside and tossed them around like pebbles. And Elijah stood safe and unafraid with the hurricane roaring round him. He did not feel that God was in the wind.

Next, the ground underneath the prophet began to tremble... then to shake... then to shudder... and with a mighty crack, the mountain split in two. Elijah stood safe and unafraid on the heaving soil. He did not feel that God was in the earthquake.

All at once there was a blaze of flame and a rush of heat as every tree, plant and blade of grass caught fire. Elijah stood safe and unafraid while the flames licked all around him. He did not feel that God was in the inferno either.

Finally, the wind dropped, the earth juddered to a halt and the flames died away. Elijah was left alone in the silence of the mountainside. Then he heard a still, small voice speaking quite clearly into his mind – and he felt the Lord was there. Deeply afraid, he hid his face in his cloak and listened. "Go to Damascus in Syria and find two men: Hazael and Jehu. Anoint them as future kings: Hazael, king of Syria, and Jehu, king of Israel. They will wreak terrible destruction on King Ahab and his sinning subjects, and I will be avenged by them for the wrongs the Israelites have done me. When you have finished in Syria, go and find Elisha, the son of Shaphat. He is to be your assistant and will take over from you when your work for me is done. And do not be discouraged. There remain 7,000 people in Israel who have not worshipped Baal and who are true to me."

Elijah set off for Syria with renewed energy and hope. No matter how gloomy things looked, God had shown him that He was always there and would deal with things in His own good time. And with Elisha for a companion, Elijah would no longer have to face the sinning Israelite nation on his own.

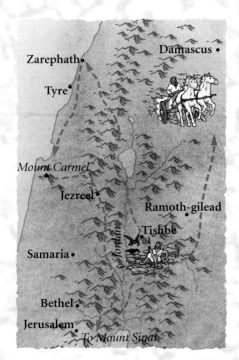

ELIJAH WAS UPSET WHEN HIS LIFE WAS THREATENED. HE PANICKED AND RAN AWAY. HE WAS VERY TIRED. PEOPLE MAKE BAD DECISIONS WHEN THEY ARE TIRED. WHAT THEY NEED TO DO IS STOP AND PRAY.

The journey of Elijah
Elijah travelled all over Israel to follow God's commands. He first heard God speak to him in Tishbe, and had his competition with the Baal prophets after going to Zarephath. He then fled to Mount Sinai, before going up to heaven on the chariot of fire.

❖ ABOUT THE STORY ❖

Elijah was used to seeing God act in spectacular ways. Wind represented His powerful Spirit, the earthquake was a sign of His judgement and fire was what He had spoken through on Mount Carmel. Elijah had to learn that God works in many different, quieter, ways too. God had quietly kept other people faithful to Himself, but Elijah had been too busy to notice.

Ahab Strikes a Deal

WHEN Ahab was king of Israel, the strongest nation in the region was Syria, under King Benhadad. Benhadad wanted to take Ahab's kingdom for himself. He gathered together his armies, marched into Israel, and soon reached Samaria. King Ahab's capital city was besieged; thousands of soldiers were ready to attack.

Ahab despaired. But a prophet arrived with a message from the Lord. "I will give these enemies into your hands. By this, you will know that I am the one true God. Send the servants of your district governors out to fight."

The king was mystified, but armed the 232 servants and pushed the shocked men outside the city walls to face the full might of the Syrian army.

Ahab couldn't believe his eyes. The servants hacked their way through the enemy lines. He sent reinforcements and soon Benhadad's men were either dead or scattered.

Ahab was overjoyed, but the prophet warned him that Benhadad had escaped and that Syria would attack again. Sure enough, in the spring, the Syrians appeared again. Once more the prophet told Ahab: "The Lord will again give you victory to prove He is the one true God."

By sunset, the smaller army of Israel had slain 100,000 Syrians. The stunned invaders tried to flee to the city of Aphek, but in the jostle to get through the gates the city wall collapsed, crushing many to death. King Benhadad was one of the lucky few who made it through. To try and escape with his life, the defeated king offered to return all the Israelite cities he had conquered, and let the Israelites trade with Syria. Ahab accepted, and the deal was sealed.

The Israelite king was triumphant, but a prophet gave him a grave message. "The Lord is angry with you for sparing this enemy," he said. "God will take your life instead of his, and your people instead of his." Ahab's heart sank, and he resented the word of the Lord.

❧ ABOUT THE STORY ❧

Nothing seems to be enough to convince Ahab that the Lord is all-powerful. Unconvinced by the contest on Mount Carmel, the Lord shows Ahab his power by helping him win two great victories against armies that were better trained and far outnumbered his own. Rather than humiliating Ahab in front of his own people the Lord helps him, but the king still does not accept the word of the Lord and remains completely unrepentant.

Syrian prince
This statue from around 800BC shows a Syrian prince, seated on a throne, with his feet on a footstool. He is armed with a dagger and wears a necklace with symbols of the sun and moon. It is possible that King Benhadad might have looked like this.

Trading places
In return for saving Benhadad's life, Ahab was allowed to set up trading places in Damascus. The jewellery being bought and sold there might have looked like these necklaces, made of gold, lapis lazuli and cornelian.

Naboth's Vineyard

IN Samaria, next door to King Ahab's palace, there was a beautiful vineyard which belonged to a man called Naboth. Every day the king would look out of his window and dream of the wonderful fruits and vegetables he would grow for himself if only he owned the fertile earth.

One day a royal messenger knocked on Naboth's door. "The king wants your vineyard," he said bluntly. "You can either swap it for any vineyard you want or the king will pay you good money for it."

Naboth pondered for a moment. "This land has belonged to my family for generations," he thought. "I wouldn't part with it for any sum of money, and besides, the Lord says that it's a sin to sell someone your birthright." Naboth looked at the messenger. "Tell the king he can't have my vineyard," he said firmly. "It's God's law that I can't part with it."

The king was extremely annoyed. He lay in his bedroom in a mood, refusing to eat anything. "Cheer up!" Jezebel laughed. "I'll get you the vineyard." The wicked queen wrote a letter to each of the elders in the city. She forged Ahab's name and sealed each letter with the king's royal seal. The plot was set.

Some weeks later there was a great ceremony in the public square. As Naboth stood on the platform in front of all the citizens, two men began to lie that they had heard him curse both God and the king. "Treason! Treason!" cried the corrupt elders and nobles, stirring up the crowd into a frenzy. And the innocent, bewildered Naboth was dragged outside the city and stoned to death.

The delighted king trotted off to claim the vineyard. However, as he strutted round it the prophet Elijah came striding up to him. "The price you have paid for this vineyard is your very soul," the furious prophet thundered. "Because of your crimes against the Lord, you and all of your family will be wiped out. The dogs will lick up your blood and the birds will peck at your bones."

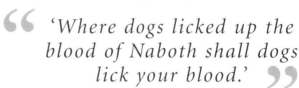

66 *'Where dogs licked up the blood of Naboth shall dogs lick your blood.'* 99

Ahab was terrified at the words of the great prophet. He wept and tore his clothes. He put on sackcloth and fasted, all to try and earn some mercy from God. When the Lord saw that Ahab was at last taking some notice of Him, He promised to show him a little mercy, but as for complete forgiveness – it was far too late for that.

Breaking the law
According to God's law, it was forbidden to sell land that had been inherited from one's ancestors. The picture above shows Ahab and Naboth in the vineyard.

Ahab's seal
This is a picture of Ahab's seal. It is a bronze ring and the inscription on it reads "Ahab, king of Israel". Jezebel would have used this seal to forge Ahab's signature on the letters she wrote.

❖ **ABOUT THE STORY** ❖

Ahab knew that the law said he couldn't take Naboth's vineyard. But Jezebel, who cared nothing for God's law, believed the king could do anything. But she knew that simply taking the vineyard would cause a riot, so she lied and murdered to get it. The Bible has many stories about people who misused their power, and shows that God's law is to be obeyed by everyone, however famous, rich or powerful they are.

The Death of Ahab

IT didn't take long for Elijah's prophecies of disaster to start striking the royal family. And it was King Ahab himself who met his doom first. The king of Israel had become friendly with his rival, King Jehoshaphat of Judah. Ahab suggested that he and Jehoshaphat should together attack Syria to win back the city of Ramoth-gilead, which was in the hands of King Benhadad. "What do you think?" Ahab asked the king of Judah. "You can consider my forces your own," Jehoshaphat assured him. "Only let's first consult the Lord about this plan."

King Ahab called all the prophets in Israel to the palace. "We want to know whether we should fight the Syrians for Ramoth-gilead," King Ahab said. The prophets all agreed. "The Lord says yes..." said some. "The Lord will give you victory..." urged yet more. One of them, Zedekiah, even approached the thrones wearing a horned battle helmet! But for some reason, Ahab felt uneasy about the prophets' enthusiasm. He looked around the room. Someone was missing.

"Where's Micaiah?" the king said slowly. "Bring him here at once." Ahab explained why to Jehoshaphat. "Micaiah is a troublesome prophet," he sighed. "He never tells me what I want to hear. But because of this, I tend to believe him more than the rest. They just seem to agree with everything I say."

When Micaiah arrived, he at first went along with the other prophets.

Preserved armour
This coat of mail found at Nuzi, in Iraq, dates from around 1400BC and is made of overlapping bronze scales. This is the sort of armour Ahab would have worn.

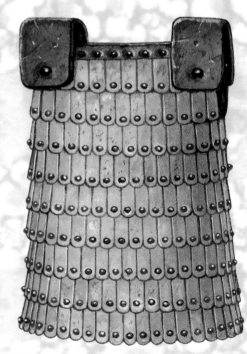

Coat of mail
Coats of mail were worn by archers who were unable to protect themselves with shields. They were more protective than leather armour and lighter than plate armour. Their weak point was the joints of the sleeves, which is probably where the arrow that killed Ahab entered.

❧ ABOUT THE STORY ❧

This story shows how weak Ahab was. He knew Micaiah told the truth, but he was afraid to call the battle off – after all, he had suggested it himself. As a result, he lost his life and Israel and Judah lost the battle. The point of the story is that it is better to lose face and listen to God than to ignore God and bring trouble on oneself and others.

"Go and triumph," he told the king, "God will grant you victory." But Ahab looked him in the eye.

"Come now, Micaiah," he insisted. "Tell me the truth."

Just as Ahab feared, Micaiah then prophesied doom and gloom. "I have seen all Israel scattered upon the mountains like sheep with no shepherd," he began.

Ahab groaned and turned to Jehoshaphat. "You see, I told you so. He never has a good word to say for me."

Micaiah continued, "I saw the Lord in heaven, wondering how He could persuade you to attack the Syrians. One of the angels said He'd put lies in the mouths of your prophets so they'd advise you to go to battle."

Zedekiah flew into a fury. He struck Micaiah across the face. "How dare you say that God lies to us and yet speaks truthfully through you?"

"You'll see that I'm right on the day that you run and hide in the face of defeat," Micaiah answered.

At the mention of the word "defeat", King Ahab decided he'd listened to quite enough. "Arrest this man!" he cried to his guards. "Keep him in prison on bread and water until I return victorious and decide what to do with him."

Micaiah remained completely unruffled. "If you return victorious, my name's not Micaiah," he said calmly.

Despite the Israelite king's outward show of confidence, he was inwardly very worried by Micaiah's words. Ahab let Jehoshaphat go into battle dressed in his king's robes and riding in his royal chariot, while he disguised himself as an ordinary soldier. Benhadad of Syria had ordered his chariot regiment to attack no one but the king of Israel, and they nearly killed Jehoshaphat by mistake, thinking that he was Ahab.

However, one of Benhadad's archers, firing at random, delivered the king of Israel's mortal wound. An arrow pierced a chink between the plates of metal and embedded itself deep in his flesh. A faithful horseman carried the wounded king out of the fighting, and all day he lay in his chariot, watching his troops being slaughtered. After sweltering and bleeding all day in the hot sun, that evening King Ahab died and his troops disbanded and fled.

> ❝ *They washed the chariot by the pool of Samaria, and the dogs licked up his blood.* ❞

Ahab's body was taken home to Samaria and buried there. But it was at a spot near to where Naboth had been stoned to death that his chariot was washed clean. And as Ahab's blood streamed out of the chariot floor, stray dogs came and licked it up, just as Elijah had said they would.

Micaiah
Micaiah was a prophet during Ahab's reign. Apart from this story of his meeting with the king, little else is known about him. He may have been brought out of prison to prophesy in this case. He had obviously prophesied regularly before as Ahab was already aware of his gloomy, but truthful and accurate, predictions.

Cleaning the chariot
The above picture shows people cleaning out Ahab's chariot after his death. The blood is being licked up by stray dogs, fulfilling Elijah's prophecy.

Elijah's Chariot of Fire

ELIJAH sighed. He had to go on a journey, and he knew it would be his last. "God is sending me to Bethel," he told his assistant, Elisha. "Don't come with me. I won't need you this time." But Elisha sensed what lay behind his master's words and he insisted on keeping Elijah company.

When the two companions reached the far-off town, Elisha found out that he wasn't the only one who knew what was about to happen. The prophets living at Bethel whispered to him worriedly. "Do you know that the Lord is going to take Elijah from us?" they gasped.

"Yes, I know," Elisha reassured them. "Keep it to yourselves." And he hurried back to his master.

"Why don't you stay here, Elisha?" the older prophet urged. "The Lord has told me that I've got to go further on, to Jericho."

"You're not getting rid of me that easily," smiled the young man, striding out determinedly.

They drew near to Jericho and saw the prophets of the city waiting for them. Once again, Elisha was beckoned aside. "The Lord is going to..." they began.

"Hush, now," interrupted Elisha. "I know. Now try to keep it quiet." And he dashed back to his master.

"Honestly, Elisha," insisted the older prophet, "I really think you should stay here. God now says that I've got to go all the way to the River Jordan."

"As long as the Lord's above and you're alive down here, I'll never leave you," said the faithful young man. And the companions went on down the road, followed by a group of about 50 prophets, who hung back nervously.

Elijah and Elisha reached the Jordan. Elijah took off his cloak, rolled it up and struck the waters with it. The river parted, leaving a dry path. The two men crossed without even getting their feet wet.

Then Elijah turned to Elisha and smiled sadly. "You know that I'm going to be taken from you," he said. "Is there anything you'd like to ask me or do for you?"

"Master," Elisha said, "I need a double share of your spirit in order to do your job."

Crossing the Jordan
The crossing of the River Jordan that Elijah and Elisha made reminds us of the miracle that Moses performed when he parted the waves of the Red Sea. When Elisha also performed the same miracle, it showed that he had indeed taken over from Elijah.

❧ ABOUT THE STORY ❧

This great vision was God's way of telling Elisha that he was called to a very special job, carrying on the work that Elijah had started. Elijah wasn't able to promise the "double share" of his power, because only God could give that, but he believed God would answer Elisha's prayer. There was nothing magical about Elijah's cloak, but it is symbolic of the fact that Elisha is taking over Elijah's role.

Elijah shook his head. "That's something I can't promise to give you," he replied. "However, if God allows you to see me taken up to heaven then I'm sure He will give you what you ask."

Elisha saw everything. It started as a glimmer in the sky that swirled and glowed until it became a flaming chariot drawn by horses of fire that landed between them. Elisha watched in awe as Elijah got in and raised one hand in farewell. Then the horses began to gallop in circles until everything was a blazing whirlwind. The chariot rushed upwards and was gone.

> ## *Behold, a chariot of fire and horses of fire separated the two of them.*

Elisha knew that he'd never see his master again and began to mourn. Then he noticed Elijah's cloak lying on the ground. Rolling up the cloak, he cried aloud, "Where is the God of Elijah?" He struck the waters of the River Jordan and once more the river parted to let him through.

When the 50 prophets saw Elisha's miracle, they knew that the spirit of Elijah had come on him, and they bowed down before him. But they found it hard to accept that the great prophet was really gone. "May we go and look for Elijah?" they begged. Elisha was reluctant to let them go, but realized they hadn't seen what he had seen.

After three days of searching, the prophets returned. They knew in their hearts that Elijah was in heaven and wouldn't be coming back.

A first-born son
Elisha is not being greedy or arrogant when he asks Elijah for a "double share". A first-born son usually inherited a double portion of a parent's estate, so it is more that Elisha wants to be recognized as Elijah's spiritual heir.

Elisha, Elijah and the prophets
The Bible tells us that a group of prophets followed Elijah and Elisha round the country. The "prophets" in this case are not the same as Elijah and Elisha. They are people who try to live good lives, but God does not speak directly to them.

Elisha and the Women

ELISHA travelled and spread the word of God, working many miracles that established his reputation as a great prophet.

In Jericho, he purified the foul-tasting water that gushed from the city's main spring.

Elisha also helped a woman so poor that she had only a single jar of oil. She was deep in debt, and her creditor was about to take her children into slavery as settlement. Elisha told her to borrow empty jars and begin pouring her own oil into them. To her astonishment, as long as there were jars to be filled, the oil kept flowing. She had more than enough oil to sell to pay off her debts.

In Shunem, a rich woman made Elisha and his servant, Gehazi, welcome in her house. The prophet wondered how he could repay her kindness. Then Gehazi mentioned that the wealthy couple didn't have a child. "This time next year, you will have a son," Elisha told them. And to the couple's great joy, they did.

Some years later, Elisha was praying at Mount Carmel with Gehazi when the woman came hurrying up, weeping her heart out. "My son is dead!" she sobbed. "He was brought home this morning with a bad headache and by lunchtime he was lifeless in my arms! You're a holy man, please do something!" At once, Elisha hurried to the woman's home.

> **❝** *As he stretched himself upon him, the flesh of the child became warm.* **❞**

When they got there, Elisha quietly shut the door to the dead child's room and prayed. Then he stretched his hands out over the small, stiff body. Elisha sensed his skin gradually warming up and felt gentle breath on his face. "A-choo!" the child sneezed. "A-choo! A-choo!" God had answered the great prophet's prayers to bring the dead boy back to life.

Oil jar
The Bible refers to the use of oil a great deal, and it usually refers to olive oil. Oil was used for cooking as much in Elisha's time at it is now, but it was also an offering to God, used for trade and as fuel for lamps.

MIRACULOUS STORIES OF PROPHETS HEALING THE FAITHFUL REMIND US THAT GOD PROTECTS HIS PEOPLE. THESE STORIES ENCOURAGE FAITH WHEN TIMES ARE HARD. ❧

The widow's oil
This is an illustration of the story based on a picture in a 13th-century Spanish Bible. Many Bibles throughout history have been very lavishly illustrated, not only with pictures but with decorated letters.

Naaman the Leper General

WHEN the Syrians took some of the Israelites captive, they heard the amazing stories of Elisha. The general of the Syrian army, Naaman, was particularly interested. He had leprosy, a terrible skin disease. His wife's Israelite maid was sure that Elisha would be able to cure him, so Naaman asked the king if he could go to find the prophet.

> *He was a mighty man of valour, but he was a leper.*

When Naaman and his royal entourage arrived at Elisha's house, Naaman was annoyed to find that the prophet wouldn't come out but sent a servant instead. "Elisha says to tell you to bathe seven times in the River Jordan," Gehazi said. "Goodbye." And he shut the door.

Naaman was furious. He'd come all this way to see the holy man, and he'd brought magnificent gifts, too: sacks of silver, bags of gold and ten very expensive robes. "All Elisha had to do was pray a bit!" he raged. "If it's just a matter of washing, we've got better rivers back at home!" Humiliated, he was about to head straight back to Syria, when one of his attendants stopped him.

"Sir, you've nothing to lose," he said. "You've come all the way here, and it's an easy thing to do. Why not try?"

Once... twice... three times Naaman washed himself in the Jordan. The sores were there just the same. Four... five... six – nothing. But as he rose from the waters for the seventh time, he knew something was different. He looked down and saw that his skin was as smooth as a child's.

Naaman jumped for joy, then ran to thank Elisha. "Now I know that your God is the true God," he said. "May I take some earth to worship him when I return home?"

"Of course," said the delighted prophet, but he wouldn't accept a single gift that Naaman tried to press upon him.

When Naaman had left, Elisha noticed that Gehazi was missing. Instantly, he knew his servant had gone to tell Naaman that his master had changed his mind about the gifts, so he could take them for himself.

When Gehazi returned the prophet knew what he had done and was unforgiving. "Now you have Naaman's wealth, you can have his leprosy too," Elisha thundered, and the horrified servant felt his skin begin to bubble.

Aramean architecture
The Syrians were known at this time as "Arameans", and Syria was called "Aram." The picture shows the base of a column from an Aramean palace. The sphinx is a mythical animal that is seen in art and architecture all over the world. Solomon had sphinxes, called cherubim in Israel, in the temple he built at Jerusalem.

Earth from Israel
At this time people believed that a god could only be worshipped on their "home" land. In order to carry on worshipping God, Naaman asks Elisha if he can take some of the earth of the Promised Land home with him to make a holy place in Syria.

> ❖ **ABOUT THE STORY** ❖
>
> *It was important that Elisha and Gehazi did not take any gifts, because Naaman needed to learn that God does not do things for people just because they are generous. God's love, forgiveness and help cannot be bought. The healing is an example of what the Bible calls grace – God's undeserved and unearned kindness. This story reminds us that God loves everyone, including those we consider to be enemies.*

Saved from the Syrians

THE king of Israel relied on Elisha to help him with the continuing Syrian attacks. The prophet sent detailed warnings to the palace, outlining the Syrians' battle plans. He'd tell the king exactly where and when the Syrians would hit next, so the Israelites were always ready.

The Syrian king grew frustrated. "It's as if the king of Israel can read my mind!" he raged.

"Elisha the prophet knows the secrets you whisper in your bedchamber," his servants replied. "It's he who tells the king."

"He has to be stopped!" the king roared. "Where is he?"

"In the Israelite city of Dothan," came the answer.

"Go there at once and seize him," the king bellowed.

In Dothan, Elisha's servant woke up and flung open the door. "Master, master, look!" he screamed. "The Syrian army is right here, in Dothan!"

Stretching into the distance were gleaming chariots and armoured men. "Never mind," he reassured Gehazi. "There are more of us than there are of them." Elisha prayed, and Gehazi could see chariots and horses of fire all around their house. Then Elisha prayed again. "Lord, please strike the Syrians blind – just temporarily." And he set off down to the Syrian camp.

Samaria
This piece of ivory furniture from Samaria is decorated with a carving of a lion fighting with a bull. The city was besieged and captured by the Assyrians in 722BC and this signalled the end of the northern kingdom of Israel.

Siege craft
During a siege, the attacking army surrounded the city. The army would try to cut off supplies of food and force the inhabitants to surrender.

The blinded Syrians were stumbling about, terrified. When Elisha arrived and told them to follow him, they were only too pleased to hear someone who seemed to know what was going on, and they marched on until Elisha told them to stop. There was a short silence while he prayed, and then suddenly the soldiers found they could see again. To their horror they found they were in Samaria, the capital city of Israel.

The King of Israel was just as confused as the troops. "What shall I do?" he asked Elisha. "Shall I kill them?"

> ❝ *The king said to Elisha, 'My father, shall I slay them?'* ❞

"No," laughed the prophet. "Show how great you are by giving them a huge feast and then sending them all home."

After that the Syrians didn't attack Israel again for a long time. But eventually King Benhadad decided to lay siege to Samaria and starve the Israelites into defeat so he surrounded the city. No one could get in or out. Traders and merchants bringing food and wine to the city were turned away, and people got hungrier and hungrier.

Inside Samaria, things grew desperate. The people would eat anything – weeds, mice, beetles. Each day the Israelite king walked around the city walls. When he even saw people arguing over eating each other, he stormed off to Elisha. "Your God has done this to us!" he yelled.

"Tomorrow there will be plenty of food on sale in this city, and all at the right price," Elisha yelled back. "Trust me." Then he began to pray.

Later that night, four starving lepers sneaked out of the city to the Syrian camp. They were dying anyway, so weren't risking much by asking the enemy for food. But they couldn't see a soul or hear a sound. The camp was deserted.

The Lord had filled the ears of every soldier in the camp with the sound of a mighty army on the move. Thinking that a huge army of Israelite reinforcements was heading straight for them, the panicking soldiers hadn't hung about to strike camp. They had just fled, leaving everything exactly where it was.

The lepers went wild, dashing from one storehouse to the next, shoving food into their mouths, cramming it into their pockets, running off and hiding it. Then they thought they'd better go and tell the king. And the next day, food was on sale in Samaria just as Elisha had said – more than enough for everyone.

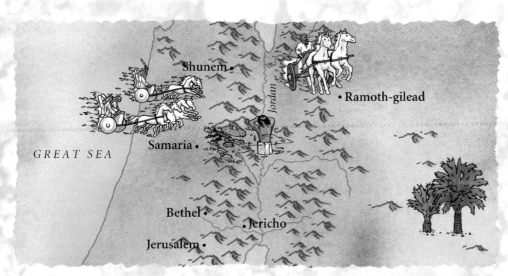

The journeys of Elisha
After Elisha witnessed Elijah being carried to heaven by the flaming chariot, he travelled around a great deal, but he spent a lot of time in Samaria. In the capital city of Israel he brought God's message to the kings and people. It was near Samaria that Elisha's servant saw the vision of the heavenly army.

❖ About the Story ❖

In the days of Elisha there were far fewer maps. Most people who travelled had little idea what the places they were aiming for looked like. The roads were mostly tracks and there were no signposts. So the Syrians were blind in the sense that they were lost! Also, they didn't really know what Elisha looked like – there were no photographs – so they didn't recognize him. They hardly expected their enemy to walk up and introduce himself!

Jehu the Avenger

A commander in the Israelite army called Jehu was sitting in the officers' room one day when a messenger came from Elisha, asking to talk to him in private. Jehu took the rather agitated man out of the room. The man took out a bottle of sacred oil and said, "I anoint you king of Israel. You will strike down every last one of the royal family belonging to King Ahab, fulfilling the great Elijah's prophecy." Then he dashed away.

Now Jehu knew that King Joram of Israel, Ahab's son, lay very ill in bed, but he certainly wasn't dead yet. And why ever would he, Jehu, be chosen as the next king?

"Is everything all right?" his friends asked, as he returned pale-faced to the mess.

"Yes, everything's fine," Jehu replied, his mind obviously elsewhere.

"So why did that mad fellow come to see you then?" the other officers began. They pressed him so hard to find out what had happened, that eventually Jehu gave in and told them. Roaring with delight, they laid their cloaks down so Jehu wouldn't have to get his feet dirty, and took him out to show the other soldiers. They trumpeted loud fanfares to proclaim Jehu their new ruler, then raced off to get rid of King Joram.

The king's guard on the watchtower in Jezreel looked down and saw a group of charioteers in the distance, speeding towards the city in a cloud of dust. The racing chariots showed no sign of slowing, and the lookout soldiers guessed that Jehu was at their head – he was well

known for driving everywhere at top speed.

King Joram realized that if one of his highest-ranking officers was dashing to see him, it must be serious; and he raised himself up out of his sick bed to go out and meet him.

"You're too ill to go alone," said Joram's nephew, King Ahaziah of Judah, who had come to visit his sick uncle. "I insist on coming too."

Joram was too weak to argue. "Prepare our royal chariots," he croaked to his servants, as he staggered out on Ahaziah's arm.

Face to face the chariots thundered nearer and nearer. When they were within shouting distance, King Joram gathered his remaining strength and yelled, "Do you come in peace, Jehu?"

"How can I come in peace," came the reply, "when your mother, Queen Jezebel, is worshipping idols, practising black magic and leading our whole country into sin?"

Joram's heart began to pound. "Treachery, Ahaziah!" he cried, and the two kings wheeled their chariots back in the direction of the palace. But it was too late. Jehu reined his horses to a halt, drew his bow and fired an arrow that pierced Joram right between the shoulder blades. The king sank down dead in his chariot and his driverless horses careered over the bumpy ground. Jehu paused just long enough to order his men to catch the chariot and fling Joram's body on to the ground, abandoning it to the birds and the

beasts. Then he pursued the fleeing king of Judah and shot him dead, too.

Next, Jehu turned back to the city of Jezreel. Queen Jezebel was waiting for him at the palace, adorned in her finest regalia and hanging over the balcony, screaming insults. Jehu looked up at the trembling servants who stood next to her. "Are you with me?" he shouted. The men didn't hesitate to please their new king. They grabbed hold of the queen and hurled her out of the window.

Jehu had had a busy day. He strode into the palace and instructed the servants to prepare him something to eat and drink. He rested and ate his meal, recovering from his exertions. By the time he felt refreshed enough to get round to ordering the servants to clear away the queen's body, stray dogs had eaten her and there was nothing left.

> " *Jehu slew all that remained of the house of Ahab in Jezreel.* "

The avenging king's work wasn't over. During the months that followed, he ordered his officers to bring him the heads of all of Ahab's 70 other sons. Then he laid plans to kill all Ahab's counsellors, friends and priests. Finally, the whole of King Ahab's house lay dead, just as Elijah had prophesied.

Face at the window
This ivory carving is believed by some to be Jezebel looking out of her palace at Jezreel.

J EHU WAS FOLLOWING GOD'S ORDERS WHEN HE WENT OUT AND TOOK REVENGE ON AHAB'S FAMILY FOR ALL THE WRONG THEY HAD DONE. IT IS NATURAL FOR PEOPLE TO FEEL ANGRY ABOUT THOSE WHO DO WRONG. THE NEW TESTAMENT SAYS THAT FOLLOWERS OF JESUS ARE NOT TO TAKE REVENGE LIKE THIS. THERE'S A BETTER BUT MUCH HARDER WAY TO RID THE WORLD OF EVIL: BY LOVING OUR ENEMIES.

❧ ABOUT THE STORY ❧

This bloodthirsty story comes from a time in history when there was not the kind of legal and police system we have today. People who were wronged had to take revenge themselves. Ahab and Jezebel broke God's law so blatantly that God took His revenge through Jehu, and there was no way he could be stopped. This story shows that Ahab and his supporters got what they deserved in the end.

The End of Israel

KING Benhadad of Syria was ill – so ill that he thought he might be dying. He remembered how the Israelite prophet Elisha had cured Naaman of leprosy, and told his servant, Hazael, to ask him if it was God's will that he should recover, too.

Elisha knew just why Hazael had come. "You can tell your king that he will get better," the prophet said, "but God has told me that he's going to die." Hazael was more than a little confused by this answer, but he didn't question it because Elisha was staring at him so strangely. Then the prophet began to weep. "I am grieving because you will bring great suffering to Israel," Elisha explained. "You will set on fire our fortresses, slay our men, batter our women to death and crush our children."

Hazael was appalled. "What am I, a wild animal?".

"You are to be the next king of Syria," Elisha said quietly.

On the long journey back to Damascus, Hazael had plenty of time to think about what the prophet had said. The day after he returned, he took a blanket and suffocated Benhadad while he slept. Then he took the throne for himself.

Meanwhile, in Israel, King Jehu was busy putting right the wrongs of King Ahab and his son King Joram. He did his best to wipe out the worship of Baal and other pagan gods from his land, directing his subjects back to the Lord. But he didn't go quite far enough. He allowed King Jeroboam's two golden calves to remain on their altars at Bethel and Dan. And the Lord began to punish Israel, using the king of Syria to do so. Hazael continually attacked Israel and took more and more land. When Jehu and Hazael died, their sons carried on in their footsteps. Jehu's son Jehoahaz continued the worship of the calves at Bethel and Dan, and angered the Lord still further. In turn, God continued to give Hazael's son military success. The king of Syria slaughtered so many of Jehoahaz's

❧ ABOUT THE STORY ❧

The fall of Israel was a very sad event. The ten northern tribes were never re-united. The Bible writers say that this last defeat was God's punishment for the nation's refusal to worship Him alone, and for people's desire to follow wrong religious practices.
The end was a long time coming, however; God had warned them for several centuries. This story shows that God is a judge, but that He is also very patient.

Bowing to the king
This limestone relief shows Jehu, or one of the ambassadors of the king, bowing down in front of the conquering King Shalmaneser, which was the usual gesture of defeat. Behind the kneeling figure, Israelite attendants carry the gifts requested by Shalmaneser. The stone dates from around 840BC and originally stood at Nimrud in Assyria.

Winged sphinx
This statue of a winged sphinx was a common image in Assyrian art. Statues like this were put at the gates of their palaces as they believed they had the power to ward off evil spirits.

troops that in the end there were no more than 10,000 foot soldiers, 50 horsemen and 10 chariots left in the Israelite army. By the time King Jehoahaz died, the whole land of Israel was very nearly destroyed by the might of the Syrian army.

It was left to Jehoahaz's son, King Jehoash, to fight back. By now Elisha was a very old man. As he lay dying, he called Jehoash to him for the last time. "Take a bow and arrows and open the window to the east," the frail prophet asked Jehoash. Then Elisha laid his hands over the king's hands and told him to shoot an arrow out of the window in the direction of Syria. "That is the Lord's arrow of victory, the victory you shall have over your enemy," the holy man told him. "Now take the other arrows and strike the floor with them." Jehoash hit them on the floor three times. Elisha's face fell. "You should have struck more times, for then you would have defeated Syria completely," he told the king. "Now you will win only three battles." Nevertheless, these three battles were enough to recover several Israelite cities and keep the Syrians at bay.

Over the years that followed, the Israelites fell back into worshipping pagan gods and ignoring the Lord. Weird idols and strange altars reappeared all over the countryside, with all sorts of seances, black magic and even human sacrifice taking place. And the Lord made sure that each Israelite king had an increasingly hard struggle to hold on to his lands.

> " *So Israel was exiled from their own land to Assyria.* "

At the same time, a greater threat than Syria was rising: the cruel, merciless Assyrian Empire. They conquered country after country, and soon the Assyrian King Shalmaneser turned his eyes towards the Promised Land. Shalmaneser said he would leave Israel alone as long as King Hoshea, the last king of Israel, paid the Assyrians a vast amount of gold and silver each year. The desperate Hoshea sent messengers to Egypt begging for help, but Shalmaneser heard of his plot and the vast Assyrian army swooped down to lay siege to Samaria. The capital city was besieged for three nightmarish years before it finally fell. The kingdom of Israel was no more.

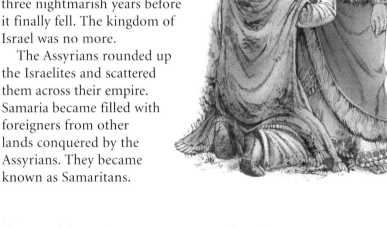

The Assyrians rounded up the Israelites and scattered them across their empire. Samaria became filled with foreigners from other lands conquered by the Assyrians. They became known as Samaritans.

Idol worship
The Samarian golden calves were set up by Jeroboam, the first king of the divided Israel, to try to stop his subjects going to the temple in Jerusalem to worship.

Assyrian Empire
The Assyrian Empire, at its height, stretched across the whole of the 'fertile crescent'. This is a crescent-shaped area of land that is very good for growing all kinds of crops. The crescent followed the routes of the three great rivers of the area: the river Nile in Egypt, and the rivers Tigris and Euphrates in present-day Iraq.

Kings of Judah

WHEN Jehu the avenger killed King Ahaziah it left the kingdom of Judah without a ruler. The king's mother, Athaliah, wanted to be queen. So she set about killing everyone else in the royal family. Soon, Athaliah ruled unchallenged over Judah – or so she thought. For an heir still remained. Ahaziah's sister had smuggled one of his sons, Joash, into the temple in Jerusalem, where her husband, Jehoiada, was high priest. There the little boy grew up unharmed, while his grandmother wreaked havoc as queen.

When Prince Joash was seven years old, Jehoiada

told his secret to the senior army officers and some elders of Judah. Under heavy guard, the young boy was crowned the new king of Judah.

"Treason!" Athaliah cried, when she saw her subjects bowing to the child. Jehoiada told the guards to take her out of the temple, and they killed her in her own home.

At first Joash was a good king who loved the Lord. He was upset that the temple built by Solomon had fallen into disrepair, so he set up a collection box for donations of money to restore the building. But when the high priest died, evil officials talked Joash into worshipping pagan idols. The king even sent money from the temple fund to King Hazael of Syria, to pay him not to attack. Prophets warned the king that his sins would bring Judah down, but he refused to listen. Once, Jehoiada's son, Zechariah, climbed to the top of the temple and began preaching. "Why have you all forsaken the Lord?" Zechariah shouted. "God says that because you've abandoned Him, He's going to abandon you."

Leprosy
This picture shows King Uzziah in the temple, burning incense on an incense altar. For this sin, he was struck down with leprosy. Today, leprosy is known as a contagious disease that affects the skin, the inside of the mouth and the nerves. The Hebrew word for leprosy is less specific. Some of the features of leprosy described in the Bible do not occur in the disease that we call leprosy today.

Household gods
This is a statue of an Assyrian god called Lahmu, which means 'the hairy one'. Lahmu was one of the household gods who guarded homes and kept out evil spirits. The Assyrians put figures of these gods under the floors of their houses. Lahmu is just one example of the pagan gods the Judeans turned to at this time.

The crowds began to drag Zechariah down. King Joash chose not to call a stop to the riot. Instead, he watched as the prophet was beaten to death. The king went to check he was really dead. Zechariah's eyes suddenly opened. "May the Lord see and avenge!" he whispered.

That year the Syrians attacked Jerusalem. They slaughtered many people and plundered the capital. Joash was killed by his own men. They knew that he had brought the trouble upon them.

Under Joash's son, King Amaziah, the country went from bad to worse. He worshipped pagan idols as well as the Lord. And instead of attacking Syria, he turned on his neighbour, Israel. As God's punishment, Judah was defeated and Amaziah captured. The wall of Jerusalem was broken and the treasures in the temple seized.

Amaziah's son, King Uzziah, determined to do better. He worshipped only God, and the Lord helped his army win many victories over his enemies. But success went to his head and Uzziah grew arrogant. When he tried to burn incense in the temple, a job only priests were allowed to do, the Lord punished him by striking him with leprosy.

> *And the Lord smote the king, so that he was a leper to the day of his death.*

Uzziah's grandson, Ahaz, was the worst king of all. He abandoned all pretence of worshipping the Lord and turned openly to worshipping the pagan gods. He worshipped idols and even burned his own son alive as a sacrifice. He smashed all the holy objects in the great temple in Jerusalem and replaced the great altar with a pagan one, then he eventually locked its doors forever.

God was furious. First He allowed the king of Syria to march into Judah and take hundreds of captives back with him into Damascus. Then He let the king of Israel massacre Judah's army and return to Samaria with over 200,000 prisoners. Other tribes in the Promised Land such as the Edomites and the Philistines took towns and villages in Judah. Eventually Ahaz found himself facing the might of the ruthless Assyrian King Tiglath-Pileser.

❖ ABOUT THE STORY ❖

The kings of Judah had a great advantage over the kings of Israel – the temple was in their capital to remind them of God and His laws. But even good kings were weak, led astray by their officials and forgetting that God had helped them succeed. These stories are in the Bible to show how important it is for leaders to live in God's ways. When they don't, the whole country suffers.

King Tiglath-Pileser
This stone relief from Nimrud in Assyria shows King Tiglath-Pileser standing in his chariot with a driver and an attendant. The relief dates from around 740BC.

Damascus
The kingdoms of Israel and Judah were often attacked by the Syrians, and many of their treasures ended up in Damascus, the Syrian capital. This picture shows goods for sale in modern-day Damascus.

Isaiah Shows the Way

In the year that King Uzziah died, the prophet Isaiah had a vision in the temple. He saw the Lord sitting on a throne. Above Him were angels called seraphim who sang a beautiful song in praise of God:

"Holy, holy, holy is the Lord of hosts, The whole earth is full of His glory." The temple trembled and was filled with clouds of smoke.

> ❝ *'Holy, holy, holy is the Lord of hosts.'* ❞

"Help!" cried Isaiah. "I have seen the King, the Lord of hosts. How can I live with being the sinning, flawed person I was before?"

One of the seraphim flew to the prophet, touching his lips with a burning coal that he'd taken from the altar. "Your sins have been forgiven," the angel told him.

Then came a voice that made Isaiah's heart leap. "Who is there that will take my message for me?" God asked.

Without a moment's hesitation, the eager prophet sprang to his feet. "Here I am, Lord!" he cried. "Send me."

"Then go and speak to my people," said the Lord. "But you will find they will not listen or understand till they have been scattered far from the Promised Land."

God spoke to the prophet throughout his lifetime. He spoke of trouble, but also of great hope. "For to us a child is born," Isaiah said, joyfully, "to us a son is given." He was speaking of the coming Messiah, Saviour of the world.

Seraph
A seraph has six wings, two to fly, and a pair each to cover its face and feet. The task of the seraphim Isaiah saw was to guard the throne of God.

Isaiah's vision revealed God's holiness – His perfection. Bible writers tell us that God can never do wrong, and that we are to try to become like God, holy in speech and conduct.

Isaiah
Isaiah was a prophet who lived in Jerusalem in the 8th century BC. He prophesied during the reigns of several kings, from Uzziah to Hezekiah. Most of his prophecies concentrated on the futures of Judah and Jerusalem. Isaiah is important as the prophet who foretold the coming of the Messiah, the Saviour of the Jewish people.

King Hezekiah the Good

JUDAH had held out against the Assyrians for 20 years after Israel had been conquered. God was rewarding Judah's good king, Hezekiah, who had destroyed all the pagan altars and kept the Lord's laws. Then the Assyrian king, Sennacherib finally attacked. Hezekiah was afraid and offered Sennacherib all his gold and silver to keep out of Jerusalem. Hezekiah even had to strip the temple itself in order to make the payment. But the ruthless Assyrian went back on his word and marched on Jerusalem anyway.

Sennacherib's spokesman tried to talk the citizens into surrendering, speaking in Hebrew, to make sure that everyone understood. "Hezekiah may say that your God will save you, but no nation has been saved from the Assyrians by their god. Make peace instead," he shouted.

The king told his subjects not to listen to the Assyrian lies, and went to the temple to pray. "Don't worry," Isaiah told him. "The Assyrians will never be allowed to enter Jerusalem, for it is God's city and he will certainly defend it."

That night, the Lord sent an angel over the Assyrian camp, and many of Sennacherib's troops died. Then news came that the African country of Ethiopia had suddenly attacked Assyria and the king was needed back home. And on returning to his capital, Nineveh, Sennacherib was murdered by his sons.

The saving of Jerusalem was not the only miracle God worked for the good Hezekiah. Once, when the king was very ill and was near death, he begged the Lord to repay his faithfulness with a little more life. Isaiah brought the news that his prayers had been answered, God was granting him 15 more years of life.

But no matter how hard the king tried not to sin, he could not lead a blameless life. Years later, when the king of Babylon's son came to visit, Hezekiah proudly boasted about all the treasures he once again possessed. He showed the pagan prince every single precious gem, piece of gold and chest of spice he owned.

Isaiah was not pleased. "God says the time will come when all you have shown to this prince will be carried off to his kingdom," he prophesied, "and your sons will be servants in the Babylonian king's palace."

God's angel of death
This medieval-style picture shows an angel flying over the Assyrian camp, striking the soldiers dead. God sent the angel to save the king of Judah, Hezekiah, because he had been a faithful worshipper of God.

❧ ABOUT THE STORY ❧

This story shows that God is completely fair and just in every possible way. When Hezekiah most needs the care and support of the Lord, God is there for him, and is able to give him as much extra life as He wishes, to reward Hezekiah for his loyalty. But when Hezekiah makes a mistake, he is punished by God. It may seem harsh to punish the king for this mistake, but God has very high standards of behaviour for all His people.

Josiah and the Law

WHEN King Hezekiah of Judah died, his 12-year-old son, Manasseh, came to the throne. Manasseh was as bad as his father had been good. He not only rebuilt all the pagan altars that Hezekiah had destroyed, but built new ones too. He even set up statues of idols in Jerusalem's great temple! He had witches and wizards as counsellors and he took part in all sorts of evil rituals.

The next king, Amon, was just as wicked and cruel as his father. The people killed him, and put his eight-year-old son Josiah on the throne instead.

Like his great-grandfather, Hezekiah, Josiah loved God even when he was a very young boy. It saddened him to see how the temple had been dishonoured and vandalised over the years, and at the age of 26 he ordered the great house of the Lord to be repaired.

Craftsmen cleared every dusty corner, restoring the building wherever possible, and knocking down and rebuilding wherever it was not. Sacred objects, that had been flung aside for years, again saw the light of day and were polished up, good as new.

One day, the high priest, Hilkiah found a soft cloth. Inside a hole was a bundle wrapped in richly embroidered material. When Hilkiah unwrapped the package, he gasped. Inside lay an ancient scroll containing laws that God had given to Moses long ago in the wilderness. Trembling, he took it straight to the king.

Josiah read the scroll at once. He didn't stop until he'd taken in every single word. And he was horrified. King after king in Judah had led the people in breaking every law there was to break. And the scroll told of the dreadful punishments that God promised to those who sinned. Josiah broke down and wept, tearing his hair and ripping his clothes. "My people!" he cried. "Is it too late to be forgiven for our sins?" The king sent his officials to ask a prophetess, Huldah, what he could do to put things right. Her answer was solemn: "All you have read in the holy scroll will come true. Your people have sinned and the Lord will take vengeance upon them. But because you are full of repentance, God will allow you to live in peace. Your eyes will not see the misery of Judah's punishment."

> ❝ *And when the king heard the words of the book of the law, he rent his clothes.* ❞

Josiah ordered everyone in Judah to come to a great meeting at the temple. Loud and clear, Josiah read the scroll of the law to his subjects. His face was stern, his eyes deadly serious. You could have heard a pin drop. Not a sneeze, not a cough, not a whisper came from the huge throng while the king was reading. Then Josiah rolled up

Scroll of law
The Hebrew laws, also called the law of Moses, are God's instructions to His people as to how they must worship God and live their lives.

Josiah and Huldah
This picture shows Josiah's officials asking advice from the prophetess, Huldah, as to how they could make amends for past errors.

At last, the Lord was the one and only God worshipped in Josiah's kingdom, and the king led his people in a festival which had been forgotten for many years – the feast of the Passover – which they celebrated just as it said in the scroll of the law. Everyone in the country spoke about the wonderful things the young king had done. But it was not to last, because 13 years later Josiah was killed in battle and his reforms were to die with him.

the scroll and held it aloft, so everyone could see. "From this day onward," he thundered, "I swear with all my heart and soul to live by every single law in this scroll and walk in the path of the one true God." The crowds before him leapt to their feet. "We are with you!" they cried. "We will obey the Lord!"

Then Josiah told the priests to burn the pagan idols in public. He ordered all the heathen priests in Judah to be slain, and then went the length and breadth of the country, smashing every single one of their altars into dust. He cleared the places where human sacrifices had been offered and filled them with the bones of the dead, and no one went there any more.

Josiah
This picture shows Josiah reading the scroll. Although Judah was ruled by Assyria, their hold on the land was weakening. This meant Josiah could ignore the Assyrian gods he was told to worship.

Assyrian bronze demon
This is a bronze statue of an Assyrian demon, called Pazuzu, who was believed to carry disease. It is 15cm high and dates from around 800BC.

❧ **ABOUT THE STORY** ❧
In this story Josiah tries to make up for the way that his father and grandfather led the people away from God. When Hilkiah finds the scroll of the Laws of Moses, Josiah is determined to reform the people of Judah. While he is alive he inspires his people to live as God wants them to, but Huldah the prophetess makes it clear that Judah has to be punished, and the reforms are lost when Josiah dies.

Jeremiah's Warnings

JEREMIAH was the son of a priest, and a quiet young man. He was stunned when he heard the Lord talking to him. "I want you to speak for me to the people," God said, "to remind them what dreadful fates will befall them if they continue to do wrong. It will be difficult, because they won't want to listen and they won't believe you. But don't get downhearted. Tell them everything I say, and I will give you the strength to cope."

The Lord told Jeremiah to go to a potter's house and watch him moulding his clay. As the wheel span, the water jar the potter was making suddenly collapsed into an ugly, squat shape. The potter stopped what he was doing and squashed the clay into a wet ball. Then he threw it back on to the wheel and began again, shaping it into another quite different vessel that stood tall and upright and beautiful. "Go and tell the people of Judah that they are like clay in my hands," the Lord told Jeremiah. "At any time, I can crush a nation that is becoming evil and destroy it. But if it repents, I can change my mind and allow it to flourish into something strong and good."

Jeremiah bought one of the potter's earthen flasks and set out for the valley of Hinnom, where many of the locals had turned once again to pagan worship. In front of all the people, he raised the flask up above his head and then dashed it to the ground, where it smashed loudly into a thousand tiny pieces. "The Lord says that the day is coming when this place will be called the Valley of Slaughter," he cried. "Because you have forsaken the one true God, your enemies will slay you here in your homes. The Lord will shatter Judah like this broken flask, so no one can repair the kingdom."

So Jeremiah's mission began, travelling from village to village with the same message, for the Lord wanted to give His people one last chance to mend their ways. But everywhere he went, he was shouted down by the angry locals and chased out of town – some of them even tried to kill him. Yet the lonely prophet didn't give up, and the Lord gave him enough courage to stand and preach in Jerusalem in the temple itself: "Listen to the word of God!" he shouted, above all the jeers and insults. "The Lord will destroy this very city and all the towns through the whole of Judah. For you stubborn, stupid people are refusing to heed his warnings."

> " *'Behold, like the clay in the potter's hand, so are you in my hand, O house of Israel.'* "

The high priest, Pashhur, pushed his way through the mob. "How dare you cause this commotion in the house of the Lord!" he spat, striking and kicking Jeremiah until he lay cowering on the ground, and then hauling him away for a night in the stocks. But Jeremiah had a personal prophesy ready for Pashhur when he came to release him the following morning: "The Lord says that you will bring terror unto yourself and onto all your friends. Your enemies will kill all those you love while you look on, helpless. Judah will fall into the hands of the king of Babylon, and you, Pashhur, and all your family shall be carried away to live there in captivity. You will die in exile for failing to lead the people in the true ways of the Lord."

When God saw that Jeremiah wasn't having much success with talking to the people, He told him to write down every single word He'd said on a scroll. Perhaps then the warnings would seem more 'official' and the people might take notice of them. So Jeremiah called his loyal servant, Baruch, and dictated everything God had ever said to him. It was a long and tricky job. Everything had to be remembered perfectly and written down just so. But finally it was finished. "Baruch, you must read this to the

people," Jeremiah told the exhausted scribe. "I can't do it; I am not allowed to go to the temple. If I do the officials will arrest me. Go to the temple and, slowly and clearly, read out the whole scroll. Don't miss out anything."

One of the men who heard Baruch reading in the temple was Micaiah, a high-ranking official in the king's government. The words left him shaking in his shoes and he went straight to the royal court to tell his superiors what he'd heard. Baruch was immediately sent for and told to read the scroll all over again. The nobles were just as worried as Micaiah. "Are you sure this has all come from the mouth of the man of God?" they asked.

"Every word came from Jeremiah's lips and was written down by my hand," Baruch assured them.

"Then go and hide with your master, out of reach of King Jehoiakim's anger," the nobles urged him. They took the scroll to the king's secretary for safekeeping, and nervously went to Jehoiakim's chamber to tell him the most importants bits. To their surprise, the king seemed to take it all quite calmly. "Really?" he remarked, looking concerned. "All Jeremiah's work, eh? He says it's the word of God, does he?"

When the king asked if he could see the scroll for himself, the nobles were pleased. "Of course," they agreed. "We're so glad you're taking an interest in it. We really do feel that there's something in these words of Jeremiah's." But to the nobles' horror, as each chapter of the scroll was read out to the king, Jehoiakim merely cut it off and threw it into the fire.

And when the last piece had burned away, the king sighed and wiped his hands. "That's sorted that," he said.

The Lord spoke to Jeremiah. "Never mind," He consoled the dejected prophet. "You'll just have to write it all out on a new scroll." And Jeremiah began to dictate to Baruch all over again.

Jeremiah

Jeremiah is seen here with his scribe Baruch. Jeremiah was first called as a prophet in his early twenties. His prophesying continued for 40 years and spanned the reigns of the last five kings of Judah: Josiah, Jehoahaz, Jehoiakim, Jeconiah and Zedekiah. Jeremiah's prophecies did not always please the kings and priests of the time and, as a result, he was persecuted, plotted against and imprisoned. He spent much of his life struggling with the dilemmas that his prophetic calling imposed upon him.

❧ ABOUT THE STORY ❧

Jeremiah is sometimes called 'the weeping prophet'. The state of his country and the attitudes of the people upset him terribly. His message was not all doom and gloom; he offered hope to people who trusted God. The fact that he was made to suffer by people who rejected his message reminds later readers that following and serving God is sometimes very hard. It is sometimes necessary to face imprisonment and even death.

The End of Judah

KING Nebuchadnezzar of Babylon conquered nation after nation, growing so strong that he crushed even the mighty Assyrian Empire. He swept into Judah and surrounded Jerusalem, leaving King Jeconiah (Jehoiakim's brother) begging for mercy. Nebuchadnezzar agreed to leave Judah alone, but on drastic terms. First, Jeconiah and the royal family would be taken into captivity in Babylon, along with all the elders and priests. Secondly, Nebuchadnezzar would also take into exile many of Judah's skilled craftspeople, whom he could use in his own kingdom. Thirdly, Judah would have to pay a massive yearly tribute of treasure in return for peace. And fourthly, Nebuchadnezzar got to choose his own king: the youngest of the good King Josiah's sons, Zedekiah, who would have to obey his every word if Judah was to be left alone.

The stunned people left in Judah could hardly believe what had happened. They were deeply shocked at losing their leaders, and their own future hung in the balance.

Jeremiah wrote a letter of comfort to the exiled people in Babylon: "God says make the most of this bad situation. Do all your usual things and enjoy life. Don't grumble and be nasty to the Babylonians. Look after their cities and the Lord will look after you. For He has told me that in 70 years' time, He will bring you back to the Promised Land where you will again live happily."

Jeremiah started wearing an oxen's harness to show the people in Judah that being captured by the Babylonians was not a bad thing. They would be happy living under someone else's rule, as the ox was. "This is the Lord's work," the prophet said. "Judah's punishment is unfolding as it should."

The Lord showed the prophet a vision of two baskets outside the temple: one full of plump, juicy figs and the other full of overripe, stinking fruit. "The exiles in Babylon will eventually ask me for forgiveness and I will make sure that they flourish like the good figs," God explained. "But anyone who struggles against my will and tries to remain in Judah will rot like the fruit in the second basket." After this, Jeremiah went to King Zedekiah himself to warn him to put all thoughts of rebellion out of his head. "You must not try to resist Nebuchadnezzar," he warned, "or you will lose everything."

"Just whose side do you think you're on?" cried Zedekiah, and locked him up. But Jeremiah's faith didn't waver. He believed that the Lord would one day restore Judah and, to prove it, he invested a large sum of money in buying a piece of land.

> *I have given all these lands into the hand of Nebuchadnezzar, the king of Babylon.*

Even under house arrest, Jeremiah kept on sending out messages. "Anyone who stays in Jerusalem will die by sword, starvation and disease," he told them. "But those taken into exile by the Babylonians will live and prosper."

"This is ridiculous," thought the nobles of Jerusalem, "we have to shut him up." They threw Jeremiah into a deep, dark, mud-filled pit and left him there to die. But the king secretly sent a servant to haul him out and bring Jeremiah to him. "I need you to tell me the truth," he said to the prophet in private.

"Promise not to kill me and I will," replied the exhausted, starving prophet. The king anxiously agreed.

"God says that if you surrender to Nebuchadnezzar, the lives of you and your family will be spared and this city will survive," said Jeremiah. "However, if you try to fight against the Babylonians, Jerusalem will be burned to the ground and you will not escape from their hand."

Several years later, despite all Jeremiah's warnings, Zedekiah made a deal with the Egyptian army to try to defeat King Nebuchadnezzar and the Babylonian army. But the Egyptian king went back on his word and withdrew his troops, leaving Jerusalem to stand alone. The Babylonians pounced and Zedekiah barricaded the city. It withstood the siege for two years before the starving people finally gave in. The king was caught and forced to watch his sons slaughtered before he was blinded. He was led in chains to Babylon, along with many of his subjects. Only a few of the very poorest people were allowed to remain in Judah. Nebuchadnezzar's army smashed the walls and pulled down the temple before burning the city, just as Jeremiah had said they would.

Babylonian Empire
After the Assyrian Empire, the Babylonians became the greatest military force in the region. They conquered the Assyrians to occupy the important area of fertile ground around the River Tigris in the east, and the River Jordan in the west.

❧ ABOUT THE STORY ❧
The final destruction of Jerusalem took place in 587BC. This incident is one of the most important in the whole of the Old Testament. It marks the end of Judah as an independent country; there were never again any real kings to rule it and it was always dominated by a larger nation. Its destruction showed people that God had meant what He said – He hated rebellion against Him.

Ezekiel and the Exiles

WHEN the Babylonians were taking their captives from Judah into exile, they asked Jeremiah whether he would like to go or stay. Times were dangerous in the tiny, weak country, and he chose to stay to help Gedaliah, the governor the Babylonians had appointed to rule over the few people who remained. But the pagan tribe of the Ammonites saw their chance to take back land they had lost centuries ago to Moses and Joshua and they murdered Gedaliah. "Stand your ground against the Ammonites," Jeremiah told the terrified Judeans. "If you remain in Judah, the Lord will one day make you strong again. But if you are tempted by the thought of fleeing to Egypt, and wilfully abandon the Promised Land, you'll have only

death to look forward to." But the people of Judah fled, forcing Jeremiah to go with them, and the last remnants of the nation were swallowed up by the Egyptian civilization.

Meanwhile, among the exiled people of Judah – now called "Jews" by the Babylonians – a new prophet had arisen, a man called Ezekiel. Before Jerusalem had fallen, the Lord had told him that it would be up to him to try to keep the Jews together as a nation and turn them back to the one true God.

It was an extremely difficult task. The Jews were now scattered throughout a foreign country, among a strange people who had their own religions and customs. The Jews had no Promised Land, no elders, no kings. And the great temple in Jerusalem, where they thought God lived, had been destroyed.

Ezekiel had to teach the Jews two very important lessons – first, that God is everywhere, and secondly, that God judges everyone on who, not what, they are. For at first the Jews thought that simply being one of God's race of chosen people was enough to be given back the Promised Land one day.

"Here you are among pagans," Ezekiel said. "You're worshipping their idols, eating their food and sacrificing to their gods. Do you really think that the Lord will reward you? Each one of you is responsible for yourselves. If your father has sinned, you won't necessarily be damned for it. If your children commit crimes, God won't consider it to be your fault. The Lord is here, watching you in exile, and judging each one of you on your own, purely on what you do and how you live."

Ezekiel
The prophet Ezekiel was taken to Babylon as an exile. Five years after this, he received his call as a prophet. His prophecies were not generally popular but he still managed to reach a position of honour.

The Exile
This map shows Babylon, where the exiles were taken. This was a very important time in the history of the Israelites. In Babylon, under the leadership of prophets like Ezekiel, they became a united nation. This was where they were first called Jews.

> " *As I prophesied, there was a noise, and behold, a rattling; and the bones came together, bone to its bone.* "

Gradually, the Jews began to take Ezekiel's teaching to heart. Far from their homeland, living among strangers and surrounded by foreign religions, they began to pull together as a nation and turn back to worshipping the one true God. And as soon as they did so, they began to enjoy life and prosper, just as Jeremiah had hoped they would. Jewish craftsmen began to be recognized for their skilled work. Jewish farmers were employed by Babylonian landowners at excellent rates of pay, and Jewish officials rose to prominent positions in government.

God was pleased and he began to grant Ezekiel visions of the restoration of the Jewish people and the rebuilding of the temple in the Promised Land. "The Lord has shown me that our nation lies dead like a skeleton," Ezekiel told the people. "But we have only to ask God to breathe on us and we will live. The scattered parts of the skeleton will connect together, bone to bone. And the Lord will join the two peoples of the Promised Land into one kingdom with one king, and raise us up to life as one nation."

❧ ABOUT THE STORY ❧

Prophets like Jeremiah had been told by God that the Israelites would prosper living in Babylon, and also that the nation of the Jews would be properly created after the Israelites had been taken far from their homeland. Under the leadership of Ezekiel this begins to happen. God's long term plan for his chosen people is coming to fruition, and the Jews are learning to love God and live by his laws, and they are reaping the benefits.

The father of Judaism
This picture shows Ezekiel teaching the Jews in exile. He is thought of as the founding father of Judaism as it is today, as it was he who drew together the exiles from Israel and Judah and made them into a faithful and devoted people.

Nebuchadnezzar's Dream

IT wasn't just God who was pleased with the way the Jews worked hard and lived good lives in Babylon. King Nebuchadnezzar was pleased too. So pleased that he took the most promising young people to the palace to learn Babylonian culture and language.

Four of the students were Daniel, Shadrach, Meshach and Abednego. They worked hard and God rewarded them with exceptional talents in letters and wisdom, and the gift of understanding dreams for Daniel. At the end of the course they amazed the king who gave them important jobs on his royal staff.

The king often had bad dreams and would ask his advisers to tell him what they meant. These "wise men" consulted oracles and conjured up spirits, then told Nebuchadnezzar what they thought he wanted to hear. But after one dream the king decided to test them. "This time, I don't just want an interpretation," he said. "I want you to tell me what I dreamed, too."

Panicking, the advisers made a wild stab at lying. The king was enraged. "Put them all to death!" he fumed. Unfortunately, that included Daniel and his three friends. When Daniel heard, he ran to the king. "I'm sure I can tell you about your dream," he begged.

Nebuchadnezzar remembered how Daniel had impressed him before. "Come back tomorrow," he demanded, and Daniel dashed home to pray.

Next day, he returned confidently. "No human, however wise, can tell you your dream," Daniel began. "But last night the Lord showed me. You dreamed of a huge statue –

Brick-making
The furnace in the story was probably used for making bricks. A brick is a piece of straw and mud or clay (usually rectangular) that is dried hard in the sun or baked in a kiln. In Bible times, bricks were used more than any other material for building. At first, bricks were shaped by hand, but later wooden moulds were used. In Babylon, bricks were often stamped with the king's name. The picture, from a tomb near Thebes, shows brick-makers at work.

Book of Daniel
This is a fragment on a Greek papyrus manuscript of the book of Daniel from around AD250. This Greek version of the Hebrew Old Testament originally contained the books of Ezekiel, Daniel and Esther and was one of 11 books from a Christian library found in Egypt.

the head was gold, the chest and arms silver, the belly bronze, the legs iron and the feet half iron, half clay. A huge rock smashed the statue into pieces that blew away on the wind. Then the rock grew into a great mountain which filled the world."
Nebuchadnezzar gasped. "The body parts stand for five empires," Daniel explained, "that will come after yours. But God's kingdom will eventually destroy all human empires and will stand for ever."

> ❝ *The mystery was revealed to Daniel in a vision of the night...* ❞

After that, Daniel was appointed chief royal adviser and his three friends were made provincial governors. The other district officials were filled with jealousy. But they didn't have long to wait to get their own back.

Nebuchadnezzar made a huge golden statue. He ordered a fanfare to be played at certain times, and whenever the people heard the music, they were to fall down in the direction of the idol and worship it – or be thrown in a furnace. The jealous district officials told Nebuchadnezzar that Shadrach, Meshach and Abednego refused to pay homage. They were arrested and brought to Nineveh.

"Do what you will. We cannot bow down to an idol," the friends told the king. The king ordered that the furnace be made seven times hotter than usual, and that the friends should be bound and thrown into the blazing furnace immediately.

But when Nebuchadnezzar went to check that the men had been burned to a cinder, he was utterly baffled. The servants who had thrown the Jews into the white hot flames were killed by the searing heat. But inside the furnace, the three men were walking around freely, chatting to what looked like an angel. "Come out!" Nebuchadnezzar roared. The three men stepped out of the blaze without a single hair on their head singed.

The shocked king sent a decree through the whole of Babylon. "No one may say anything against the God of the Jews, for no other god is as powerful as theirs."

The meaning of the dream
The kingdoms described in Daniel's interpretation are believed to be Babylon (represented by gold), Persia (silver), Greece (bronze) and Rome (iron). The rock that grew into a huge mountain represents the everlasting kingdom of God.

> ❧ **ABOUT THE STORY** ❧
>
> *These stories were included in the Bible to encourage the exiles to stand firm for God and not to lose their faith when they were being threatened in Babylon. The stories showed that God could save His people from terrible things, just as He had done in the past. People in ancient times were very interested in dreams; Daniel's experience reminded them that God understood everything even if people did not.*

Belshazzar's Feast

THE next king to seize the Babylonian throne was Belshazzar. He loved to show off just as much as Nebuchadnezzar, and was especially fond of holding massive feasts to impress everyone. Belshazzar planned one grand banquet for a thousand guests. The huge banqueting hall was decorated with the richest hangings and ornaments from the royal treasure houses. Hundreds of waiters, musicians and dancers were booked. Belshazzar employed the very best chefs in Babylon and brought rare delicacies from the furthest corners of his empire for their elaborate menus. He ordered the most expensive wines from his cellars. The king took care of every single detail.

The feast was a complete success. The guests applauded and cheered the performance of the entertainers. They gasped as the waiters brought in platters of magnificent food and placed jewelled pitchers of wine on every table. Then Belshazzar called for silence. "Ladies and gentlemen," he announced proudly, "tonight is a very special night. You are in the greatest city in the world, being entertained by Nineveh's top performers, tasting the best food and wine that money can buy." Belshazzar's guests gave a loud cheer. "It is only right," the king continued, "that you should be eating and drinking from the finest plates and cups." Belshazzar turned to his servants. "Bring out the holy goblets we mighty Babylonians took from the Jews' temple in Jerusalem!"

The guests loved it. "Let's drink to our own gods!" they cried, drunkenly. "Here's to the gods of gold and silver!" They turned to toast the king himself and raised their glasses. "Cheers Belsha..." Their voices died away as they saw that the king was pale-faced and still, staring like a statue at a mysterious hand writing on the wall. The ghostly finger traced several words and Belshazzar sank wobbly-legged into his seat. "Guards! Guards!" he cried. "Fetch my advisers immediately!"

Belshazzar's magicians were totally baffled. Not one of them could tell what the mysterious writing said. "Call Daniel," advised the queen mother. "My husband Nebuchadnezzar used to say he was the wisest man in the entire world."

> *They drank wine, and praised the gods of gold and silver.*

The king promised to make Daniel the third most important man in the empire. "Keep your promotion," replied Daniel. "You're not going to be pleased with what I have to tell you. The first word – *mene* or 'number' – means that you have reached the full number of days God is granting you as king. The second word – *tekel* or 'weight' – means that God has weighed out what you are worth in His eyes, and it isn't much. The third word – *parsin* or 'divided' – means that your kingdom will eventually be split up. God is going to give half to the Medes and half to the Persians."

The party was definitely over. That very night, King Belshazzar was murdered. And Cyrus, king of the Medes, took the empire of Babylon for himself.

MANY PEOPLE TAKE FAITH IN GOD LIGHTLY AND MAKE FUN OF PEOPLE WHO WORSHIP GOD. THIS STORY REMINDS BELIEVERS THAT ONE DAY GOD WILL JUDGE EVERYONE ON EARTH. ❧

Hanging Gardens
The Hanging Gardens of Babylon did not literally 'hang', but were built on the roof on stepped levels called terraces. King Nebuchadnezzar is said to have built the gardens to please his wife, who missed the greenery of her home in the mountains of Media. The Hanging Gardens were well known throughout the ancient world and in the 2nd century BC were listed as one of the Seven Wonders of the World.

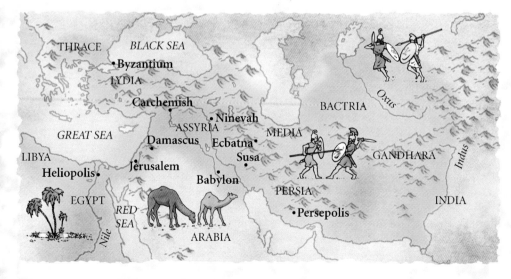

Persian Empire
The Persian Empire stretched from Egypt in the west right across to the banks of the river Indus in what is modern Pakistan. Persia was the largest of the three empires, the others being the Assyria and Babylonia, that ruled Palestine and beyond.

❖ **ABOUT THE STORY** ❖
This mysterious event is often pictured as a hand without an arm. It can be explained in one of two ways. It may have been a vision entirely in Belshazzar's mind. Possibly a servant was writing orders for the feast on the wall (which is what the words were usually used for) and somehow his body was obscured. In either case Belshazzar, half drunk and with a guilty conscience, knew God was using it as a message to him.

Return from Exile

KING Cyrus was a man with new ideas of how to run an empire. He told all the peoples who had been captured by the Babylonians that they were free to go home. He had a special message for the Jews. "It is your God who has made me emperor over all the earth. Now go and rebuild His house in Jerusalem. Anyone who wishes to remain in Babylon can help by giving money and supplies to those who are returning." Cyrus even gave back the treasures Nebuchadnezzar had taken from the temple.

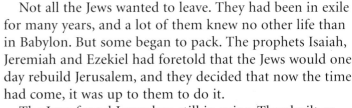

Not all the Jews wanted to leave. They had been in exile for many years, and a lot of them knew no other life than in Babylon. But some began to pack. The prophets Isaiah, Jeremiah and Ezekiel had foretold that the Jews would one day rebuild Jerusalem, and they decided that now the time had come, it was up to them to do it.

The Jews found Jerusalem still in ruins. They built an altar out in the open air for the Feast of Tabernacles, and offered prayers and sacrifices. Then work on the temple began under two new leaders: Jeshua (a priest) and Zerubbabel (a descendant of King David). The day the foundations were finished was a day of great emotion. The priests led the celebrations with singing and dancing, and there were tears of sadness from those who remembered the former great temple of Solomon, as well as tears of joy.

> *The returned exiles celebrated the dedication of this house of God with joy.*

The work went on, very slowly. The peoples brought to the Promised Land by the conquering Assyrians and Babylonians came to look. "We want to help," they volunteered. "We've been following your religion as best we can. Let us help with the building and then we can all worship your God together." But the Jews wouldn't have any of it. During their years in exile, they'd followed their religion very strictly. They were afraid that if they let foreigners join in – some of whom still worshipped pagan idols – they would be led into breaking

Samaritans
After the Assyrians captured Samaria and the Israelites were sent away, Samaria was filled with people from other lands who became known as Samaritans. The Jews always resented them for taking their kingdom. Here the Jews are sending away the Samaritans.

> ❖ **ABOUT THE STORY** ❖
> *The exiles returned from Babylon to Jerusalem in 538BC, but the temple was not finished until 516BC – almost exactly 70 years after Nebuchadnezzar had destroyed it. This was the second Jewish temple to stand in Jersualem; the Temple of Solomon was the first. The second temple was not as big or grand as Solomon's first temple. It stood until the Roman General Pompey destroyed it in 63BC.*

some of their laws. "You can have nothing to do with our God or our temple," the Jews told the Samaritans. The rioting that broke out was so bad that the exiles were forced to down tools, and the temple was left unfinished.

With the passing years, times grew harder in the Promised Land. "Look at what's happening," a prophet called Haggai told the Jews. "Our crops are failing, the water is drying up, our clothes are falling to bits and money seems to run through our fingers. It's because we've built ourselves houses to live in, but we haven't finished off the house of the Lord."

"The Lord has told me that we should be strong and complete the building of the temple," another prophet, Zechariah, agreed. "He says that as soon as we've done it, there'll be bumper harvests and plenty of rain, and we'll live peacefully and prosper."

This encouraged the Jews to go back to work. But the envious Samaritans went to the governor of the province to cause trouble. "Who gave you permission to build here?" he demanded angrily.

"We're building at the command of Emperor Cyrus himself," the Jewish elders explained. "If you write to the new king, Darius, he'll tell you it's the truth." When the governor received a reply from Nineveh that, yes, Darius had indeed found such a decree signed by Cyrus, the Samaritans were forced to back off and the temple was finally finished. The Jews celebrated by holding the great feast of Passover and sacrificed 12 goats among the many offerings – one for each of the scattered tribes of the Promised Land. At last, the surviving Jews felt they had made a new beginning.

Palestine after exile
When the Jews returned to Israel their great ideas for rebuilding the city and the temple gradually became less important. They felt that building houses and farming the land for food were more urgent. The prophet Haggai reminded them that God would care for them if they rebuilt the temple in His honour.

Haggai's message
The prophet Haggai told the Jews that their lives would not improve until they got their priorities right and started putting God first, instead of themselves.

Rebuilding Jerusalem

THE Promised Land remained a province of the empire of the Medes and Persians for many years, under Darius's successor King Ahasuerus and then King Artaxerxes. Stories about the few Jews who had left the comfort and security of Babylon and had returned to their homeland used to make their way across the empire to the many people who had stayed in Babylon and Persia. The news was not always good. Rumours reached a priest called Ezra that the Jews in Israel were slipping into bad habits, mixing with the pagans and becoming lazy in their worship of the Lord. He at once begged the Persian King Artaxerxes to let him go to sort it out. Now Ezra was very persuasive. The king found himself not only giving permission for Ezra, his fellow priests and a couple of thousand Jews to return to the Promised Land, but also found himself giving money to help them on their way. He wrote an official decree that told the provincial governor to support Ezra in any laws and judgments he thought fit to impose on the people.

The minute Ezra arrived in the Promised Land, people came running to him to tell of Jews who had married into the pagan communities and were living according to their ungodly customs – it turned out that the priests and the community leaders were the worst offenders of all! Ezra sat down in front of the temple and wept, crying out in a loud voice, confessing everything the people had done wrong. It was as bad as he had feared. But the determined holy man didn't stay downhearted. He made the priests swear to amend their ways and called everyone to attend a meeting of the utmost importance. Soon a crowd of Jews stood in the open square of the temple, while Ezra told them in no uncertain terms that they had to give up everything to do with pagans and turn back to God's law.

It wasn't just Ezra whom King Artaxerxes allowed to return to the Promised Land with his blessing. Some years later the king noticed that his butler was moping around with a long face and he asked him what was wrong.

"Sir, I've heard that my countrymen, the Jews, have raised a new temple in Jerusalem," Nehemiah explained. "But the city all around it is a disgrace. It's still lying utterly in ruins."

> **Come, let us build the wall of Jerusalem, that we may no longer suffer in disgrace.**

"I shall write a letter to the provincial governor, Sanballat, to tell him that I'm putting you in charge of rebuilding the city, and you must go at once," said the king. "Just promise me that you'll come back as soon as you've finished."

Of course, Sanballat and Tobiah, his second-in-command, gave Nehemiah a very frosty reception. The king had sent them a Jew who had been given equal powers to their own, and they had been given no part to play in the rebuilding of the important walled city. Nehemiah knew from the start that the government officials were going to make life difficult for him, so he surveyed the ruins of Jerusalem late at night, sorting out in secret what needed to be done.

As soon as Nehemiah got down to work, Sanballat and Tobiah did their best to cause trouble. First, in front of the provincial army, they taunted and ridiculed the Jews as they scuttled back and forth over the charred heaps of rubble. Then, as the walls began to take shape, they tried different tactics. "The ramparts and turrets are for shutting you out of the city," the officials told the local people, trying to make them angry. "Are you going to just sit back and watch?"

Sanballat and Tobiah were delighted when the furious Samaritans began to attack the workers on the walls at every opportunity. But Nehemiah simply split the working Jews up into teams, and put two teams on each shift: one to stand watch with weapons and fight if necessary, the other team to carry on building the walls.

Under Nehemiah's leadership, the Israelites finished the walls in only 52 days. Even the local people who had tried to tear them down were impressed. "Their God must have had a hand in it," they whispered, as they stood beneath the towering walls in awe and watched the Jews sing and dance their way right round the city in a great ceremony of dedication.

While the Jews were completing the inside of the city, they didn't take any risks with the Samaritans, who were getting more and more worried as the city neared completion. Each day, they kept the gates firmly shut against attack as they built house after house, until there were enough people living inside Jerusalem to defend it. Then, just as Sanballat and Tobiah had feared, they cast out anyone who wasn't Jewish through and through. At last the descendants of the kingdoms of Israel and Judah felt they could hold their heads up high again. They were back in the Promised Land, one nation under one God.

Ahasuerus and Darius
This section of a stone relief shows the Persian King Darius on his throne. Behind him stands his son, Ahasuerus, who was also known as Xerxes. This relief was found in Persepolis, in Iran. It is around 2.5m high and dates from 521 to 486BC.

❖ ABOUT THE STORY ❖

Nehemiah is one of the great heroes of faith in the Bible. His job in Persia was very important – he had to make sure the king wasn't given poisoned wine! He combined his practical common sense with a deep faith in God which he expressed through prayer. Whenever a problem arose, Nehemiah didn't just think up a solution, he prayed for God's help and wisdom too.

Daniel and the Lions

DANIEL was one of the Jews who felt too old and settled to leave Babylon. Instead of returning to the Promised Land, Daniel remained at the palace, a trusted adviser to King Cyrus of the Medes and Persians. Cyrus's successor, King Darius, relied on Daniel even more. Darius made Daniel one of the most powerful people in the

whole empire. He appointed him as one of three ministers to rule over his kingdom. Daniel did a much better job than the others. Darius began to trust him more, consulting him privately and giving him special responsibilities. The two other ministers were jealous. They began to seek a way to bring about Daniel's downfall, eager to find any little mistake they could blow up into something big. But Daniel was such a God-fearing man that he seemed to live a perfect life. He didn't lie or swear. He didn't gossip and spread rumours. He always dealt with people fairly, and was polite and helpful. The two ministers were soon at their wits' end.

They plotted together, and went to King Darius with a clever plan. "We need a new law," one of the men told him, looking serious. "Nobody should be allowed to ask for anything from any god or man except you for a period of 30 days."

"And anyone who breaks the law should be flung into a den of lions," added the second, eagerly. "All the district officials agree."

"Oh all right then," Darius sighed, stamping his royal seal on the law. The two men hurried away to spy on Daniel, rubbing their hands with glee.

It wasn't long before they were back at the palace, demanding to see the king.

"We think you should know about Daniel," they said. "He gets down on his knees three times a day and prays to his God, facing Jerusalem. What are you going to do about it?"

King Darius realized he had been tricked and was furious. "Get out of my sight!" he roared, kicking

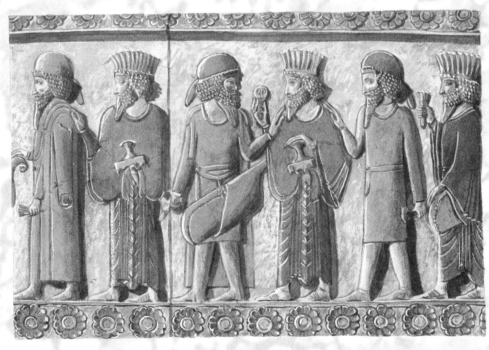

King Cyrus
This marble head from the 6th century BC shows King Cyrus, who ruled Persia from 558 to 530BC. It was Cyrus who conquered the Medes in 549BC.

Medes and Persians
This stone relief dating from around 485 to 465BC shows a row of Medes and Persians. The Medes are wearing rounded hats and short tunics, whereas the Persians are dressed in full-length robes and tall crowns.

the two ministers as they grovelled before him. The worried king spent all day striding back and forth, desperately trying to think of a way to get Daniel off the hook. But it was no good.

"The law's the law," the officials insisted.

So Darius very reluctantly sent his guards to arrest his best minister.

The king shuddered as he stood at the top of the pit, listening to the lions roaring hungrily below. He turned to the old man who stood beside him and placed his hand on his arm. "Daniel, my friend," he said to his trusted adviser. "May your God – whom you serve so faithfully – save you." The royal guards lowered Daniel down towards the snarling lions, then blocked off the pit with a huge stone. Darius marked the entrance with his royal seal, so no one would dare tamper with it, and then trudged back to the palace. The sad and anxious king wouldn't eat or talk to anyone. He shut himself up in his room and spent a sleepless night alone, worrying, and furious that he'd been tricked by his ministers.

> " *The king said to Daniel,*
> *'May your God, whom you*
> *serve continually,*
> *deliver you.'* "

As soon as the sun rose, Darius was back at the pit, demanding it be uncovered. "Are you down there, Daniel?" he cried, as the guards began heaving away the stone. "Are you all right?"

To his great relief, a familiar voice came floating up from the darkness. "My king, I am alive. An angel has been here with me, and the lions have done me no harm."

The emperor nearly wept with joy. "Quick," he yelled at his guards. "Get him out of there at once!"

Later on, the lions got their dinner after all. The king ordered that the two wicked ministers be thrown into the pit along with their families, and the animals tore them to bits. Then Darius sent a proclamation out to every corner of the Medean empire announcing to all the nations that Daniel's God should be worshipped by everyone as the one true God. "He saves all of those who believe in Him," wrote the emperor, "and His kingdom will last for ever."

Lion of Babylon
This picture shows a detail from a reconstruction of the gateway into Babylon. Lions were associated with kings and power.

Marduk
In this picture from a carved cylinder found at Babylon, the Babylonian god, Marduk, is shown standing on a creature which has the body of a serpent. This creature was his symbol. Marduk wears a crown and holds a rod and a ring, which are symbols of authority.

❖ ABOUT THE STORY ❖

The book of Daniel was written especially to encourage Jews to be faithful to God at a time when they were being persecuted by people who did not believe in God. No one finds it easy to admit they believe in God when they know they could be killed for it. Daniel's example was meant to show them that even in such terrible situations, God could still help and rescue them, but that even if He didn't, they should still be faithful to Him.

Esther the Beautiful

DURING the reign of the next emperor, King Xerxes, there were still many thousands more Jews living in Babylon and Persia than had returned to the Promised Land. The civilization of the Medes and Persians was still the greatest in the world, and Xerxes was immensely proud of his empire, which stretched all the way from India to Ethiopia. He decided to hold a massive banquet in his capital, Susa, to celebrate his magnificence. First, he invited every single one of the princes, army chiefs, nobles and governors in his empire to a feast the likes of which no one had ever seen before. In immense marble halls bedecked with banners of the finest silks, his honoured guests lay on golden couches and ate off jewelled platters while every single one of the priceless valuables in Xerxes' treasure houses were paraded before them on velvet cushions. It took 180 days for the stunned VIPs to admire all Xerxes' splendours. Then the generous king threw his doors open to his subjects too, holding a magnificent garden party for a further week in the grounds of the palace itself. The ordinary people were stunned, they had never seen such magnificence! There were refreshing fountains tinkling in the sunshine, the perfume of sweet-smelling flowerbeds, mosaics underfoot of mother-of-pearl and precious stones – and as much free wine as everyone could drink!

By the seventh day the king was feeling exceedingly merry. "I've not only got the most beautiful palace in the world," he thought, "I've also got the most beautiful queen too." He summoned his seven chamberlains and ordered them to go and fetch the queen at once. "Tell her to put on her best dress," he demanded. "I want to show her off to everyone."

Now Queen Vashti was giving her own party for all the women, in another part of the palace. She was a strong, independent woman, besides being beautiful, and she refused to come. "I can't leave my guests so rudely," she told the chamberlains. "Whatever would they think? And besides, I don't want to be paraded about like something from one of my husband's treasure houses."

When the chamberlains told the king that Vashti wouldn't come, he was mad. Xerxes' courtiers were far too frightened of the raging emperor to tell him to calm down. In fact, they all nodded their heads and agreed that he was very right to be so angry. "Whatever are you going to do about Vashti?" the most senior of them urged. "You can't possibly let her go unpunished. What will happen if other women get to hear of it? We'll have wives all through the empire rebelling against their husbands. And where will that leave us?"

> " *Let the maiden who pleases the king be queen instead of Vashti.* "

"You're right," decided Xerxes. "Vashti will have to go. Kick her out and find me a new queen to take her place – one who's even more beautiful."

A royal proclamation soon went out through all the land, announcing a competition. All the young maidens in

the kingdom were to present themselves at the palace. The most beautiful would be chosen to stay for lessons in skincare, hairstyling, make-up and how to behave like a queen. And at the end of a year, the king would choose the one he liked best to replace Vashti.

In the back streets of Susa there lived a servant in the royal household called Mordecai, an old Jewish man who was one of those who had chosen to stay in Babylon rather than return to the Promised Land. Mordecai was the guardian of his orphaned cousin Esther, whom he had brought up as his daughter. "No one could be more beautiful or queenly than you," he told her, giving her a hug. "Hurry along to the king's palace and enter the competition– but make sure you don't tell anyone you're Jewish. The king might not be so keen on that."

Esther easily made it on to the short list of the most beautiful maidens in the country and she was hurried off to new living quarters in the palace, where all the young women were to be groomed for a year. Every day, Mordecai would make sure he had an errand to do that would take him past her chambers. And every day, he was more and more pleased with what he saw of Esther's progress. She was such a well-mannered and good-natured girl that she quickly became the favourite of Hegai, the courtier in charge of the competition. He made sure that Esther had the very best face creams, the finest food from the royal kitchens and the most skilled maids to help her with her hair and advise her on her clothes.

The time came for the young women to parade, one by one, in front of the king. They were all trying very hard to impress him. In the end, though, there wasn't much of a competition at all. Esther was by far the winner, and the delighted Xerxes held a lavish great banquet in honour of his lovely new queen.

Make-up and jewellery
Wealthy women wore jewellery, like this gold armlet which is decorated with griffins, a mythical animal with an eagle's head and a lion's body.

THIS STORY SOUNDS A BIT LIKE THE STORY OF CINDERELLA – SOMEONE FINDING THEIR DREAMS COME TRUE, AND GETTING FAMOUS AND RICH. BUT THIS STORY IS NOT JUST ABOUT ESTHER HAVING FUN AND ENJOYING HER NEW ROYAL LIFE. IT REMINDS US THAT WHEN GOD DOES ALLOW SUCH THINGS, HE GIVES US RESPONSIBILITIES TOO. ESTHER WOULD HAVE A VERY DIFFICULT, BUT ALSO IMPORTANT, JOB TO DO AS QUEEN.

❧ ABOUT THE STORY ❧

This story is really about God's protection of His people and the timing of His purposes. It seemed pure chance that Esther was chosen, and she kept very quiet about her nationality. But God knew that soon she would be the only person who could avert a tragedy. The Bible shows God working behind the scenes so that everyone is in the right place at the right time when it really matters.

Esther Saves the Jews

NOT long after Esther had become queen, Mordecai heard two palace servants in the palace plotting to kill the king. He hurried to tell his daughter and she went straight to her husband. Xerxes ordered the men to be arrested, tried and hanged.

After this, the king decided he could do with a right-hand man. He chose Haman, who was an arrogant man who ordered everyone to bow when they saw him coming.

"I'm not paying homage to anyone but God," Mordecai said. Haman wanted revenge for being embarrassed. He decided to punish not only Mordecai, but his entire race.

"Sir," Haman said to Xerxes one day, "there are a people in your empire who refuse to live by your laws. They ignore your government officials and only take notice of their own priests and elders.

If you don't put a stop to it, you'll soon have a full-scale rebellion on your hands. Why don't you let me exterminate them?"

"Order what you think best," Xerxes said, handing him his royal seal. "Have these troublemakers wiped out."

"The prime minister's proclamation includes you," Mordecai wrote to Esther. "Go to your husband and beg him to do something."

But it wasn't that simple. Esther replied, "It's the death penalty for anyone who enters the king's presence uninvited. But if I am to die for my people, then so be it."

After three days of fasting and praying, the brave young queen went to the king. Luckily his face brightened into a smile. "What can I do for you?" he said, and held out his sceptre to her, ushering her in.

Festival of Purim
The Jewish festival of Purim is held in spring to commemorate the defeat of Haman's plot to massacre the Jews. At the festival, the book of Esther is read aloud and it is customary for the congregation in the synagogue to cheer Esther's name, but shout and boo whenever Haman is mentioned.

The king's sceptre
Esther was risking her life when she went to see the king. This was an offence punishable by death, unless the king held out his sceptre. This law allowed the king some privacy and protected him from would-be murderers.

Casting lots
Haman threw lots, rather like modern dice, to determine a day to carry out his plan to exterminate the Jews. Small stones and pieces of pottery, like the ones above, were often used as lots. The word *purim* is the plural of the word *pur*, which means "lot".

"Sir," Esther said, "will you have dinner with me tomorrow? And will you bring the prime minister?"

The king was delighted. Haman smirked smugly.

"No one else in the entire empire is as important!" he bragged to his friends. But one thought left him glowering. "Still that Mordecai refuses to bow."

"Don't put up with it," everyone urged. "Get the king to build a gallows and hang him. Then you can enjoy tomorrow's dinner unspoilt."

The king had been unable to sleep and he'd been reading his official records all night. "Look here," Xerxes remarked to his advisers, "there's no record of how we rewarded Mordecai for foiling that murder plot. We must put things right straightaway." The King called Haman. "If you were king, how would you reward your most loyal servant?" the king asked.

> ❝ *And Haman said to himself, 'Whom would the king delight to honour more than me?'* ❞

Haman thought the king was talking about him. "Dress the hero in your robes and crown and set him on your horse. Then give him a parade through the streets with a noble leading the way, shouting, 'The king is delighted to honour this man!'" he said.

The king clapped his hands. "Brilliant!" he cried. "Hurry along and do it for Mordecai the Jew."

It was the beginning of the end for the miserable Haman. That night, at dinner, Esther made her plea. "Oh my king, I am Jewish," she sobbed, "and orders have been given for me and my people to be put to death."

Xerxes was outraged. "Whose orders?" he bellowed.

"His!" Esther wept, pointing at the evil prime minister. Just as Haman had wanted, the king demanded that gallows to be built as quickly as possible – but it was the prime minister who was hanged on them, not Mordecai. Esther confessed that the faithful servant was her foster father and Xerxes rewarded him with Haman's old job. At once, Mordecai sent out an edict which cancelled the former prime minister's commands and, thanks to Esther, thousands of Jewish lives were saved.

Esther
This painting shows Queen Esther dressed in her royal robes. She was very brave and risked her life to save her people. But the Bible does not commend her when she encourages the Jews to massacre their enemies.

ESTHER PUT GOD AND OTHERS BEFORE HERSELF. SHE COULD HAVE DONE NOTHING AND DIED WITH HER PEOPLE. INSTEAD, SHE RISKED HERSELF TO SAVE THEM. IT IS AN EXAMPLE OF HOW GOD WANTS US TO LIVE. ∾

❧ ABOUT THE STORY ❧

The Medes and Persians had very strict laws. Once a law was made, no one – not even the king could change it. So when Haman was hanged, the order to kill the Jews still stood. The new law which Mordecai drafted allowed the Jews to defend themselves against anyone who attacked them. That way, no one would bother to comply with the original law.

Jonah and the Whale

IN the days of the great Assyrian Empire, there was a prophet, Jonah, who was not very pleased when God called him. "Jonah, I want you to go to the Assyrian capital, Nineveh," the Lord told him. "Preach to the pagans there. They're doing nothing but sinning against me." Now Nineveh was a long way away, the Assyrians were a hard, cruel race and Jonah – a Jew – didn't really care about foreigners anyway. "I'll run away to somewhere the Lord can't find me," he thought, packing a bag. Soon he was boarding a ship and setting off on a long voyage in quite the opposite direction to Nineveh – to Tarshish in Spain.

No sooner had the ship left harbour and reached open waters than the skies darkened and the wind began to blow up. Great gusts whipped up the sea, rain lashed the masts and the ship was tossed up and down the towering waves, threatening to break up at any moment. Terrified, the sailors threw as much of their cargo overboard as they could to lighten the load, but the ship still bowed and cracked in the full force of the storm. "On your knees!" cried the captain. "Each one of you beg your gods to save us!" and he ran around the ship to check that everyone was praying.

Then the sailors superstitiously cast lots to find out which of the passengers had brought the wrath of the gods upon them. They picked Jonah, who was soon surrounded by the angry crew. "Which god do you serve?" they demanded. "What have you done to bring this storm raging down upon us?"

"I'm a Hebrew," Jonah gulped. "The only thing that's going to save everyone is if you throw me overboard." Even though the sailors were desperate, they weren't murderers, and they did their best to row to shore. But it was impossible. With every stroke of their oars, the wind seemed to blow more strongly. In the end, they had no choice but reluctantly to throw Jonah off the ship. As soon as the prophet had splashed into the water, the gale began to die down and the waves to subside. And as Jonah drifted away from the ship on the swell, he heard the captain and the sailors praying once more – but this time to the one true Lord, not to their pagan gods.

> **❝ *... and Jonah was in the belly of the fish three days and three nights.* ❞**

Just when Jonah thought things couldn't get any worse, they did. One minute he was bobbing up and down in the water like a cork; the next minute, he was swimming around inside a dark, wet cave – a huge fish had swallowed him up. For three days and nights Jonah was in the pitch black darkness of its belly. "Oh Lord," he prayed, "I'm dreadfully sorry. If you get me out of here, I promise to obey you in future." A little circle of light appeared in the distance and very quickly widened. There was a rumbling and a roaring and a rushing of water, and the fish coughed him out of its mouth. Choking and spluttering, the prophet felt himself dropped onto a firm bed of sand. "Thanks be to God!" he cried as the waters drew back leaving him in warm sunlight blinking on the dry land.

happened. The sun set on the 40th day and still nothing had happened. "We have been saved," cried the people of Nineveh. "God has forgiven us!" They sang and danced and rejoiced, offering prayers and sacrifices to God – all except Jonah, who stomped off into the desert. "Why have you spared them, Lord?" he moaned up to heaven, stacking a few sticks together as a shelter from the heat. "They aren't even Jewish! If you're going to save sinners like these, I'd rather be dead than serve you."

God taught Jonah one last lesson. Overnight, a broad, shady tree grew over Jonah that guarded him from the burning sun till evening and kept him cool. But next morning, the disappointed prophet found that the tree had withered away. And Jonah needed its protection more than ever. All day long, not only did the sun blaze down but a scorching wind also blew across the sands. "Lord, the death of that tree is the last straw," Jonah groaned. "Please let me die."

"How can you be so upset about the death of a tree you didn't plant or water," the Lord scolded, "when you're cross with me for not killing the thousands of people in Nineveh?" Jonah finally realized that God created all the people of the world, and He cares for people from all nations, not just his own; that the Lord's kingdom stretches over the whole earth.

The Lord's voice boomed at him: "Now are you ready to go to Nineveh for me? Tell those pagans that unless they beg my forgiveness for their sins, in 40 days' time I will destroy the city." Jonah trembled before the power of God, and set off at once.

The city of Nineveh was so big that it took Jonah three whole days to work his way across it, shouting himself hoarse as he went. But to his great surprise, the ruthless Assyrians listened to what he had to say. When the king himself got to hear Jonah's message, he sent out a royal proclamation ordering everyone to begin praying and fasting at once. When dawn broke on the 40th day nothing

A reluctant prophet

Jonah tried to escape from the purpose that God had for him by fleeing on a boat from the port of Joppa. He could not escape the will of God, though, and when the sailors threw him overboard to try to save their ship, he was swallowed by a big fish, which left him on the shore. From there he went to Nineveh.

The Old Testament Prophets

ELIJAH was a prophet of Israel who lived in the 9th century BC, during the reign of King Ahab. Nothing really is known about his background. Six episodes in the life of Elijah are related in the Bible: his prediction of drought, the contest on Mount Carmel, his flight to Mount Horeb, also called Mount Sinai, the story of Naboth, the oracle about King Ahaziah, and Elijah's ascent to heaven. All these episodes, except for the last, are concerned with the clash between the worship of the God of Israel and that of Baal. It was King Ahab's wife, Jezebel, a Phoenician princess, who encouraged Baal worship among the Israelites.

In the first episode, after Elijah announces to King Ahab that there will be a drought, he escapes, first to the brook at Cherith and then to Zarephath, in Phoenicia, where he performs a miracle by healing a sick boy. In both places God provides for Elijah.

In the second episode, Elijah presides over a contest between God and Baal on Mount Carmel. Elijah's sacrifice to God bursts into flames, whereas the sacrifice of Baal's priests remains unlit. After this victory, there is a mighty storm as God puts an end to the drought by bringing the rain. In doing so, He shows Himself to be superior to Baal.

Elijah then flees to Mount Horeb, the mountain where God gave Moses the Ten Commandments. Elijah's journey to this holy place is important as Elijah is returning to one of the most important places in the Jewish faith.

The fourth episode tells the story of a man called Naboth. He refuses to sell his vineyard to King Ahab because he knows it is forbidden by God to sell inherited land. When Ahab has Naboth stoned to death and takes his vineyard, Elijah announces that he will be punished.

In the fifth episode, Elijah reveals that God will punish King Ahaziah for worshipping the Syrian god, Baal-zebub.

Finally, Elijah is taken up to heaven in a chariot of fire and his role as prophet passes to Elisha.

It was Elijah that was to appear to Jesus, along with Moses in what is called the Transfiguration. Elijah remains to this day one of the most important of the Old Testament prophets; a place is still set for him at the table for some of the Jewish feasts.

Elijah and Moses
Elijah has been compared with Moses. Elijah is accompanied and succeeded by Elisha, just as Moses was by Joshua. Elijah's demonstration of God's power on Carmel was like Moses receiving the law on Mount Horeb.

The chariot of fire
This picture shows Elijah being taken away to heaven in a chariot, watched by Elisha. The taking of someone to heaven, while still alive, is called a translation. Only two people in the Bible are said not to die: Elijah and Enoch.

ISAIAH was a prophet in Judah from around 740-700 BC. Most of his prophecies concentrated on Judah and, in particular, on its capital, Jerusalem. He prophesied from the reign of King Uzziah to the reign of King Hezekiah.

These were troubled times for the Jewish people as, not long after Isaiah was called as a prophet, the Assyrians took over the state of Judah, making it part of their empire.

Isaiah's prophetic life began when he had a vision in the temple at Jerusalem, of God sitting on a throne, surrounded by angels called seraphim. God told him to go out and speak to the people, passing on the message that they should put their trust in Him alone, they should not worship other gods, they should keep His laws, and should listen to His prophets.

Isaiah's vision
Isaiah had a holy vision of Jesus in a kingdom where the wolf would lie down with the lamb.

From ancient times, Isaiah has been thought of as the greatest of all the Old Testament prophets. He has been called, amongst other things, "the prophet of holiness" and "the eagle among the prophets". He is perhaps most important as the prophet who foretold the birth of the Messiah, who would be descended from King David and would come to save the Jewish people. Isaiah prophesied that the present Assyrian Empire of violent rule would be replaced by a peaceful kingdom of God. He described the Messiah as a king of Israel who would free his people from the Assyrians. Christians, though, believe that Isaiah's words foretell the coming of Jesus Christ, who would save everyone, Jews and Gentiles alike, from sin.

Isaiah says, "For unto us a child is born, unto us a son is given: and the government shall be upon His shoulder: and His name shall be called Wonderful, Counseller, the mighty God, the everlasting Father, the Prince of Peace."

❦ KINGS OF ISRAEL AND JUDAH ❧

The single nation ruled by Saul, David and Solomon split into two after Solomon died.

Israel (north)	Judah (south)
Jeroboam *931-910BC*	Rehoboam *931-913BC*
Nadab *910-909BC*	Abijah *913-911BC*
Baasha *909-886BC*	Asa *911-870BC*
Elah *886-885BC*	Jehoshaphat *870-848BC*
Omri *885-874BC*	Jehoram *848-841BC*
Ahab *874-853BC*	Ahaziah *841BC*
Ahaziah *853-852BC*	Athaliah *841-835BC*
Joram *852-841BC*	Joash *835-796BC*
Jehu *841-814BC*	Amaziah *796-767BC*
Jehoahaz *814-798BC*	Uzziah *791-740BC*
Jehoash *798-782BC*	Jotham *750-732BC*
Jeroboam II *793-753BC*	Ahaz *735-716BC*
Zechariah *753-752BC*	Hezekiah *729-687BC*
Shallum *752-752BC*	Manasseh *696-643BC*
Menahem *752-742BC*	Amon *643-640BC*
Pekahiah *742-740BC*	Josiah *640-609BC*
Pekah *752-732BC*	Jehoahaz *609-609BC*
Hoshea *732-723BC*	Jehoiakim *609-597BC*
	Jehoiachin *597-597BC*
All dates for kings are approximate.	Jeconiah *597-597BC*
	Zedekiah *597-587BC*

❦ PROPHETS ❧

The Old Testament prophets worked in specific regions. Some even prophesied in foreign countries.

Israel	Judah
Samuel *1050-1010BC*	Joel *810-750BC*
Elijah *870-852BC*	Isaiah *740-700BC*
Micaiah *870-852BC*	Micah *742-687BC*
Elisha *855-798BC*	Zephaniah *640-610BC*
Amos *760–780BC*	Huldah *610-605BC*
Hosea *760-722BC*	Habakkuk *605BC*
	Jeremiah *626-587BC*
All dates for prophets are approximate.	Ezekiel *593-570BC*
	Nahum *630-612BC*

Jeremiah   Ezekiel   Samuel   Micaiah

The Book of Psalms

THE Book of Psalms in the Old Testament, also known as the Psalter, is a collection of 150 religious verses which are sung or recited in both Christian and Jewish worship. According to tradition, 73 of the psalms were written by King David, a musician and a poet. Other authors named in the titles are King Solomon and the prophet Moses.

*O Lord, our Lord, how majestic is Thy name in
all the earth!*

*Thou whose glory above the heavens is chanted
By the mouth of babes and infants, Thou hast founded a
bulwark because of Thy foes,
to still the enemy and the avenger.*

*When I look at Thy heavens, the work of Thy fingers
the moon and the stars which Thou hast established;
what is man that Thou art mindful of him,
and the son of man that Thou dost care for him?*

*Yet Thou hast made him little less than God, and dost
crown him with glory and honour.
Thou hast given him dominion over the
works of Thy hands;
Thou hast put all things under his feet,
all sheep and oxen,
and also the beasts of the field,
the birds of the air, and the fish of the sea,
whatever passes along the paths of the sea.*

*O Lord, our Lord, how majestic is Thy name in
all the earth!*

Psalm 8; A psalm of David

*The Lord is my shepherd, I shall not want;
He makes me lie down in green pastures.
He leads me beside still waters; He restores my soul.
He leads me in paths of righteousness for His name's sake.*

*Even though I walk through the valley of the
shadow of death,
I fear no evil; for Thou art with me;
Thy rod and Thy staff, they comfort me.*

*Thou preparest a table before me in the
presence of my enemies;
Thou anointest my head with oil, my cup overflows.*

*Surely goodness and mercy shall follow me all
the days of my life;
and I shall dwell in the house of the Lord for ever.*

Psalm 23

*Make a joyful noise to the Lord, all the lands!
Serve the Lord with gladness!
Come into His presence with singing!*

*Know that the Lord is God!
It is He that made us, and we are His;
We are His people, and the sheep of His pasture.*

*Enter His gates with thanksgiving,
and His courts with praise!
Give thanks to Him, bless His name!*

*For the Lord is good;
His steadfast love endures for ever,
and His faithfulness to all generations.*

Psalm 100

TIMELINE 1000BC TO 400BC

• Solomon's kingdom is divided into Israel in the north and Judah in the south. Jeroboam rules Israel, and Solomon's son Rehoboam rules Judah.

DECORATIVE FURNITURE FROM SAMARIA, CAPITAL OF ISRAEL

1000BC

• Ahab becomes king of Israel, with Jezebel as his queen.

ELIJAH'S CONTEST WITH THE PROPHETS OF BAAL

900BC

• Isaiah is prophet to King Ahaz and King Hezekiah.

• Samaria falls to the invading Assyrians.

ISRAEL'S CAPITAL, SAMARIA, IS CAPTURED, AND IS OCCUPIED BY THE ASSYRIANS

800BC

The Trials of Job

THE Book of Job tells the story of a rich man called Job, who was faithful to God and blessed by him. One day, a member of God's heavenly council suggests that Job's faith should be tested. He makes a bet with God that if Job were to suffer great misfortune, he would lose his faith. To find out if he is right, God gives permission for Job to be robbed of his wealth, his ten children and his health. Job's family and friends assume that his misfortunes are God's punishment for some terrible sin, and throw him out of the town.

As Job sits outside the city gates, three of his friends (known as Job's comforters) come to console him. After seven days of silence, Job pours out his feelings in a bitter lamentation and there follows a long, heated discussion about the reason for his plight which forms most of the book. Although his friends' lack of understanding drives Job to distraction, it also turns him to God. Despite his suffering, he refuses to curse God and continues to pray to Him. In the end, Job's prayers are answered. He is made twice as wealthy as he was before, he is cured of his disease, he has ten more children and goes on to live a long and happy life.

The book of Job has been called "one of the most original works in the poetry of humankind". It deals with human experience in general and, in particular, with suffering. Although in the end Job's misfortunes disappear, the story seems to contradict the basic principle that those who have faith in God will have good fortune, and people that do not will suffer. The question Job keeps asking is why God is treating him in this way. One suggestion is that Job needed to realize that he did not know everything about God, and that he could not predict God's actions. By the end of the story, Job has understood that God's wisdom and greatness are such that no human can ever fully grasp them. Job's mistake was that his idea of God was too small. When he realizes the greatness of God, his problems disappear.

Discussing the problem of suffering
This picture shows Job with his three comforters. The phrase "a Job's comforter" has come to mean a person who makes a situation worse, while apparently trying to give comfort.

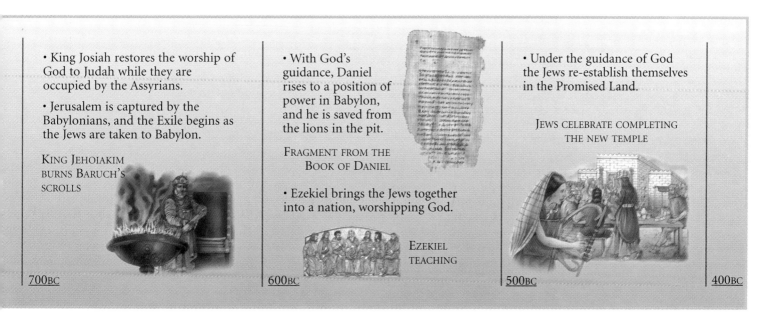

• King Josiah restores the worship of God to Judah while they are occupied by the Assyrians.

• Jerusalem is captured by the Babylonians, and the Exile begins as the Jews are taken to Babylon.

KING JEHOIAKIM BURNS BARUCH'S SCROLLS

700BC

• With God's guidance, Daniel rises to a position of power in Babylon, and he is saved from the lions in the pit.

FRAGMENT FROM THE BOOK OF DANIEL

• Ezekiel brings the Jews together into a nation, worshipping God.

EZEKIEL TEACHING

600BC

• Under the guidance of God the Jews re-establish themselves in the Promised Land.

JEWS CELEBRATE COMPLETING THE NEW TEMPLE

500BC

400BC

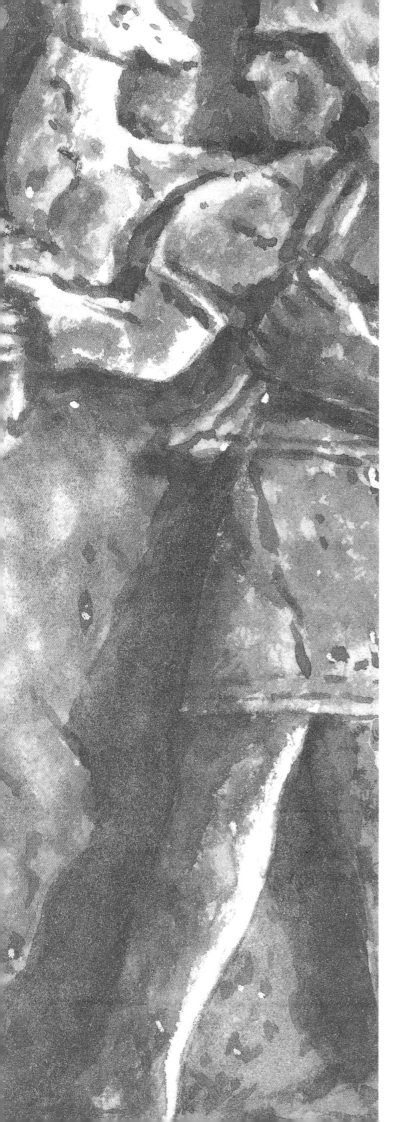

PEOPLE
AND
PLACES

WRITTEN BY
NIGEL RODGERS

———

GLOSSARY

People and Places

Aaron Older half-brother of Moses, famous for his persuasive speeches. His rod turned into a serpent. While Moses was on Mount Sinai, Aaron made the Golden Calf which the Israelites worshipped. Despite Moses' anger, Aaron still became chief priest.

Abel Second son of Adam. Killed by brother Cain because God preferred his sacrifice to Cain's.

Abigail Beautiful wife of Nabal who angered David by rudeness. After God killed Nabal, became David's wife.

Abner Captain of Saul's army who remained loyal to Saul. Killed by Joab, David's captain.

Abraham (Abram) First patriarch of Israel. Born in Ur, Mesopotamia, with wife Sarah and nephew Lot moved to Canaan, which God promised to his descendants. First son was Ishmael by Hagar, second Isaac by Sarah in her old age. Willing to obey even God's seeming command to sacrifice Isaac but saved by angel.

Absalom King David's favourite son, led a revolt against his father. Defeated, his long hair caught in a tree while he fled and he was killed by Joab, against David's orders.

Adam First human created by God. Eve was created from his rib. Like Eve, he was tempted by the serpent and ate from the Tree of Good and Evil, then was expelled from Garden of Eden for this.

Ahab King of Israel (north kingdom) 869-850 BC who worshipped Baal, killed in war against Syria.

Amnon David's eldest son. He raped his half-sister Tamar, later killed by Absalom in revenge.

Amos One of the first prophets, who warned Israel of coming doom.

Ararat Mountain in eastern Turkey where the Ark landed.

Assyria Powerful kingdom with capital at Nineveh in what is now northern Iraq that destroyed Israel (north kingdom).

Baal Canaanite god proved powerless by Elijah.

Babel Legendary tower raised so high in Shinar, kingdom of Nimrod the hunter, that God destroyed it.

Babylon Great city on the river Euphrates in what is now Iraq; centre of an empire which destroyed Jerusalem and carried off Jews to captivity.

Balaam Sent by the Moabites to curse Israel, his ass (donkey) refused to pass an angel until he agreed not to harm the Israelites.

Bathsheba Wife of Uriah until David fell in love with her and had Uriah killed. She bore David a son, Solomon, who succeeded him.

Beersheba Town in Judah (Palestine) where Abraham and Jacob lived.

Belshazzar Last king of Babylon, who was feasting and caught unawares when the Persians conquered the city.

Benjamin Youngest son of Jacob by Rachel, kept behind by Jacob when his brothers went to Egypt but called for by Joseph. Descendants formed tribe of Benjaminites.

Bethel Town near River Jordan where Jacob had his dream.

Bethlehem Town in Judah, home of Jesse and David.

Byblos Phoenician city which gave its name to the 'bible' (Greek: book).

Cain Elder son of Adam and Eve who was a farmer. God refused his offering but took his brother Abel's, which so angered Cain he killed Abel. God put a mark on Cain's brow and he became an outcast.

Carmel Mountain range in northwest Israel by the sea Canaan Land (approx modern Palestine/Israel) promised by God to Abraham and his descendants.

Damascus Capital of Syria, traditionally in Solomon's kingdom.

Daniel Captive in Babylon, won King Belshazzar's favour by deciphering writing on wall. Later thrown to lions but survived uneaten thanks to God.

David Chosen by Samuel, killed Philistine Goliath with sling although only a boy. Charmed King Saul with harp-playing until Saul grew jealous and forced David into revolt. Succeeding Saul as king, united all 12 tribes of Israel, captured Jerusalem and brought the ark there. Took Bathsheba for his wife after having her husband killed, but otherwise led blameless life.

Deborah Israel's only female prophet gave judgement under a palm tree.

Delilah Samson's wife, who discovered the secret of his strength was his uncut hair and cut it while he slept, before giving him to the Philistines who blinded him.

Eden Legendary garden in Mesopotamia where Adam and Eve lived before the Fall.

Edomites Descendants of Edom or Esau, the Israelites' neighbours and nearest kin.

Egypt Strongest and richest power in the Near East that enslaved nearby peoples, including the Israelites, to increase its wealth.

Eli Prophet and priest at the holy city of Shiloh whose descendants sinned and so did not become prophets.

Elijah Prophet and opponent of evil King Ahab, he defeated 450 priests of Baal in competition to set alight sacrificial bullock. Swept up to heaven in a chariot of fire.

Elisha Prophet and Elijah's chosen successor, he anointed Hazael and Jehru as kings. Cursed a group of children who were then eaten by bears.

Endor, Witch of Against God's laws, consulted by Saul when in despair and summoned Samuel's ghost from the world of the dead for him.

Esau Isaac's elder son and a hunter, he was supplanted by Jacob, who was his brother and also a farmer. Later reconciled with Jacob.

Esther Daughter of Mordecai, she became wife of the Persian king Xerxes (Ahasuerus) and saved the Jews of the Persian empire from a plot by the minister, Haman, to have them massacred.

Eve First woman and mother of all humanity, created by God from Adam's spare rib. Tempted by the serpent in the Garden of Eden, she ate from the Tree of Good and Evil and urged Adam to do so. This led to the Fall and expulsion from Eden.

Ezekiel Israelite Prophet during the Babylonian captivity.

Euphrates River in Mesopotamia (present-day Iraq) on which Babylon was sited, by whose waters the Israelites sat down and wept.

Galilee Region and Lake in northern Israel.

Gath One of the five Philistine cities, home of Goliath.

Gaza Philistine city on coast where Samson was blinded.

Gideon Judge who delivered Israel from the Midianites who were attacking Israelite homes and plundering them. Choosing only 300 out of 32,000 followers, he defeated the Midianites in a surprise attack.

Gilead Region east of the River Jordan.

Goliath Philistine giant warrior whom no Israelite dared face until David appeared with his sling and killed him.

Hagar Servant of Sarah and Abraham, she became Abraham's concubine and bore Ishmael. Driven out by jealous Sarah, she was comforted by an angel. The Arabs are said to be Ishmael's descendants.

Ham Cursed for seeing his father Noah drunk and naked, his descendants became the Hamites of North Africa.

Hannah Mother of prophet Samuel.

Hebron Highest town in Palestine, 30km southwest of Jerusalem. Abraham, Sarah and Jacob are buried there.

Hezekiah King of Judah who turned to the prophet Isaiah for help against the Assyrians besieging Jerusalem.

Hiram King of Phoenician city of Tyre, supplied the cedar wood for the building of the Jerusalem temple.

Isaac Son born in old age to Sarah and Abraham, who later almost sacrificed him at God's command. Married Rebekah and had two sons: Esau and Jacob. Tricked in old age by Rebekah into giving Jacob, not Esau, his blessing. His grandsons were the 12 patriarchs of Israel.

Isaiah Prophet and counsellor of kings of Judah. Foresaw the destruction of Jerusalem and the coming of a Messiah.

Israel Name of a) Jacob and b) kingdom of Israel, which split after Solomon's death to become two kingdoms of Judah and Israel.

Jacob Favourite son of Rebekah, who helped him trick his father Isaac into blessing him. He had a dream of a ladder to heaven. Worked 20 years for his brother Laban, and married both Leah and sister Rachel. Returning home, he wrestled with a man whom he discovered was God and who renamed him Israel.

Jehu King of Israel, former general of Ahab, restored the worship of God and founded short-lived dynasty.

Jeremiah Prophet in the kingdom of Judah famous for his denunciations of his age, which led to imprisonment. Foretold the Babylonian Captivity.

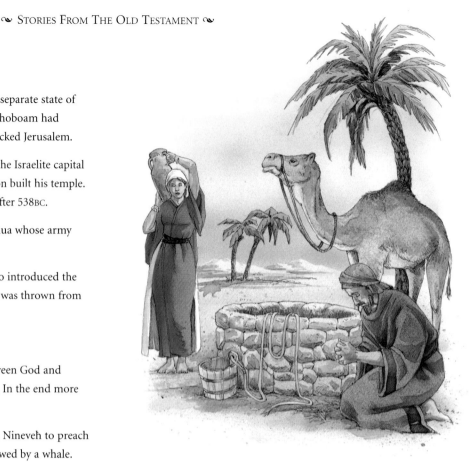

Jeroboam Servant of Solomon who formed separate state of Israel with 10 out of 12 tribes of Israel when Rehoboam had angered his people. Although larger than Judah, this lacked Jerusalem.

Jerusalem After being captured by David it became the Israelite capital and holy city. David brought the Ark there and Solomon built his temple. Destroyed by the Babylonians in 587BC, rebuilt partly after 538BC.

Jericho City near the river Jordan conquered by Joshua whose army marched round it blowing trumpets.

Jezebel Wife of Ahab, daughter of king of Sidon, who introduced the worship of the god Baal into Israel. After Ahab's death was thrown from a window at Jehu's orders and eaten by dogs.

Joab David's nephew and most successful general.

Job A virtuous man who became object of a bet between God and Satan. Burdened with sufferings, refused to curse God. In the end more than his original wealth and health restored to him.

Jonah Reluctant prophet who tried to avoid going to Nineveh to preach by taking a ship but was thrown overboard and swallowed by a whale. Escaped from whale and then went to Nineveh.

Jonathan Son of Saul and close friend of David. Supported David against Saul and was finally killed fighting Philistines.

Jordan River flowing into Dead Sea, on the eastern boundary of Canaan.

Joseph Elder son of Jacob. Betrayed by his brothers into slavery in Egypt, rose to prominence there. When his brothers came seeking food, he played tricks on them. Finally whole family moved to Egypt.

Joshua Moses's successor, who led people of Israel into the promised land of Canaan and divided it between the 12 tribes. Notable for commanding the sun to stand still and for causing the walls of Jericho to tumble down by commanding trumpets to be blown in front of them.

Josiah King of Judah who tried to reverse the country's religious and political decline, adopting book of Law. Killed fighting Egyptians.

Judah One of Jacob's 12 sons and a patriarch, whose tribe settled around Jerusalem. After Solomon's death it became a separate kingdom, small but strongly religious, until crushed by Babylon in 587BC.

Laban Brother of Rebekah, who employed nephew Jacob for 20 years and tried to cheat him out of marrying his daughter.

Levi Third son of Jacob who founded a priestly caste.

Lot Nephew of Abraham who settled in the Jordan valley. Wife was turned into pillar of salt because she looked back at the city of Sodom.

Manasseh Elder son of Joseph, whose tribe was divided east and west of the river Jordan to Gilead and Bashan.

Micah A country prophet of the kingdom of Judah who championed the poor and preached repentance.

Midianites People descended from Abraham's marriage to Keturah who raided and pillaged the Israelites' homes. Camel-riding semi nomads, southern neighbours of the Edomites.

Miriam Sister of Aaron, half-sister of Moses, led the Israelites in dancing and music-making while celebrating escape from Egyptians.

Moab Son of Lot, ancestor of Moabites who lived east of River Jordan.

Moses Born in Egypt where he was saved from a massacre of Israelite babies by being hidden in bulrushes. Brought up by Pharaoh's daughter, exiled after killing an Egyptian for maltreating an Israelite, he heard God's voice in the burning bush and returned as Israelite leader. After many trials, led Israelites out of slavery in Egypt, parting waters of Red Sea on way. On Mount Sinai received Ten Commandments from God. After 40 years leading his people through the wilderness, died within sight of the Promised Land .

Nabal Wealthy shepherd in Carmel, married to Abigail. Insulted David but saved from him by Abigail. Later killed by God.

Naboth Owned and refused to give up a vineyard coveted by King Ahab. Falsely accused of blasphemy by Jezebel and then stoned to death.

Nebuchadnezzar King of Babylon, he captured Jerusalem in 587BC and carried off Israelites to captivity.

Nineveh Capital of Assyria on River Tigris (Iraq).

Noah Righteous man favoured by God who told Noah to build a huge ark in which he took two of each kind of animal and plant. The ark survived the Flood and brought all in it to safety. Afterwards Noah planted vines and, drunk, fell asleep. He was seen naked by son Ham, cursed him and his descendants.

Persia (Iran) Empire which overthrew Babylon and let Jewish captives return to Jerusalem.

Pharaoh Title of rulers of ancient Egypt.

Philistines Confederacy of pagan peoples settled on southwest coast of Palestine (giving it its name). Often at war with Israelites.

Phoenicians Canaanite people settled on coast of modern Lebanon, great seafarers and merchants. Chief cities Tyre, Byblos and Sidon.

Rabbah Ammonite city besieged by David, modern Amman (Jordan).

Rachel Younger, prettier daughter of Laban, with her sister Leah married to Jacob. Died giving birth to Benjamin, her second son.

Rahab Prostitute in Jericho who helped Joshua's spies and so helped to prevent a general massacre in the city.

Ramah Burial place of Samson, north of Jerusalem.

Rebekah Cousin and wife of Isaac, had twin sons, Esau and Jacob. Tricked Isaac into giving his blessing to Jacob, her favourite son.

Red Sea Sea between Egypt and Arabian Peninsula which Moses parted when he led the Israelites out of slavery in Egypt.

Rehoboam Son and successor of Solomon, whose hard policies drove ten of the 12 tribes to break away and form kingdom of Israel.

Reuben Eldest son of Jacob, opposed his brother's plot to kill Joseph.

Ruth Moabite, ancestress of David. Devoted to her first mother-in-law Naomi, she later married Boaz, an older cousin.

Samaria Capital of north kingdom of Israel, destroyed by Assyrians.

Samson Judge renowned for great strength. Broke Nazirite vows by eating honey from a lion's carcass and telling Delilah, his wife, that his strength lay in his hair. While sleeping Delilah cut off his hair. Captured and blinded by Philistines in Gaza until God restored his strength and he pulled down the temple.

Saul Chosen by Samson as first king of Israel, but displeased God by not killing all the Amalekites after defeating them. Grew moody, despite David's music, drove David to revolt and finally committed suicide.

Sheba, Queen of Fabulously wealthy queen from what is now the Red Sea area who visited King Solomon and perhaps became his lover.

Shem Eldest son of Noah from whom the Semites are descended.

Shiloh Chief holy place of Israel until David captured Jerusalem.

Sidon Phoenician city (now Lebanon).

Sinai Peninsula dominated by mountain on which Moses received the Ten Commandments.

Solomon Son of David and Bathsheba, built first Temple at Jerusalem. Asked God for wisdom and also granted wealth. Wrote Song of Solomon and many other books.

Tyre Wealthy Phoenician city (now Lebanon); under King Hiram sent cedar and fir wood for building the temple at Jerusalem.

Ur City in Mesopotamia where Abraham born.

Uriah A soldier of David, married to beautiful Abigail whom David wanted. Sent into front of battle and killed.

Zechariah Prophet who urged Jews to return from Babylonian captivity and rebuild Temple.

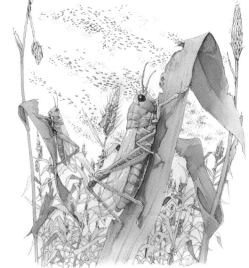

Glossary

altar

A table or flat-topped block used for religious ritual. In the Old Testament, altars were mainly used for making sacrifices or offerings to God.

altar of witness

A replica of the altar in the tabernacle at Shiloh. It was built by the tribes of Reuben, Gad and Manasseh to bear witness to future generations that even though they were separated from the rest of the tribes of Israel by the River Jordan, they all worshipped the same God.

Ark of the Covenant

A box built to hold the stone tablets of the Ten Commandments. It was the symbol of God's presence among his people.

Asherah

A Canaanite goddess, worshipped at the time that the Israelites invaded Canaan. She was worshipped as an Asherah pole, a figure carved from wood.

Baal

Baal is the main god of the Canaanites. He was a fertility god, and the people believed that he made the crops grow. He was also a thunder god, and he is often pictured holding or throwing a bolt of lightning.

birthright

The birthright was a father's blessing to his oldest son. It gave the son leadership over his brothers, but also the responsibility to take care of the family after his father's death.

Canaan

The area east of the Mediterranean, in what is modern Israel and Palestine. The area got its name from Canaan, son of Noah, who was the ancestor of the tribes that lived there.

commandments

The Ten Commandments were the most important of the laws that God gave to Moses on Mount Sinai. They were the terms of the covenant between God and his people and were produced on two stone tablets. There were probably two copies. At this time when a covenant or agreement was made between two people or countries, they took a copy each so they both knew what they had to do.

covenant

A promise in which God enters into a special relationship with His people. He promised His protection and the land of Canaan to Abraham and his descendants if they would be faithful to him.

Dagon

The main god of the Philistines. He was often represented as a fish god, but it is more likely that he was a corn god.

diviner

Someone who believes that they can tell the future by looking at different everyday objects.

grace

The grace of God is the fact that God loves all the men and women that he created even though no-one on earth is completely without sin.

dowry

A gift given by a man to his future father-in-law before his marriage, to compensate the father for his daughter's loss.

Exile

The period that the Israelites spent under the domination of foreign kings after Judah and Israel were conquered.

Exodus

The name given to the journey that the Israelites made from Egypt to the promised land. Exodus itself means "going out", which describes how the Israelites left Egypt behind.

faith

A complete trust and unquestioning belief in something or someone. Followers of God are devoted in such a way that they will do anything that is asked of them, believing that if God has requested something then it must be right.

Holy of Holies

The very centre of the tabernacle, where the Ark of the Covenant is kept.

Fall of Man

Humans' first disobedience to God. Adam and Eve lived in Paradise with God, with no sin to spoil their lives. When they listened to the serpent instead of God, and ate the fruit from the Tree of the Knowledge of Good and Evil, they fell from the sight and blessing of God.

idol

A statue of a person, god or animal. Idolatry is worshipping the statue, which is forbidden to the Israelites in the Ten Commandments. The Israelites often ignored this rule, and had to be reminded not to worship idols by prophets from God.

Israel

The nation that descended from Jacob, who was renamed Israel after wrestling with an angel by the river Jabbok. The new name, which means "he who has wrestled with the Lord", was a sign that God was still with him.

Jew

The name given to the Israelites while they were in Exile in Babylon. It was originally used to mean people from Judah, but after the Exile it came to mean people of the Jewish faith.

Judah

The southern part of the divided kingdom. To punish King Solomon for disobeying Him, God split Solomon's kingdom into two. Solomon's son, Rehoboam, ruled over the southern part, called Judah, while Jeroboam ruled the northern part which kept the name Israel.

Judges

Leaders of the Israelite nation for almost 200 years between the death of Joshua and the time of Samuel. They were people such as Samson and Ehud who kept the Israelite nation free from the domination of neighbouring tribes and rulers.

manna

The main food of the Israelites for the 40 years that they wandered in the desert. The Bible says that after the dew had gone in the morning, there was found on the ground a small round thing, whitish, like coriander seed, and with a honey taste. The Israelites used it in cooking.

miracles

Acts performed by God, either Himself, or acting through someone. They happen not only to show God's power to people, but they also form part of God revealing Himself to His creation, humans.

Nazirite

Someone who is dedicated to the service of God by special vows. Nazirites were not allowed to drink alcohol, or to eat raisins or vinegar. They were forbidden from cutting their hair, and had to avoid going near dead bodies.

Passover

The annual commemoration of the night that God killed all the first born children of Egypt to make Pharaoh release the Israelites, but he "passed over" the homes of the Israelites, leaving them unharmed. This festival is remembered with a meal of lamb and bread made without yeast.

Patriarch

The four Patriarchs in the Old Testament are Abraham, Isaac, Jacob and Joseph. They are the male heads of the family, with whom God made or renewed his covenant.

Promised Land

Abraham, the ancestor of all the Israelites was promised a large area east of the Mediterranean Sea, then called the Great Sea, where his descendants could live in freedom. When Moses led the Exodus from Egypt, he was leading the Israelites to this Promised Land.

Prophets

Men or women called by God to speak for Him and to communicate His will to the people. The prophets first emerged as a group in the time of Samuel. They offered guidance to the Israelites and warned them of troubles ahead.

rhabdomancy

A way in which people believed that they could tell the future by throwing arrow heads into the air, and then trying to read the future from the way that they landed. The word comes from *rhabdos*, the Greek word for a rod or wand

sacrifice

An offering made to God as a way for a man to give God something that belongs to him. Only the best can be offered to God, such as the first born lambs, or the finest wheat. Sacrifices are not a person's attempt to earn favour from God, but a way to honour Him.

sin

A rebellion against God, but it is also described in the Old Testament as not doing what God wants one to do.

tabernacle

The tabernacle, or tent of meeting, was the focus for the Israelites' worship of God while they were in the desert. The Ark was put into the central room of the tabernacle, and a cloud descended. A bright light shone from the tent, showing that God had taken up residence among His people. When the Temple was built at Jerusalem, a room was made for the tabernacle.

temptation

Thoughts and ideas that make people feel they want to sin. Christians are told to be always on their guard against temptation, but they are also told that God will help them and that temptation need never become too great to bear.

Index

Page numbers in **bold** refer to
illustrations.

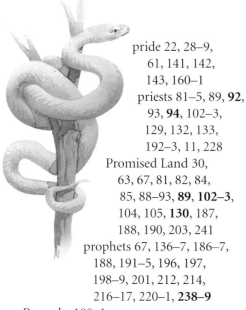

This edition is published by Southwater

Southwater is an imprint of
Anness Publishing Limited
Hermes House
88-89 Blackfriars Road
London
SE1 8HA
tel. 020 7401 2077
fax 020 7633 9499

Distributed in the UK by
The Manning Partnership
251-253 London Road East
Batheaston
Bath BA1 7RL
tel. 01225 852 727
fax 01225 852 852

Distributed in the USA by
Anness Publishing Inc.
27 West 20th Street
Suite 504
New York
NY 10011
tel. 212 807 6739
fax 212 807 6813

Distributed in Australia by
Sandstone Publishing
Unit 1, 360 Norton Street
Leichhardt
New South Wales 2040
tel. 02 9560 7888
fax 02 9560 7488

© 2000 Anness Publishing Limited

Previously published in four separate volumes: *Noah's Ark*, *Samson
and Delilah*, *David and Goliath* and *Jonah and the Whale*

Publisher: Joanna Lorenz
Managing Editor, Children's Books: Gilly Cameron Cooper
Project Editors: Peter Harrison, Jennifer Williams
Designer: Joyce Mason

10 9 8 7 6 5 4 3 2 1

PHOTOGRAPHIC ACKNOWLEDGEMENTS
Page: 6, (BL), Jean-Léo Dugast, Panos Pictures; 13, (BL), Hutchison Library; 18,
(BR), Hutchison Library; 27, (BL), The Stock Market; 35, (BL), The Stock Market;
38, (BL), The Stock Market; 42, (BL), Jeremy A Horner, Hutchison Library; 46,
(BR), Hutchison Library; 47, (BR), Hutchison Library; 70 (B/L) Erich Lessing/
AKG London; 93 (B/L) The Stock Market; 94 (B/L) Erich Lessing/ AKG London;
96 (B/L) Jean-Léo Dugast/ AKG London; 105 (B/C) Erich Lessing/ AKG London;
106 (B/C) Erich Lessing/ AKG London; 111 (B/R) Erich Lessing/ AKG London;
112 (B/R) Erich Lessing/ AKG London; 128 (B/L) Sonia Halliday Photographs;
133 (B/R) Richard T. Nowitz/ CORBIS; 154 (B/R) Erich Lessing/ AKG London;
162 (B/R) H Fenn/ Mary Evans Picture Library; 166 (B/L) John Spaull/ Panos
Pictures; 186, (BL), Bryan Knox, Sonia Halliday Pictures; 234 (BL), The Stock
Market.

Every effort has been made to trace the copyright holders of all images that
appear within this book. Anness Publishing Ltd apologises for any unintentional
omissions and, if notified, would be happy to add an acknowledgement in
future editions.

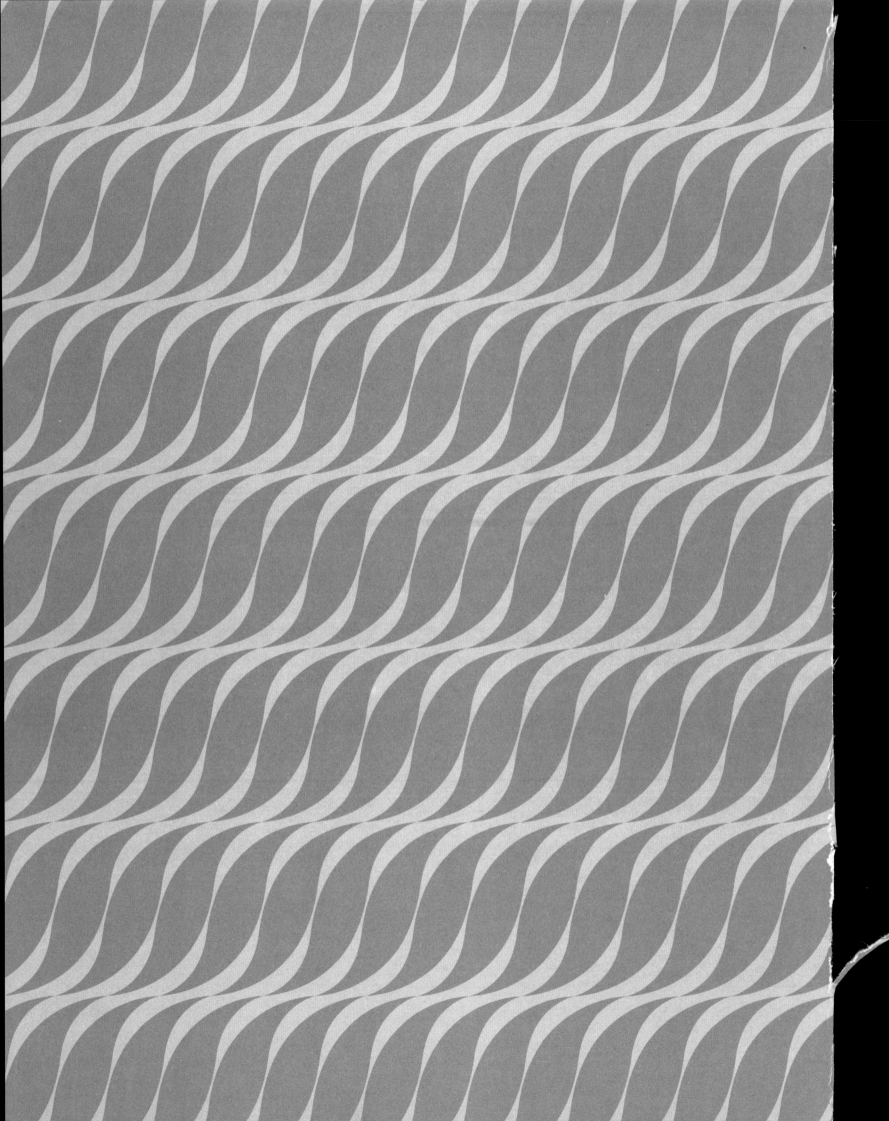